a Taste of
HAIDA GWAII

a Taste of

HAIDA GWAII

FOOD GATHERING *and* FEASTING

at the EDGE *of the* WORLD

SUSAN MUSGRAVE

whitecap

The information in this book is true and complete to the best of the author's knowledge. All recommendations are made without guarantee on the part of the author or Whitecap Books Ltd. The author and publisher disclaim any liability in connection with the use of this information. Opinions expressed in this book do not necessarily repre-sent the views and opinions of Whitecap Books. Whitecap Books does not review or endorse the contents of the websites listed in this book. Whitecap Books assumes no liability for any content or opinion expressed on these websites, nor does it warrant that the contents and links are error or virus free.

Whitecap Books is known for its expertise in the cookbook market, and has produced some of the most innovative and familiar titles found in kitchens across North America. Visit our website at www.whitecap.ca.

EDITOR: Jordie Yow
DESIGN: Andrew Bagatella
FOOD STYLING: Susan Musgrave
PROOFREADER: Jackie Wong
PHOTOGRAPHY: Photo credits appear on page, except pages ii, 62, 92, 154, 270 and 358 by Michelle Furbacher; page v and 18 by Peter Sloan; pages viii, 220 and 246 by Guy Kimola; page 352 by Kathleen Hinkel. Section break ornaments by Dejahlee Busch
COVER: Photography by Michelle Furbacher except sunset, snowy owl and Alphabet Soup by Guy Kimola and Copper Beech exterior by Peter Sloan. Illustrations by Dejahlee Busch
MAP DESIGN: Andrew Bagatella

Printed in China

Library and Archives Canada Cataloguing in Publication

Musgrave, Susan, 1951-, author
    A taste of Haida Gwaii : food gathering and feasting at
    the edge of the world / Susan Musgrave.

Includes index.
ISBN 978-1-77050-216-1 (pbk.)

1. Cooking, Canadian--British Columbia style. 2. Food--
British Columbia--Haida Gwaii. 3. Cookbooks. I. Title.

TX715.6.M868 2015   641.59711'12
C2014-908071-9
17 18 19   5 4 3

We acknowledge the financial support of the Government of Canada and the Province of British Columbia through the Book Publishing Tax Credit.

Nous reconnaissons l'appui financier du gouvernement du Canada et la province de la Colombie-Britannique par le Book Publishing Tax Credit.

TO JULIA MCNAMARA

LADY OF THE MANOR

2011–2014

DIXON ENTRANCE

North Island

Lepas Bay

Naden Harbour

Old Massett
Massett

GRAHAM ISLAND

Masset Inlet

Port Clements

Cape Ball

East Beach

Rennell Sound

Yakoun River

Tlell River

Tlell

HECATE STRAIT

Queen Charlotte

Skidegate

Sandspit

Copper Bay

MORESBY ISLAND

Cumshewa Inlet

Tasu Sound

Gowgaia Bay

GWAII HAANAS

INSET MAP

TOW HILL ROAD,
NORTH BEACH,
AND
ROSE SPIT

North Beach

Tow Hill Road

1. Rose Spit
2. Tow Hill
3. Naikun Village
4. Hiellen Village
5. Blow Hole
6. Agate Beach
7. Yakan Point
8. Moon Over Naikoon Bakery
9. Sangan River
10. Chown River
11. George Point, Naden Harbour
12. Masset Sound
13. Watun River
14. Juskatla
15. Beitush Road, Tlell
16. Chinukundl Creek (Miller Creek)
17. Skidegate Landing
18. BC Tel Point
19. Alliford Bay
20. Cape Knox
21. Tasu
22. Rose Harbour
23. Skidegate Narrows

N
W   E
S

Living on Haida Gwaii,

"a remote archipelago" that lies equidistant from:

Luxor (6200km) • Machu Picchu (5000km)

Ninevah (7600km) • Timbuktu (5000km)

LOCATIONS SHOWN ON MAP ARE MENTIONED IN BOOK

CHAPTER ONE: For Starters

Yes, I'll marry you.

TOP: The author, as solemnizer, on beach at White Creek PHOTO BY GUY KIMOLA; BOTTOM: PHOTO BY MICHELLE FURBACHER

WILL WRITE FOR FOOD: INTRODUCTION TO THE AUTHOR

When applying last year to be Haida Gwaii's new Marriage Commissioner, I was asked, "What qualifies you for such a position?" I replied, honestly: "I've been married three times. Third time lucky because he's spent most of our 25-year marriage in prison."

What qualifies me to write a book about food gathering and feasting on Haida Gwaii? As a criminal lawyer once said to me, "If you don't have an area of expertise, claim one."

My job of choice would be not Marriage Commissioner or writer, but food critic. I've written one restaurant review and I am including an excerpt here lest the editors of the Michelin Guide happen to pick up this book and wish to offer me gainful employment. I'd like to say, "Will write for food." But it would be great if I could get my airfare and hotel paid for, also?

The review was entitled, "Ondaatje on the Hook: The Poet as Restaurant Critic."

> *We weren't brought menus, which meant the chef was going to surprise us. As an appetite-whetter we were served small bowls of delicate savoury broth with a sprinkling of herbs, croutons and the first chanterelles of the season. With this came a bottle of Cotes de Saint-Mont 1998 which Patrick* [Patrick Lane, my guest] *said, "has a plum quality with the edge of a knife." At least, I think that's what he said. By the time I had fished out my notebook he'd forgotten his exact words— very important when it comes to nailing down the qualities of a fine wine. He thought he might have said "an icy edge" but I'm sticking to my story: a plum quality with the edge of a knife. I'm the one who has been asked to take over the* Globe and Mail's *restaurant critic's job this week while she is on hiatus.*
>
> *Our waiter, noticing our almost-empty glasses, tops us up, and I notice we've made a serious dent in the bottle before we've even finished the pre-appetizer course. "Nice and tight," Patrick declares, of the croutons, "like a woman. Keeping the tension in the crouton is hard work." Then, after a reflective pause, "I should be writing this!" Little does he know, he is.*

Next comes a Dover sole so delicate it could slip through your breath (my line, not Patrick's.) "This sole looks like Ondaatje on the hook," Patrick says, not to be out-done. At least, when I look at what I've written, it appears that's what he said. It could have been "Ondaatje on the book," but that wouldn't have made sense. Unfortunately, not much is making sense by this point. The evening seems to be slipping from our hands.

Finally, Patrick says something normal. "This is the best Dover sole I've had in my life!" I can tell he means it because he has even eaten the skeleton.

That was the last note I took.

I know we had a second bottle of wine, and that it was red: I meant to make a note of the name. At that point I decided to pace myself, which meant making sure I drank glass for glass with my companion so I would get my share, and as a result I am unable to remember the nuances of what we had to eat. I can safely say that Pierre [Pierre Koffel, chef at Deep Cove Chalet on Vancouver Island, my favourite restaurant on the planet] *can cook lamb so it melts in your mouth; you don't even need teeth in order to eat it.*

They say the mark of a good writer is one who can make you drool and your gastric juices begin to ferment by describing the smells and tastes of a memorable feast. I'd like to be able to describe our final course in the kind of elegant language a sober restaurant critic might use, ("then came an apple upside-down tart with warm thyme-infused honey") but by this time we had dropped the last vestiges of the discreet charm of the bourgeoisie. Dessert was something with puff pastry, poached pear and blackberry sauce. No little seeds that get caught in your teeth, either. It was yummy. I would have asked for a second helping but that might not have been . . . professional."

Living on Haida Gwaii, "a remote archipelago" that lies equidistant from Luxor[*], Machu Picchu, Nineveh[†] and Timbuktu, I can't just row around the point to dine at the Deep Cove Chalet anymore, but I have learned to fend for myself, and for my guests at Copper Beech House, in the culinary department.

When it comes to wild food, measurements are hardly precise. My editor has done his job and tried to pin me down and I have resisted, in some cases, without getting too snarky, except when I was editing under the influence of influenza

---

[*]   Luxor, site of the Ancient Egyptian city of Thebes, not the Egyptian-themed hotel and casino in Las Vegas.

[†]   Ninevah is an ancient Mesopotamian city on the eastern bank of the Tigris River and capital of the Neo-Assyrian Empire.

TOP LEFT: North Beach on summer day PHOTO BY SUSAN MUSGRAVE; TOP RIGHT: Beach and blue sky in spring PHOTO BY JANIE JOLLEY; MIDDLE LEFT: Stormy beach in winter PHOTO BY JANIE JOLLEY; MIDDLE RIGHT: North Beach on summer day PHOTO BY CHARLOTTE MUSGRAVE; BOTTOM: Masset Inlet in fall PHOTO BY GUY KIMOLA

MUSHROOMS

DEADLY POISON
DEADLY POISON
DEADLY POISON
DEADLY POISON
DEADLY POISON
DEADLY POISON
DEADLY POISON
DEADLY POISON
DEADLY POISON
CURE FOR ACUTE PARANOIA
DEADLY POISON
DEADLY POISON
DEADLY POISON
DEADLY POISON
DEADLY POISON
DEADLY POISON
DEADLY POISON
DEADLY POISON

Mushrooms PHOTO BY DAVID SHRIGLEY

over Christmas. Then I became very ill-tempered and wrote things like, "Why must people shorten a perfectly good word like macaroni, it's not that much of a mouthful," or "If people need to be told how much salt to add to the water when they boil pasta, they shouldn't be reading this book." (This is why I am not in marketing, but am the mere writer of the book.) When I say, for instance, 2 lb of cockles, I can't tell you how many cockles that will be because it will depend on the size of the cockles you have. Haida Gwaii cockles tend to be big but there are over 200 species of cockles on the planet, and some will be smaller than ours. When I say "a leg roast of venison," it is hard to say "a 3 lb leg" because when you go out to shoot a deer you don't know how big his legs are going to be. If you gather bladderwrack to steam your mussels in a pot, I ask you to rely on common sense when it comes to quantities. Obviously a wheelbarrow full would be too much, a coffee mug full not enough.

As far as recipes go, I view them—as I view stop signs—as suggestions. In some cases (such as making sourdough bread) it is important to take the suggestions to heart, and follow the instructions to the letter of the law. That is, stop, look both ways for three seconds, then proceed with caution. When you make a soup or a stew—throw caution to the wind. Be creative. Experiment. Except with wild mushrooms. Never never experiment with wild mushrooms. What could be worse than dying and having your friends say, "I told you so?"

MISTAKES ARE MADE

"The only real stumbling block is fear of *failure*. In cooking you've got to have a what-the-hell attitude."
—Julia Child

It wasn't always this way. That is, I didn't learn to cook until I had left home and was living in sin and in too many rooms with the English professor from Berkeley I'd met in the mental hospital where we'd both found ourselves committed.

I still hear my father's words, "You're so useless you can't boil an egg," every time I start to prepare a meal (especially if it involves boiled eggs.) I wonder why it is so difficult to put duct tape over the mouth of one's inner critic?

LEFT: PHOTO BY SUSAN MUSGRAVE

TOP RIGHT: Graffiti on school door, Masset PHOTO BY CHAR-LOTTE MUSGRAVE

I took to meal planning and gastronomy with great gusto when I lived with my lover in California. We shared a house with a famous playwright who poured ketchup over all my culinary creations. I can't remember what I cooked, or if all my recipes lacked something (like flavour) and could only be redeemed by adding ketchup. I think I got better over the years. (There's the critic again. Where's the bloody tape?)

Most of us know someone who has taken up cooking with a vengeance. They love cooking. The only trouble is cooking doesn't love them back. If you put half a cup of salt in your apple pie instead of half a cup of sugar, or a quarter cup of baking soda instead of a quarter teaspoon of baking soda in your cookie dough, it is safe to say you will not achieve the desired results.

Still, our mistakes make the best stories, and that's why we should not think of them as failures. Christmas was made memorable the year my friend at Tlell forgot to remove the paper packets of organs from the cavities of the Cornish game hens she cooked for dinner in lieu of a turkey. We each got a surprise package on our plate: the organs dried to little crisps.

My mother is famous for her ball-bearing pastry. We were eating steak and kidney pie and one by one started spitting out pieces of what we thought were shot—my oldest brother didn't find one in his helping of pie and felt terribly excluded. My mother was mortified—we could have broken a tooth! She figured out that her very ancient rolling pin had started leaking ball bearings as she'd rolled out her pastry that afternoon.

Because so many of my guests at Copper Beech House have a preference for gluten-free baked goods, I have had to adapt. I am a gluten-friendly person. I live in a gluten-friendly house, have a gluten-friendly cat, and make heaps of gluten-friendly sourdough bread. That doesn't mean I am insensitive to other

Graffiti, Masset PHOTO BY
CHARLOTTE MUSGRAVE

peoples' needs and when the gluten-free lifestyle first became popular I even bought gluten-free shampoo for our bathrooms, ever aiming to please. I picked up a large bag of (very expensive) gluten-free flour when I went off-Island (I confess the young woman at the health store didn't know what gluten was, either— she thought it had something to do with meat by-products) and when I got back to Masset I made a batch of blueberry muffins. The batter didn't look (or taste or feel) right but I wasn't used to gluten-free baking and chalked it up to my profound inexperience.

When the muffins came out of the oven they were like my spirits—sunken, heavy and demoralized. They were also unappetizing and inedible. I returned the heavy and expensive bag of flour to the healthy store on my next trip to Victoria. The clerk pointed out that I had purchased a bag of vital wheat gluten, not gluten-free flour, which might have accounted for my failure.

That word again. Not failure, but the best stories. My hope is that this book will leave you with a few memorable great ones.

NAMING THESE BEAUTIFUL, SHINING, WINDY ISLANDS

Haida Gwaii from space PHOTO
COURTESY OF NASA

Bill Reid once named these mystical islands at the western edge of civilization the "Shining Islands." How much more beautiful and apropos than "Canada's Galapagos," (which is how Haida Gwaii is described in most, if not all, magazine and newspaper articles) especially as you will not find a single blue-footed booby on any one of the 150-or-more islands.

In 1787, the islands were surveyed by Captain George Dixon, who named them the Queen Charlotte Islands after one of his ships, the *Queen Charlotte*, which was named after Charlotte of Mecklenburg-Strelitz, wife of King George III of the United Kingdom.

TOP: Snowy owl (blown off-course from the mainland in winter) PHOTO BY GUY KIMOLA; MIDDLE LEFT: Winter wren PHOTO BY JANIE JOLLEY; MIDDLE RIGHT: Kingfisher PHOTO BY PETER SLOAN; BOTTOM LEFT: Geese PHOTO BY GUY KIMOLA; BOTTOM RIGHT: Sandpipers PHOTO BY JANIE JOLLEY

GETTING TO HAIDA GWAII IN THE 21ST CENTURY

LEFT: By plane, Masset airport PHOTO BY GUY KIMOLA

RIGHT TOP: By sea, BC Ferry PHOTO BY ARCHIE STOCKER SR.

RIGHT BOTTOM: Sign on door of Masset airport PHOTO BY SUSAN MUSGRAVE

GETTING AROUND HAIDA GWAII IN THE 21ST CENTURY

LEFT: Masset bus stop PHOTO BY MICHELLE FURBACHER

TOP RIGHT: Water taxi PHOTO BY PETER SLOAN

BOTTOM RIGHT: By bicycle PHOTO BY GUY KIMOLA

Before the *Queen Charlotte* dropped anchor, the islands had been called "Xaadala Gwayee" or, in alternative orthography, "Xhaaidlagha Gwaayaai," meaning "islands at the boundary of the world." (Pre-contact the Islands were also known to the Haida as Inland Country; the mainland was The Land Out There.) American traders, who considered the islands part of the US-claimed Oregon Country, called the Queen Charlottes "Washington's Isles."

The name Haida Gwaii meaning "islands of the people" in the Haida language) was created in the early 1980s as an alternative to the colonial-era name, to recognize the history of the Haida people. On December 11, 2009, the government of British Columbia announced that legislation would be introduced in mid-2010 to officially rename the Queen Charlotte Islands as Haida Gwaii. The legislation received Royal assent on June 3, 2010, formalizing the name change.

Royal dispensation PHOTO BY MICHELLE FURBACHER

MORE THAN ORGANIC
THE NEVER-LOST ART OF FOOD GATHERING

"Only take enough for what you need. You don't need to take any more than that. Never get too greedy. If you look after it, it will always be there."
—Gandaawngaay (Herb Jones), quoting his Grandmother

Ever since Euell Theophilus Gibbons published his highly successful *Stalking the Wild Asparagus* in 1962 ("the lore here can turn every field, forest, swamp, vacant lot and roadside into a health-food market with free merchandise") foraging, wild crafting or rewilding has become more and more trendy. New York City's parks have had to ban the practice altogether since too many people had taken to gathering edible wild plants like mushrooms, American ginger, and elderberries.

Martha Stewart rhapsodized about the bliss of foraging in the woods at her home on Mount Desert Island, Maine. "It's one of the most beautiful places on earth to me," she says. "There are many kinds of moss, all sorts of ferns and ground covers. And I'm always looking down. Foragers are a downward-looking people. We love the discovery of an edible something."

Since Martha came out, stories about wild edibles have appeared in just about every major publication, including *The New Yorker's* food issue on November, 2011. When I did my own research for this book, ordering tons of material from the Vancouver Island Regional Library system that ships to Haida Gwaii, the books with the most holds on them were those on the subject of wild foods and foraging.

"Food itself means basic animal existence, but wild food is food for our imaginations as well as for our bodies," writes Terry Domico in *Wild Harvest: Edible Plants of the Pacific Northwest.* When she is kneeling in a field pulling roots, or stripping spruce buds from the end of a branch, or picking huckleberries, she says, "my body is ten thousand years in the past, feeling dim memories; my mind embraces ten thousand years of future."

Connie Green, also known as "The Mushroom Lady" who supplies the California restaurant The French Laundry with an array of mushrooms that are the highlight of their menu, says she finds herself sitting squarely "at the crossroads of the Stone Age and haute cuisine." Many's the time she has crawled out of the woods, oblivious to the twigs and leaves in her hair, and driven her bounty straight to the restaurant whose clients land their private jets near her hunting grounds, and turned it over to a delighted chef in a white uniform. (Her description was "immaculate whites" but that is not my experience of the uniforms of any chefs I have known.) "Muddy jeans and glistening stemware, old pickup

LEFT: Partially mowed lawn in Masset PHOTO BY GUY KIMOLA

RIGHT: PHOTO BY KATHLEEN HINKEL

trucks and limousines, campfires and Viking ranges . . . there isn't a hairbreadth of difference between the foragers' and the chefs' passion for their work," she writes.

On Haida Gwaii you don't see a lot of "glistening stemware" (you'll see glistening *silverware* at least at Copper Beech House where it is polished, if not daily, occasionally by volunteer guests!) and the only limousine I know of is the one Smokin' Joe parks in his front yard as a rusted-out garden attraction, but we can assume that all the wild foods we pick, harvest, or catch, though not organically certified, are *beyond* organic: eating local is the new organic; foraging is the new eating local. Wild foods grow *wildly*, wherever they choose to put down roots, not where anyone with a wad of pesky certified organic produce stickers says they are *allowed* to grow. Wild foods defy domestication.

"The forager's golden rule is that you never, ever eat a food you can't identify with 100 percent certainty," writes Langdon Cook, forager, chef and author of *Fat of the Land*. "The dangers go beyond mushrooms. The northwest has plenty of poisonous greens, such as poison hemlock—the stuff that killed Socrates.

"It looks like wild parsley. Or a wild carrot. That's a family where you really have to know your stuff."

Cook, who lives in Seattle, will try a wild food only after he finds a record of other people eating it—especially local First Nations, for whom none of this food gathering business is breaking news. Ethnographies of native life are Cook's primary source of information about potential "new" foods.

He gives an example of devil's club (his recipe for Devil's Club Stir Fry appears later in this book), a medicinal plant for the Haida and other Northwest Coast nations. "It's a prehistoric-looking plant that has big parasol-shaped leaves with spines on them," he writes. Cook eats the buds in the springtime and describes their flavour as akin to "inhaling the forest."

But you don't have to journey to a remote mountainside, or even to these mythical, misty isles (though why would you pass up the opportunity?) to gather wild foods. If you have an unmowed lawn, a vacant lot, or even just a sidewalk with weeds growing between the cracks, then you have something to start with. On a visit to Haida Gwaii, Douglas Gibson, author and publisher, told me he picks Saskatoon berries in downtown Toronto (of course he won't divulge the exact location). Becky Lerner, a journalist living in Portland, spent a week surviving on wild edibles foraged from sidewalks, parks and backyards in the city, dining on stinging nettles, dandelion, bull thistle, wapato ("duck potato"), cattail, plantain, Japanese knotweed, dock, clover, chickweed, chicory, miner's lettuce and morel mushrooms. Washington state has under development a 7-acre public plot called Beacon Food Forest—food in the edible forest section of the project will be available freely to visitors—smack-dab in the middle of downtown Seattle.

Unlike most of Canada during the last ice age, parts of Haida Gwaii escaped glaciation. Likewise, partly due to our perceived isolation we have also escaped having our land polluted by agriculture and industrialization the way much of our planet has been ravaged over the past 200 years. Foragers in cities do need to think about how they can best minimize their exposure to poisons and pollutants. The further you are from civilization (*so-called* civilization, this writer notes) the less chance you have of contamination. It's a good sign if you see lichens growing on the trees, since they are usually too sensitive to grow in polluted air.

Haida Gwaii Mosscape PHOTO BY JANIE JOLLEY

John Kallas, a Portland botanist and foraging expert, offers the following safety advice: "Don't gather food within 4 feet of an old house because of lead paint. Don't gather food within 30 feet of a highway—and even then, preferably gather uphill—because of nickel and cadmium from the batteries, petroleum chemicals wearing off tires and washing off the side of the road, coolant and gasoline. And never, ever, ever gather near railroad tracks. They've been putting pesticides and herbicides in those areas for the last 100 years."

I might add, "And don't let the Safety-First Police catch you food gathering without a hard hat or a helmet. A tree might fall on your head and kill you whilst you go innocently about picking blewits." But I will try not to make fun of the Safety-First Police. Otherwise next time they catch me berry picking without wearing sunscreen, they might not be forgiving.

MISTY MORNINGS AND CASHMERE WOODS

In a *New Yorker* dated January 12, 2012, which I bought at the Thrift Shop in Masset for 25 cents, Patricia Marx describes the thousands of delicacies found in New York markets of the 1860s: "porcupine, raccoon, groundhog, cuckoo birds, woodpecker, wild swan, about 25 varieties of duck, ox teeth, beeves palates and, of course, bung gut." Writing about the present century in appetite-whetting detail she describes the "quality grub" she finds at food megastores in New York City: "At Eli's the cheeses are evidently so valuable that some, like the drunken, goat

cheese soaked in wine ($20/lb.) and the Tête de Moine, a Swiss cheese eaten by scraping it with a knife ($20/lb.), must be kept under surveillance in vitrines."

In the Delmas Co-op in Masset, there used to be a surveillance sign in the aisle where the air fresheners were displayed. Why anyone would want to boost a Glade Sense & Spray® Automatic Freshener, which detects someone passing by and instantly releases a burst of fragrance into the air, I don't know, because a person can experience any of these scents—Misty Morning, Cashmere Woods (Cashmere around here is a brand of toilet paper), Crisp Waters, Refreshing Surf, Wandering Stream, Clear Springs and Moonlit Walk—simply by opening a window or stepping outside their front door on Haida Gwaii.

And reading Marx's descriptions of New York City grocery stores where you can find fig-flavoured goat's milk ice cream, gluten-free no-trans-fats kosher fries,

TOP LEFT: Moonlit Walk PHOTO BY JAGS BROWN

MIDDLE LEFT: Misty Morning PHOTO BY PETER SLOAN

BOTTOM LEFT: Refreshing Surf PHOTO BY GUY KIMOLA

TOP RIGHT: Crisp Waters PHOTO BY GUY KIMOLA

BOTTOM RIGHT: Clear Springs PHOTO BY GUY KIMOLA

Himalayan goji berries, biodynamic blueberry juice and uncured-bacon-wrapped mahi-mahi fillets with apricot glaze—makes me appreciate the Co-op even more for its "nothing hoighty-toighty about us" attitude. I mean, what's wrong with a store that sells plain old Heinz tomato ketchup, Hellman's mayonnaise, tooth-picks, tinfoil, paper plates and air fresheners, for Pete's sake?

But Marx's writing can be, like food, addictive: "Oh, the bagels, the thir-ty-seven varieties of olives (in oil), the fat wedges of Parmigiano Reggiano, organic popcorn, frozen Barney's Franks 'n' Blankets and how about Murray's lemony-gar-lic rotisserie chicken (you could eat it till you die), plus 600 artisanal cheeses from around the world, and, would you believe it, Velveeta and Spam, too?"

You can still buy Spam in Masset. I included a 30-year-old tin (it came in a DIY "shrine kit" I was given way back when) of the dubious meat by-product in a shadow box I made to decorate the entranceway to Copper Beech House. It was stolen the first night. The item I replaced it with, a 10-year-old tin of escargots, purchased from Field's in Masset for $1.00, was stolen, too. Either someone is really hungry or they are looking for colourful tins to include in their own DIY shrines.

On Haida Gwaii we don't have huge houses of food worship, such as New York's Fairway (with parkas available for shoppers who brave the refrigerated meat-and-dairy room) or the mega church of Costco selling salmon fillets the size of clown's feet and blister packs full of enough electric-toothbrush heads for a hammerhead shark. We don't have Gourmet Warehouses or high-end kitchen shops selling gad-gets that promise to make living simply easier, like a Dancing Can Opener that gyrates in time to the coffee grinder, or an automatic ice-crusher. In Masset we have the Thrift Shop. All you have to do is focus on what you need, and chances are excellent that you will find it for sale, for less than a dollar, on Thursday afternoon or on Saturday morning, when the Thrift Shop opens its doors. People line up half an hour before opening time to shop at what my daughter, Charlotte, maintains is one of the best little thrift shops in the world.

Recently, for instance, with bagels on my mind after reading Ms. Marx's article, I decided I couldn't live without a bagel guil-lotine. The next trip to the Thrift Shop and *voilá!* A never-used, un-bagel-blood-stained bagel guillotine. I purchased it ($1.00) and took it home, and wrote about my score on Facebook, only to be informed by Meredith Adams, friend and neighbour who lives off the grid on the property known as Moon Over Naikoon

ILLUSTRATION BY DEJAHLEE BUSCH

Thrift Shop PHOTO BY
MICHELLE FURBACHER

on Tow Hill Road, that you won't find a bagel for sale on Haida Gwaii that doesn't come already sliced.

Crushed, I donated the bagel slicer back to the Thrift Shop the next day. (I have subsequently read that bagel guillotines are the most popular items unsold at garage sales around the world.)

My two other, more useful Thrift Shop scores have been a Zwilling J.A. Henckels knife (25 cents) made in Germany and a Peugeot pepper grinder (also 25 cents) from France. The knife turned out to be my own, as did the pepper grinder.

How did I come to buy my own knife back? In the fall of 2012 I began volunteering at the Thrift Shop. I needed something to occupy my time, besides managing Copper Beech House, writing a cookbook, editing, and teaching poetry online at the University of British Columbia—oh, yes, and being Haida Gwaii's new Marriage Commissioner. Every week for our coffee break I would take some sort of baked treat for coffee time: a bran muffin, a Welsh cake (see page 58) and once a thick slab of Irish whiskey-laced tea cake in honour of Margo Hearne. (Margo, who controls the operation, is a fellow writer, originally from Ireland). I would bring my own bread board from home, and a good bread knife.

Inadvertently, I left my knife behind. The following Saturday I found a pile of knives, all priced (25 cents) on Margo's sorting table, and decided to pick through

TOP: Pepper grinder PHOTO BY MICHELLE FURBACHER; BOTTOM LEFT: At least one anatomically correct doll PHOTO BY SUSAN MUSGRAVE;
BOTTOM RIGHT: Masset Thrift Shop find PHOTO BY SUSAN MUSGRAVE

them to see if there was anything worth high grading. (From Wikipedia: "The term high grading in forestry, fishing and mining relates to selectively harvesting goods, to '*cut the best and leave the rest*.' " The practice is frowned upon by anyone who is not doing this themselves, and it is certainly not a practice Margo endorses at the Thrift Shop in Masset.)

But since the knives were already priced, this wasn't high grading, right? And that's how I spied it—slicing through the corner of my eyesight—a Henckels bread knife, with a slightly melted handle, just like the one I had at home! Turned out it *was* the one I thought I had at home. As to how my pepper grinder ended up at the Thrift Shop, I can only speculate. I tend to take it with me to potlucks (yes, and my own Georgian silver fork, and my own pillow if I venture far from home). So perhaps I left it behind and a friend donated it. I'm just happy it found its way back to me, still full of the Kampot pepper my brother brought me from Cambodia.

CHAPTER TWO: Breakfast at Copper Beech House

TOP: Haida Gwaii PHOTO BY JANIE JOLLEY; BOTTOM: David Rowing ILLUSTRATION BY GWAAI EDENSHAW

A CONDENSED HISTORY OF COPPER BEECH GUEST HOUSE

"This being human is a guesthouse.
Every morning a new arrival.

...

Be grateful for whoever comes,
because each has been sent
as a guide from beyond."

—From "The Guest House," by Jalāl ad-Dīn Muhammad Rūmī, more popularly known in the English-speaking world as Rumi, a 13th-century Persian poet, jurist, theologian and Sufi mystic

1914: A Swedish carpenter builds the house for a cannery manager living at George Point in Naden Harbour, on the north coast of what had come to be called the Queen Charlotte Islands.

1921: The cannery closes. The house is floated, on strapped-together logs through Dixon Entrance and down Masset Sound, where it comes to rest on the shores of the Watun River.

1932: A new owner sets sail again—back *up* Masset Sound. A stump puller and two oxen, Olaf and Buster, winch the house off the beach and onto its present footings, by the government docks in Masset.

Guestbook PHOTO BY MICHELLE FURBACHER

Its interior is redone with plywood (considered very chic at the time), a convenient in-house well, and a windmill for electricity. The copper beech tree is planted.

1971: David Phillips arrives in Prince Rupert from Toronto en route to China to get involved in the post-cultural revolution. After a failed attempt as a stowaway on a Greek freighter he lands on the Charlottes, and procures his own transportation. "I tried to circumnavigate the islands in a rowboat, in black dancing pumps," he said, in an interview with Taras Grescoe in 2006. "I got to the West

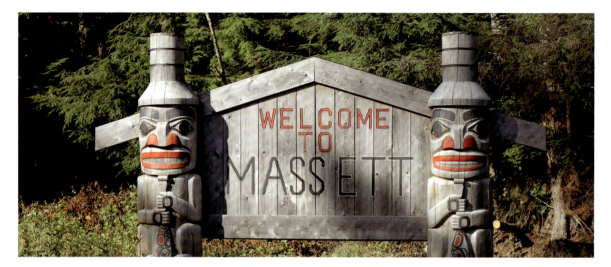

Coast, which is like the Emperor's Garden—these three-mile, deserted sandy beaches, with one rocky outcrop after another—and my boat started to sink. Fortunately, a fishing boat came along at the last minute and threw me a line."

In Masset he meets Sydney Harling Smith, living alone and in need of care; David moves in, and carefully preserves the house circa the early '30s. He takes full possession in 1986 when Sydney dies, and it becomes Copper Beech Guest House. Or, as the sign says, Copper Beech House Inn. Elsewhere it is listed as Copper Beech House B&B. I suppose it is all three of these designations, and possibly even more, but it could be said that in Masset we don't always know how to make up our minds when it comes to the "correct" spelling. For instance, the village of Masset is spelled Masset, except on the sign welcoming you to "Massett." Old Massett (two t's) used to be called "Haida," back in the '70s. Now it is usually referred to as "The Village," as opposed to the Village of Masset, which is sometimes referred to as New Masset. See what I mean?

2010: I buy the Copper Beech House from David. I keep the Persian rugs, though some of the heirloom quality furniture is too uncomfortable and has been replaced by the kind of furniture you can sink *into*, not through. The glass curio cabinet still remains, with, among other treasures, the soapstone geese, an ivory tusk, a rodent skull and a plastic Smurf. The walls are covered with the works of local Haida artists; there's an African penis gourd, antique fishing rods and a sardine can with a depiction of *The Last Supper*. And of course there are books, with several shelves dedicated to the works by writers who have stayed as guests: David

Suzuki, Margaret Atwood, Graeme Gibson, Douglas Coupland, William Gibson, Michael Turner and many more.

When I bought Copper Beech House from David, Douglas Coupland emailed me saying,

"YAYYYYYYYYYYY!!!!!!!

That's such exciting news!!!!!!!!!!!!!!!!!!!!

I can't think of a better match on so many many levels.

CONGRATULATIONS! X"

(I took that "X" to be a kiss, not the generation.)

I can't say I was cut out to be an innkeeper. I feel uncomfortable, most of the time, charging anyone for a place to lay their head. "Do not forget to entertain strangers, for by so doing some people have entertained angels without knowing it," according to Hebrews 13:2. I try not to forget, but then I think, who am I to charge angels the standard room rate plus GST and PST on top?

In Geoff Dyer's lovely novel, *Jeff in Venice, Death in Varanasi*, the protagonist goes to Varanasi and checks into an establishment called the Ganges View.

TOP: Last Supper PHOTO BY MICHELLE FURBACHER

BOTTOM: Angel PHOTO BY MICHELLE FURBACHER

"The Ganges View was one of the great hotels of the world. The reason for this, the owner said, is "because we don't really know how to run a hotel." The idea behind most hotels, especially luxurious ones, is very simple: to leech money out of guests. Every desire and whim can be catered for in an instant—and comes with a whopping surcharge. "In the course of my stay at the Ganges View I'd eaten dozens of lunches, breakfasts and dinners and had ordered endless juices, teas and doz-

ens of bottles of water. Wondering what all this might be costing, I asked Kamal—one of the smiling, gentle Nepalis who worked here—if they were keeping some kind of record of what I'd consumed. No, I was supposed to have kept a record, but they had forgotten to give me the piece of paper on which the record was kept. Kamal duly handed me the paper, and said I could start from today. As he handed me the paper, I heard a rustling behind me. When I looked around I saw a rat scurrying out of sight, behind a wardrobe.

"Don't worry," said Kamal. "He is a guest, too."

Garden at Copper Beech House
PHOTO BY PETER SLOAN

I would like to adopt this as a model for Copper Beech House. "We are one of the world's great guest houses because we don't really know how to run a guest house." I would, however, make one editorial change. "*Rodentia Non Grata.*"

BREAKFAST AT COPPER BEECH HOUSE

"I always eat eggs in the morning and night
They give me strong legs and keep my eyes bright."
—Poem fragment from my laminated placemat, circa 1956

"Breakfast. We offer you a choice. Your choice is to take it or leave it."
—Purser on board our national airline (name removed to protect the guilty) in the days when they still offered breakfast and still had pursers on board

That is *not* how we approach breakfast at Copper Beech House. At Copper Beech House, breakfast is often a leisurely all-morning-long event. If there are more than four guests we don't set the table—everyone sits in the living room with a plate on their lap. The informality leads to wonderful stimulating conversations and lets our guests get to know one another without having to worry about which knife or fork to use, or if they spilled stewed rhubarb on the white tablecloth.

We serve what I have humorously taken to calling an Off-the-Continental Breakfast (Haida Gwaii is about 100 kilometres (60 miles) off the coast of Canada, as Islanders like to say when they refer to mainland British Columbia) which includes many kinds of coffee, every kind of tea, orange juice laced with elderflower cordial, fresh fruits (including local wild berries, when in season), homemade granola, yoghurt and my 3-day Sourdough Breads (see recipes pages 76, 81 and 82). Guests usually go for the bread, partly because it takes me so long to make they would feel guilty if they didn't eat it, especially after I have reminded them of all the time and effort involved.

Eggs are from local chickens, unless marauding dogs or raccoons have eaten them (the chickens, not the eggs), first.

There are scrambled eggs (my favourite), poached eggs, fried eggs and baked eggs, cooked on low heat. Cooking eggs over high heat (frying or scrambling) changes the structure of the egg yolk, a condition known as oxidative damage. Poaching or boiling is supposed to be better for you, but I don't care. Scrambled eggs are the most comforting dish I know, next to Macaroni and Cheese, which I refuse to reduce to Mac and Cheese.

TOP LEFT: Tea Cannister PHOTO BY MICHELLE FURBACHER

TOP RIGHT: Fruits Compotes PHOTO BY MICHELLE FURBACHER

BOTTOM LEFT: Granola, fruit and yoghurt PHOTO BY KATHLEEN HINKEL

BOTTOM RIGHT: Huckleberries PHOTO BY MICHELLE FURBACHER

These days people like no eggs, also. (See "Tips" under "Crab, Chanterelle, Cara-melized Onion, Goat Cheese Omelette on page 40.) Or egg whites, which seems to be to defeat the whole purpose of eating an egg. No one ever asks, "Which came first, the chicken or the egg white?" Though this might be just the kind of philosophical conversation one could find oneself in over breakfast at Copper Beech House.

Joelle Rabu was one of our most amusing philosophical guests. Joelle, who now manages the Haida House at Tllaal, left me with this after breakfast one morning, the *Best. Quotation. Ever.* "Perception is 99% of the flaw." (It's her own, by the way.)

TOP: Philosophical Breakfast
PHOTO BY MICHELLE FURBACHER

BOTTOM: Haida Gwaii tea kettle
PHOTO BY GUY KIMOLA

SCRAMBLED EGGS

Scrambled eggs and I have history. We've been through a lot together. First there was the "I'll only eat them if they are burned" stage, which lasted until I was taken to the hospital to have my tonsils removed, at the age of five. After that there was the "over my dead body" stage, where I wouldn't eat them at all.

My mother, the morning I was admitted to the hospital, left me with a warning that if I didn't clean my plate the nurses would force-feed me by shoving a rubber tube up my nose. I know she had my best interests at heart, fearing that I would die of malnutrition if I went 24 hours without eating the hospital cuisine. I believed everything my parents told me (why wouldn't I?) and so a nurse found me, gagging over a plate load of scrambled eggs with liver mixed up in them, because every time I took a bite and tried to swallow, it came back up. I demonstrated. The nurse took the plate away and left the room saying, "No one's forcing you to eat." Still, I lay awake most of the night, waiting for her to return with the hose.

In the morning I had surgery and woke up with most of my teeth missing, a little bag of money from the tooth fairy tied to my bedstead, and a big bowl of

Egg shells PHOTO BY MICHELLE FURBACHER

A cold morning in Masset. A perfect morning for scrambled eggs. PHOTO BY GUY KIMOLA

lemon-lime Jell-O. I forgave my mother as I scarfed the Jell-O, but it had been a life lesson for me: never trust anything anyone (even your parents) tells you.

Making the perfect scrambled eggs isn't difficult. The key is whisking the eggs thoroughly and vigorously before letting them float down into your pan. Whisking incorporates air, which produces fluffier scrambled eggs. And fluffier is, if nothing else, fluffier.

A lot of people overcook their scrambled eggs. They should never be even the slightest bit brown—that means they're burnt! (Just like I liked them when I was a young gourmand. What can I tell you? Tastes change.)

The perfect scrambled eggs should be soft and just a bit moist, and of course made with a generous amount of butter and a little cream. (If you want to make anything taste delicious, use butter, cream, garlic, white wine, salt and pepper. This applies to scrambled eggs as well, though I'd omit the garlic and definitely the white wine.)

Never use water, and never milk—not skim milk (I thought this was "skin milk" when I was a kid and wouldn't touch the stuff), not 1%, 2%, not homogenized. Half and half will do, or whipping cream. (The amount of cream added is typically about 2 Tbsp (30 mL) per egg. But I have never measured. I just pour away. Until the eggs look the right colour.) It's also best not to tell anyone you've used whipping cream because in today's uber-health conscious world, it will spoil the delight they take in eating the smoothest, creamiest, loveliest scrambled eggs ever.

My mother always used evaporated milk (and that's what I still use) when we were "yachting" in the Gulf Islands. (See "Aside: All the Comforts of Home" page 37)

ASIDE: SALT
OR IN DESOLATION SOUND I DREAMED OF SIBERIA

When I was growing up we had one kind of salt: Windsor Table Salt. My mother bought it at the local grocery store and it came in a white, square box with blue and brown circles on it, but I didn't know that it had originated beneath the city of Windsor, Ontario. Salt mines, my parents reminded me every chance they could, were on the other side of the planet, in darkest Siberia, where you'd be sent to live in exile if you disgraced the family name by ending up in the Court Parade of the local daily paper, The Victoria Colonist. I was in that difficult phase between detachable mittens and handcuffs, and my parents invoked the threat of Siberia whenever I complained about having to go out on the boat for the weekend instead of going downtown and getting into trouble with boys. "You think boating is suffering," my father would say. "You should thank your lucky stars we're only going to Desolation Sound this weekend, not to the salt mines in Siberia."

In Desolation Sound I dreamed of Siberia.

"Absolutely nothing like messing around in a boat." PHOTO BY ROBERT MUSGRAVE

I adore salt. Even the most inspired combination of ingredients can result in a dish that is flavourless and dull without a judicious addition of salt. It makes everything I know taste better. Even chocolate.

I add salt to nearly everything I eat. I taste it first because you are supposed to, and if it isn't obvious by now, I always follow the rules. Applying seasoning before tasting is viewed by many as an insult to the cook: it shows a lack of faith in his or her ability to prepare a meal. My view is that the cook should always add the right amount of salt in the first place. All too often, they don't.

What does it mean when a recipe says, "Add salt to taste?" As an ingredient in dishes, salt plays two crucial roles. When we're told to "salt to taste," we're not trying to make the dish more salty. All we're trying to do is rid the dish of bitterness and make the rest of the flavours go, "tah-dah!"

TO REITERATE: salt reduces bitter flavours. It allows the aromas and tastes of the other ingredients in your dish to shine through.

We didn't have a salt shaker at home. We had an open saltcellar that sat next to the pepper grinder in the middle of the table. We used a tiny silver spoon to spoon a little salt into a tiny white pile on the side of our plate. You dipped the tip of your knife in the salt, and then touched the end of your knife to whatever combination of food (a little bit of meatloaf, mashed potato. carrot, a pea or two) you'd speared on the end of your fork. This was called *manners*, something the English invented to make other people feel inferior. (See: Beneath the Salt, page 31)

One time a non-English visitor to our house mistook the salt for sugar, and added a heaping tiny spoonful to his tea.

I have many types of salt in my pantry, and even though they come in beautiful shapes and colours, I seldom use them. There are at least as many types of salt as there are toothbrushes on the market, so I have decided only to write about the ones I use: common table salt, kosher salt, and Maldon-flaked sea salt.

TABLE SALT: a fine-grained salt used in saltshakers, the most common kind of salt found in the average kitchen. Neutral in flavour, it dissolves quickly in warm water. Most table salt is available in either plain or iodized forms. Table salt also contains anti-caking additives, which make it flow smoothly even in humid weather. (On Haida Gwaii, and elsewhere on the coast where there is a high moisture content in the air, I usually put a teaspoon of white rice in my saltshaker. The rice takes up any extra moisture and keeps the holes in the shaker from getting clogged. Except by the rice. That's another story.)

I use table salt to salt the water for cooking pasta. I rarely use it in baking any more, but if I am stuck (i.e. on a boat or in somebody else's kitchen) I use half the amount suggested in the recipe. I find table salt a bit on the salty side, ever since I started using Maldon sea salt. More on that later.

KOSHER SALT: can refer to two types of salt—one is a small flake-like form so named for its use in the preparation of meat according to the requirements of Jewish dietary guidelines. Kosher salt typically contains no additives.

LEFT: Three kinds of salt
PHOTO BY MICHELLE FURBACHER

BOTTOM LEFT: Table salt
PHOTO BY MICHELLE FURBACHER

RIGHT: Maldon (finishing) salt
PHOTO BY MICHELLE FURBACHER

BOTTOM RIGHT: Kosher salt
PHOTO BY MICHELLE FURBACHER

Beneath the Salt

IN MEDIEVAL England salt was scarce and only afford-able by the higher ranks of society. Salt was extracted from seawater through evaporation, by boiling seawater over fire.

At that time the nobility sat at the "high table" and their commoner servants at lower trestle tables. The salt was placed in the centre of the high table and only those of rank had access to it. Those at the lower tables were below (or beneath) the salt.

The term "salt" is used for the ornately designed container the salt was kept in as well as for the condi-ment itself. On his website, The Phrase Finder, Gary Martin writes that as early as 1434 the word "salt" was used in this way, e.g. "A feir salt saler of peautre." (A fine-quality pewter saltcellar). Strictly speaking, to be "below the salt" was to be below the saltcellar.

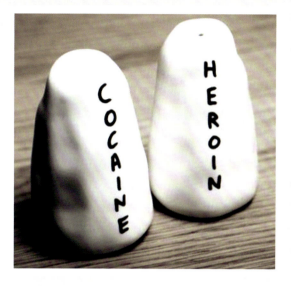

Modern times salt and pepper shakers PHOTO BY DAVID SHRIGLEY

The second type is one that has been certified as "Kosher" by a certifying body such as the Orthodox Union. The certification ensures that the product is suitable for consumption for those following a kosher diet.

I use Diamond Crystal Kosher Salt—in my bread and in stews or to mix with garlic and rub on the inside of a chicken or turkey.

MALDON FLAKED SEA SALT: I first read about this wonder-of-all-salts in one of Nigella Lawson's early cookbooks. I bought a small box for nine dollars or so, and now I don't go anywhere without it. I have a little baggie of Maldon salt in my purse that I carry with me, the way others carry other white powders in little bag-gies in their purses. To each her own.

Nigella Lawson has a blog, called "My Salt is Maldon: Another Smug Food Blog." I see she hasn't posted an entry since 2010, and I understand why. I started a blog for Copper Beech House and haven't posted anything, either, for several years. A person has only so much time.

Maldon is a brand of sea salt, harvested off the coastal town of Maldon in Essex, England. Maldon Salt has become an institution, run by the fourth gener-ation of the Osborne family, who have been hand harvesting and producing these beautiful melt-on-your-tongue salt flakes since 1882.

Maldon is really a finishing salt, best sprinkled on your food once it's on your plate on the dinner table, or scattered atop savoury sweets (Maldon sprinkled on scoops of chocolate Häagen-Dazs ice cream might be *the* perfect dessert), or even on lettuce leaves in place of a dressing, I don't squander my Maldon Salt in dishes where the salt dissolves into the liquid, heavens no. Never. Kosher salt will do for that.

ASIDE: CILANTRO

Some of my own friends, who are otherwise people of taste, claim to "hate" cilantro. I've always held this (secretly, of course) against them but now I've found out that, apparently, it's not their fault. According to a very thorough article by Harold McGee ("The Curious Cook") in The New York Times, some people may be genetically predisposed to dislike cilantro. The herb seems to inspire a primal revulsion amongst an outspoken minority of the population.

Even a culinary sophisticate such as Julia Child is not immune to cilantrophobia. In a television interview she told Larry King she would never eat any dish that had cilantro in it. "I would pick it out if I saw it and throw it on the floor."

Ms. Child is not the only hater in the hood where cilantro is concerned. There's an "I Hate Cilantro" Facebook page with hundreds of fans and even an I Hate Cilantro blog. *The Oxford Companion to Food* notes that the word "coriander" derives from the Greek word for bedbug·, that cilantro aroma "has been compared with the smell of bug-infested bedclothes" and that "Europeans often have difficulty in overcoming their initial aversion to this smell." (I can't imagine why!)*

Modern cilantrophobes tend to describe the offending flavour as soapy rather than buggy. If you are one of those who think cilantro tastes like Dove, hand lotion or the bug family of insects, read Mr. McGee's article.

No Bed Bugs on Haida Gwaii. But Dragonflies. PHOTO BY JAGS BROWN

---

* P.S. I am happy to say that I don't know what a bedbug smells like. I'd like to keep things that way. Especially since I run a guest house. I was going to say B&B but I will never again use that particular designation. Bed and Bugs. I wonder if I'm the first person to ever think of B&B that way?

Pepitas

PEPITAS ARE toasted pumpkin seeds. Pepitas can refer either to the hulled kernel or unhulled whole seed, but most commonly refers to the roasted end product.

If you are determined to make pepitas from scratch, here's what you do.

THE HARD WAY

Pick a small pumpkin from your pumpkin patch. If it is Halloween you might want to carve the pumpkin, but if not just cut it in half and scoop out the seeds. You can of course cook the pumpkin flesh and make muffins or pie.

Place the seeds in a strainer, wash and rinse very well. Dry with paper towels and place the seeds on a baking pan, or in an iron skillet. Toss with the olive oil and salt. Bake for 15 minutes or until crisp.

THE EASIER WAY

I cheat by buying a bag of unsalted pumpkin seeds and roasting them in a cast-iron frying pan until they are nicely browned. They require constant stirring so they brown evenly.

Preheat a skillet over medium heat on a stovetop and add the seeds. Stir the pepitas continually for about 15 minutes or until they start to pop and look crispy. Remove the skillet from the heat and allow the pepitas to cool before serving them.

CILANTRO PESTO MAKES 1-1½ CUPS (240-350 ML)

½ cup (120 mL) pumpkin seeds	lime juice
2 bunches fresh cilantro†, washed	¼ cup (60 mL) grated Parmesan or Asiago cheese
½ jalapeno pepper, chopped (seeds removed)	¼ tsp (1 mL) salt
2 garlic cloves	¼ cup (60 mL) olive oil
2 Tbsp (30 mL) freshly squeezed	

WHAT YOU DO

1 Toast the pumpkin seeds slightly in a dry frying pan. They toast really fast, so just turn the heat to medium-low and shake them around every half a minute or so. You will hear a satisfying pop as they begin to brown. Watch them carefully, because they burn if you turn your back to check out who has posted more insights on the I Hate Cilantro Facebook page.

---

†　Oh, and I do use the stems. Unless I'm in a wasteful mood or the stems look too coarse and I am prejudiced against them. Welcome, if not embrace, the pungency in cilantro stems. Just take into account their strong flavour and crunchiness. And whether you can be bothered to cut them off, or not.

Halloween

GUY KIMOLA, who took a lot of photographs for this book and has an amazeball eye for what makes Haida Gwaii tick, lives out of town on a secluded acreage. In an email he wrote to me, he said, "I'd never had any trick-or-treaters where I live but on Halloween a couple of years ago there was a knock at the door and I was surprised to see three little costumed critters yelling "trick-or-treat" at me. Totally off-guard, I said sorry and explained that I didn't have any candy. One little dude said that was sad and dug around in his bag and gave me a handful, then the other two also gave me some of theirs. I was quite happy taking it."

LEFT: Halloween pumpkin PHOTO BY GUY KIMOLA; RIGHT: Guy Kimola PHOTO BY GUY KIMOLA (SELFIE!)

CILANTRO PESTO (CONT'D)

2 Put all the ingredients except the olive oil into a food processor. Puree until everything is finely chopped.

3 Pour in the olive oil, a little at a time, and process until it is combined.

SCRAMBLED EGGS ON TOAST SERVES 2. (ADJUST ACCORDINGLY, DEPENDING ON HOW MANY PEOPLE YOU ARE FEEDING)

3 large brown* eggs

Pinch of salt and a generous grinding of fresh pepper

Heavy cream or evaporated milk

At least 2 tsp (10 mL) butter

1 thin (or thick; I prefer thin) slice of toast†

WHAT YOU DO

1   Make your toast, butter it and keep it warm.

2   With a fork, beat eggs with cream or evaporated milk, salt and pepper, in a small bowl, until the whites and the yolks are combined and you see a few big bubbles begin to form.

3   Heat a heavy saucepan over medium-low heat and when it is hot, add the butter. When the butter begins to foam (don't let it brown!) add your eggs. Stir gently, nudging them, folding them, until they become tender and silken, a damp gold-enrod mass. All this should take less than a minute and a half. The eggs will form large curds as they begin to coagulate; when they are 75% cooked, break these curds into smaller pieces and remove from heat while they still look as if they ought to be cooked a few moments more. Your eggs will continue cooking once they are removed from the pan and have been spooned, in all their dreamy-yellow slipperiness, onto your warm and expectant piece of toast.

4   I suspect there are people out there who prefer their eggs *not* to be served on toast. I don't know what to say to these people. Except, perhaps, "It takes all kinds."

Scrambled Eggs PHOTO BY MICHELLE FURBACHER

---

*   I use brown eggs because they always look healthier. Think brown bread versus white. The truth is, hens with white feathers and ear lobes produce white-shelled eggs. Hens with brown or red feathers and ear lobes produce brown-shelled eggs. (This makes no sense to me: why aren't the eggs red, instead of brown? And shouldn't we say "white eggshells" and "brown eggshells," not "white and brown eggs"?) And something else—a lot of people have never stopped to consider whether chickens (or any birds for that matter) have ear lobes. They do. A bird's ear has three inner chambers (like ours), but doesn't have an outer part, which is why we can't easily see them.

†   I toast the sourdough bread I make myself (see page 76), which might be even better toasted than untoasted, but the choice of what kind of bread to use is entirely up to you.

ADDITIONS

Of course I prefer my scrambled eggs unadulterated. Salt and pepper should be added to taste, but hold the dried herbs, garlic, cheese, sautéed onion or green pepper strips; no Turkish beef sausage, Chilean native fungus, or Haida Gwaii smoked salmon even. No liver, ever, under any circumstances. Maybe a couple of chives criss-crossed over the top, and of course serve with a sprig of parsley to keep the mobsters happy and my guest house from being fire-bombed (See Aside: The Parsley Racket, page 269). I know I said not to add garlic, but my daughter, Charlotte, sometimes grates raw garlic over her scrambled eggs and I swoon over every mouthful.

USEFUL TIP

Always store eggs fat end up. The pointy end has an air pocket that creates a space for bacteria to reproduce, to go forth and multiply. If you store your eggs this way it keeps the bacteria far away from the vulnerable yolk, which is more prone to bacterial infection. Storing eggs this way will also keep them "fresh" longer.

I can't say I ever recall checking to see where the pointy end is on the eggs I have bought in my lifetime. And I can't promise I will ever do so in the future, but there may be readers who might decide to look at eggs in a whole new way, armed with this knowledge.

TRUE FACT

Omega-3 eggs come from chickens that were fed flaxseed. These eggs are exceptionally yellow and wonderful in recipes such as Buttermilk Ice Cream (see page 308).

SERVING TIP

I confess to having tried out a new way of serving scrambled eggs to our guests at Copper Beech House last summer, something I had had served to me in Ireland. I made a batch of cilantro pesto (see page 33) and put two little dabs of this—to add some green, not to say that the sprig of parsley wasn't sufficient—on each plate. I didn't have the right tool so I used an extra syringe I had on hand to measure my cat's flea medicine. I kept it in the fridge, duct-taped to the pesto jar. I have often wondered if my guests have ever noticed it and thought their host was mainlining pesto.

Eggs

"FRESH" HAS to be the most over-used adjective on the planet. I once counted it 27 times in a flyer from a local grocery store.

It goes without saying that eggs should be fresh.

If you dare to test your eggs to see how fresh they really are, drop one into a glass of cold water. If it sinks to the bottom and lies on its side, it's as fresh as they claim it to be in the grocery store flyers. If the air pocket in the pointy end is a little bigger, the egg will stand up, signifying that it has probably passed its Best Before Date. If the air pocket is so big that the egg floats on the surface, you could perhaps donate it to your local museum as a "heritage egg." It is, in a plain word, old.

Another way to check for freshness is to crack an egg open and look at it, closely. A slight cloudiness in the white indicates extreme freshness. As the eggs age, the white becomes thinner and clearer.

ASIDE: ALL THE COMFORTS OF HOME

"There is nothing, absolutely nothing, like messing around in a boat," my father always quoted from *The Wind in the Willows*, a book I never liked. I'd been conceived aboard my father's first love, an old motorsailer, *Froggie*, off the rocks near Ladysmith (according to my mother after a glass or two of sherry) in a fierce southeast gale. My father had to drop the 90 lb storm anchor for the first time in his life. Family lore is that he never used it again after that night.

I grew up on the boat. My mother washed my diapers in tide pools and strung them up the mast to dry, like flags of surrender. Captain Bligh was what we called

"All the comforts of home."
PHOTO BY MICHELLE FURBACHER

our father on the good days—Bligh's crew had mutinied against him on the HMS Bounty in the South Pacific in 1789 because of the cruel and unusual punishments he doled out—when the engine didn't fail as we drifted towards the rocks, or Dad managed to steer his way out of a whirlpool. I have fun memories of trying to lure my siblings into the bilge on rainy holiday weekends while Dad tried to patch the leaks in the deck. If I complained that I couldn't sleep with a saucepan catching the drips beside my head, he would say, "What do you think this is, the Ritz?"

It would have helped me get over my fear and loathing of omelette-making sooner if I'd owned the right pan. (My father used to say, "A poor workman blames his tools.") I must have mentioned this lack-of-proper-tool to some guests because shortly after I went out and bought myself a very expensive omelette pan, I received a large box in the mail containing two more very expensive omelette pans. So now I have three. But, I tell myself, until I get the perfect lifter, my omelettes will continue to resist being lifted in one piece and will end up on the plate looking like a horse that bolted after the barn door had been closed. If that isn't mixing too many metaphors.

Enough about omelettes. Except you *must* try this one. At least once in your life. Put it at the top of your Omelette Bucket List. Guaranteed you'll die satisfied.

CRAB, CHANTERELLE, CARAMELIZED ONION AND GOAT'S CHEESE OMELETTE

SERVES 2

1 or 2 (depending on size) onions, caramelized (see page 42)	1 cup (240 mL) cooked crabmeat
1 cup (240 mL) or more sautéed chanterelle mushrooms	4 oz (110 g) goat's cheese
	3 large eggs
Butter	2 Tbsp (30 mL) water*

WHAT YOU DO

1 Get up earlier than usual so that you can caramelize your onions, or do the sensible thing and caramelize them the night before.

2 Tear the chanterelles—don't cut them—into bite-sized pieces and fry in butter until soft. (When it comes to butter, I never measure, but in this case I might say a daub of butter the size of a walnut.)

3 Set out four small bowls, one each for the caramelized onions, the chanterelles, the crabmeat and the goat's cheese.

4 In a bowl, whisk together the eggs, water, salt and pepper.

---

*   Use water, not milk (which toughens the eggs) to make a light, fluffy omelette. In scrambled eggs I use evaporated milk, or whipping cream. Never water. I have no idea why milk would toughen the eggs in an omelette, but not in scrambled eggs. I try not to think too hard about it. That way lies insanity.

5   Set one of your many expensive omelette pans on the stove, over medium heat, and add another daub of butter. (If you don't have an expensive omelette pan, you can make do with any old frying pan. That way, if your omelette doesn't turn out, you have something to blame it on.)

6   When the butter begins to foam, pour the egg mixture into the heated pan, swirl to coat the pan, and cook, without stirring, until the eggs begin to set, 2 to 3 minutes.

7   Shake pan lightly, then gently pull back cooked eggs with a rubber spatula to allow runny, uncooked portion to flow underneath the cooked part. Cook until centre of omelette is lightly set, about 1 minute.

8   Sprinkle the crab, chanterelles, caramelized onions and goat's cheese (or any combination thereof) over the eggs.

9   This is the part where life and the omelette start falling apart. *Gently fold omelette in half, slide onto a plate, and serve hot.* It sounds so easy, right? But if you are at all tentative, like me, the omelette doesn't fold in half properly, all the insides seep out into the frying pan, and by the time I get it onto the plate it looks like scrambled eggs, which I would have preferred to have made in the first place.

10 Practice makes perfect, Rome wasn't built in a day. As my father (also) used to say.

ADDITIONS
You can add 1 Tbsp (15 mL) chopped chives or 1 Tbsp (15 mL) chopped parsley.

SUBTRACTIONS
You can leave out the crab. Or the mushrooms. Or the caramelized onion. Or the goat's cheese.

TIP: At Copper Beech House I go around the room asking everyone what they would like in their omelette, and then I promptly forget.

I've learned that it's a good idea to ask everyone what they would like in their omelette and then write it down. Here's a sample, a typical Sunday in the summer at Copper Beech House (names have been changed to protect the overeaters and the picky ones)

Patricia: no crab, no mushrooms, onions, cheese

Omelette

- omelette in Dutch is *struif*
- omelette in French is *omelette*
- omelette in German is *Omelette*
- omelette in Norwegian is *omelett*
- omelette in Spanish is *tortilla*

Roger: crab, mushrooms, no onions, allergic to goat's cheese

Mary: Goat cheese only (and Roger's portion as well.)

Gordon: lots of crab, no onions, no mushrooms, cheese, no salt, no pepper, no eggs

I could go on but I am afraid readers might start skipping over the list, and, as Elmore Leonard says, "I like to leave out the parts that people skip."

(You can also skip the part where you ask everyone what they would like in their omelette, and take Air Canada's approach. "We offer you a choice. Your choice is to take it or leave it.")*

CARAMELIZED ONIONS

3–4 onions	A sprinkle of salt
2 Tbsp (30 mL) butter (or more)	1 tsp (5 mL) sugar (optional)†

WHAT YOU DO

1 Slice off the root and top ends of the onions, then peel them (or find a friend or family member who unwittingly asks, "Can I help with anything?") Slice thin.

2 Heat butter over medium-high heat in a largish cast-iron pan (for the best caramelization.) When the butter foams, add the onions.

3 **Resist the temptation to stir for the first 5 minutes or more.** Reduce your burner to medium-low heat. Cooking the onions at a relatively low temperature, called sweating, allows all the water to release into the pan and then evaporate slowly. Sweating also ensures that your onions will be soft and caramelized all the way through, and not just on the outside.

4 Sprinkle the salt over the onions. This helps to draw water and dissolved sugars out of the onion's cells. When you add salt to the onions at the beginning, it will take longer to achieve browning because of the extra water it draws out, but ultimately, your onions will have a much better flavour and will brown more evenly.

---

* I know I said I wasn't going to divulge this information, but I changed my mind.

† Sugar helps with the caramelization process. Or you can use a sweet onion, such as a Walla Walla White or Vidalia onion.

5   As soon as the onions start sticking to the pan, let them cook a little and turn brown, but for heaven's sake stir them before they burn. (If you think they are on the verge of burning, add more butter—or even a bit of water if you are desperate.) The trick is to ignore them enough so that they brown, but not so long so that they burn.

6   As the onions cook down, scrape up the browned bits from the bottom of the pan. Continue to cook and scrape, cook and scrape, until the onions begin to turn anywhere from honey-colored to deep brown, depending on how caramelized you want them to be. Let them cook for at least 20 minutes, stirring often. They will continue to caramelize and get even more caramelizeder (sic) if you let them go on cooking for another 40 minutes, on the very lowest heat, so you hear just the merest of faintest sizzle.

TIP: You can make big batches of caramelized onions and freeze them in individually sized portions. Just don't forget that they are there in your freezer. (Or you can store refrigerated for several days in an airtight container.)

PHOTO BY MICHELLE FURBACHER

LEFT: Henry White PHOTO BY PETER SLOAN

RIGHT: Onions and work socks PHOTO BY GUY KIMOLA

ASIDE: ONIONS

This was in the big snowfall of 1996: I came down with a fever. It lasted for days and I couldn't shake it. I remember lying on the chesterfield in a delirious state watching my husband shovel snow off the roof, and feeling glad that I had been stricken in such a timely fashion.

Henry White came over to borrow some morphine or whiskey (jus' kiddin') and saw that I was indisposed. He gave me his "old Haida recipe" to get rid of a fever.

2 large onions	1 pair clean work socks

WHAT YOU DO

1 Slice onion thinly, then put them in the bottom of the socks.

2 Put on the socks.

3 Go to bed.

4 In the morning discard the onions (which will most likely be cooked) in your compost or household garbage. Discard the socks, also.

5 You will be cured.*

POSSIBLY THE BEST GRANOLA 12 CUPS (2.8 L)

"The possible's slow fuse is lit by the imagination."
—Emily Dickinson

---

*   I tried it that night, in 1996. Not only was I cured, I have never had a fever since.

No Onion No Cry

FIVE WAYS OF CHOPPING ONIONS WITHOUT TEARS

- Place a match stick in each corner of your mouth
- Chew gum fast
- Hold a piece of bread (I recommend sourdough) in your mouth
- Put a spoon or fork between your lips
- Stick out your tongue and hold your breath

"Calvin: Why are you crying mom?
Mom: I'm cutting up an onion.
Calvin: It must be hard to cook if you anthropomorphize your vegetables."
—from *The Complete Calvin and Hobbes* by Bill Watterson

Just as every restaurant seems to claim their clam chowder is "famous," nearly everyone I know says their granola is the *best*. I am quite sure there is, somewhere on this battered and bartered planet, a batch of granola that is possibly as good as the granola I slave over toasting to perfection at Copper Beech House. So I do not intend to make any grandiose claims.

The impossibly beautiful Masset Inlet PHOTO BY GUY KIMOLA

6 cups (1.4 L) old-fashioned (slow cooking) rolled oat flakes

2 cups (475 mL) barley flakes

2 cups (475 mL) oat bran

1 cup (240 mL) sunflower seeds

1 cup (240 mL) large shreds of unsweetened coconut*

1 cup (240 mL) almonds, chopped (I leave the skins on)

¾ cup (180 mL) canola oil

¾ cup (180 mL) coconut oil

¾ cup (180 mL) honey, maple syrup or agave syrup†

2 Tbsp (30 mL) vanilla extract

1 cup (240 mL) toasted pepitas (pumpkin seeds)

1 cup (240 mL) chopped hazelnuts (added at end because they must be toasted to remove the skins)

1 cup (240 mL) dried cherries (you could also use raisins or cranberries or any other kind of fruit.)

* Coconuts are not indigenous to Haida Gwaii. However there have been cases where beachcombers have found them washed up on our shores, so if you want to make a 100-mile version of granola, it's not impossible. As long as you make the granola without oats, barley, almonds, canola oil, maple syrup, agave or vanilla. If you manage this, please send me your recipe. Care of the publisher. I don't want to be inundated.

† Agave tends to be sweeter than honey or maple syrup, so you may want to use a little less.

Granola

(a) A Granola person can usually be found in nature or at L. L. Bean.

(b) Despite never having held a full-time job, granolas usually manage to purchase several thousand dollars worth of over-priced outdoors equipment (i.e. skis, kayaks, rock climbing gear) which they strap to their over-burdened 1995 Subaru Legacy station wagons.

(c) A gathering of deadheads, all with a lost look on their stoned faces, often wandering in small, circular patterns while playing hacky sack.

(d) Usually tripped out, is part of the green party (sic), with new-agey views on life and death. Eats no meat, and usually no dairy, and therefore has a low iron count; is probably anemic. Is flaky and fruity, like granola. Yum.

(e) Euphemism for testicles. *She was totally checking out my granola.*

Islander Brianne Fudge bolts her Froot for breakfast. PHOTO BY MAX MITCHELL

POSSIBLY THE BEST GRANOLA (CONT'D)

WHAT YOU DO

1   Heat oven to 325°F (160°C). Line 2 baking trays with parchment paper.

2   Place the rolled oats, barley flakes, oat bran, sunflower seeds, almonds and coconut in a large bowl.

3   Combine the coconut and canola oils, honey or syrup and vanilla extract, and add to dry ingredients. Mix thoroughly.

4   Bake for 20 minutes, then stir. Bake for a further 15 minutes—or until golden. (In the last few minutes, watch your granola very carefully. It can easily burn, and burnt granola is, well, beyond redemption I'm afraid.)

5   After the granola is toasted to light brown perfection, add pumpkin seeds, hazelnuts and dried cherries.

CRACK COCAINE MADE (RELATIVELY) SIMPLE

The last time I shopped for a toothbrush I realized—you need to take a course in Toothbrushes for Dummies. Didn't there used to be one kind of toothbrush, with three variations? Soft, medium and hard bristles? Now there are aisles of everything in between. There's even a "prepasted toothbrush" for people who are too lazy to open a tube of toothpaste and squeeze some out. I shouldn't say "too lazy." Perhaps they have more important things to do—like write a cookbook.

I know you may be thinking, "What do toothbrushes have to do with crack cocaine?" You would be correct if you concluded, "nothing at all," but toothbrushes do have something in common with yoghurt,* which is really my subject matter (the crack cocaine was an attention-getting device and it worked: you're reading this, aren't you?) A person can get just as bewildered standing in front of a sea of yoghurt options in the dairy aisle as they can at their drug mart, trying to select the right sort of toothbrush for their teeth, taste buds, blood type, socio-economic position and the type of yoghurt they like to eat.

"The battle for the heart and soul of America's yoghurt preferences is a marketer's version of brutal and ceaseless trench warfare, as you, the consumer, are bombarded by wave after wave of new yoghurt products from a mind-blowing variety of yoghurt factions, all hoping to deluge your taste buds . . . to make you a yoghurt addict of their own particular yoghurt variety," writes Hamilton Nolan in "The Yoghurt Wars" on Gawker. Mr. Nolan seems particularly concerned that PepsiCo is now joining the yoghurt fray, evilly engaging in the marketing of what he calls America's new "crack cocaine."

Hotel California PHOTO BY MICHELLE FURBACHER

---

* Yogurt, yoghurt, yoghourt, yogourt, yaghourt, yahourth, yoghurd, joghourt, jogourt.
  I spell it "yoghurt" because "hurt" has always been a word I can identify with. (For further reading see my previous 27 books.) I am also drawn to the word "frozen" because it has zen in it.

Taking My Daughter for a Frozen Yoghurt Cone on her Sixteenth Birthday

WHOLESOME YOUNG FROZEN Yoghurt Seller: "Is that going to be it for you today?"

Youngest Daughter: "Yes, can I get a pack of cigarettes too?"

Wholesome Frozen Yoghurt Seller: "This is a frozen yoghurt shop, we don't sell cigarettes here."

Youngest Daughter: "I have ID though!"

Wholesome Frozen Yoghurt Seller: "This is a frozen yoghurt shop. Not only do we not sell cigarettes, but I'm pretty sure it's illegal to accept a fake ID."

LEFT: ILLUSTRATION BY DEJAHLEE BUSCH; RIGHT: PHOTO BY GUY KIMOLA

ASIDE: FROZEN YOGHURT

This dessert is supposed to be a healthier alternative to ice cream. But many frozen yoghurts have been heat-treated during processing, which kills off the live, active cultures. Go ahead and eat it, anyway. As my youngest daughter (a person of smoke) is always telling me, "Mum, we're all going to die of something."

After writing about yoghurt I went to the Co-op for my fix—I had run out of my homemade cache and was feeling lazy. (I looked for the prepasted toothbrush,

too, but didn't find one.) I stood perplexed, confronted by my choices, reading all the different nutrition facts labels. No two were the same. One 0% fat vanilla flavoured yoghurt contained 22 g (per ¾ cup/180mL) of sugar. Even the plain non-fat yoghurts had been sweetened. After 15 minutes of gruesome indecision, I bought 2 litres of milk for less than I would have paid for 650 g of yoghurt, and a tube of toothpaste. Looks like I'll be making my own yoghurt, and applying my own toothpaste to my toothbrush tonight.

Smoothies, Queen Charlotte
PHOTO BY JANIE JOLLEY

PLAIN COPPER BEECH HOUSE YOGHURT

8 CUPS (1.9 L)

I don't use a yoghurt maker. I think I have one I bought at a garage sale but it is under the stairs with the other gadgets I never use: the bread maker, the quesa-dilla maker, the electric egg cooker, the keyboard-shaped waffle iron (when you write for a living, people love to give you these clever work-related gifts) and the rice cooker. If you do have a yoghurt maker, I can't tell you how to make yoghurt. I am set in my ways, and this is the only way I know how.

Yoghurt is embarrassingly easy to make. Of course if you live in a city you will have even more options to choose from than we do on Haida Gwaii, so you might not have the same incentive to make your own. It depends on how much yoghurt you eat. And also if you want to impress people who will say, "You make your *own* yoghurt?" (I remember reading about a woman who made her own marshmal-lows—I'd always thought marshmallows came in packages the way tuna came in tins—and I thought this was above and beyond—until I read a recipe and found out how easy it really is!)

**PLAIN COPPER BEECH
HOUSE YOGHURT (CONT'D)**

WHAT YOU WILL NEED[*]

1 large pot, sterilized

1 insulated cooler

2 quart-sized (1 L) canning jars, sterilized, with lids and rings

1 hot water bottle

1 candy thermometer

2 towels

1 large aluminum bowl

INGREDIENTS

2–4 Tbsp (30–60 mL) of your favourite plain yoghurt (your starter culture)[†]

8 cups (1.9 L) whole milk

WHAT YOU DO

1   Have your starter ready. Use fresh yoghurt. I usually buy a tub of the best Greek full-fat yoghurt I can find, and then freeze it by putting 2 Tbsp (30 mL)

---

[*]   (for yoghurt, not marshmallows)

[†]   The rule of thumb is use 1 Tbsp (15 mL) of starter per 4 cups (1 L) of milk if you want your yogurt to be mild tasting. If you like a more sour taste, increase the amount to 2 Tbsp (30 mL) starter per 4 cups (1 L).

in each cube of an ice cube tray. When it's frozen, remove from ice-cube trays and store, frozen, in an airtight container. It's crucial to remember to thaw your starter several hours before you plan to make yoghurt.

2   Heat milk slowly to 180°F (82°C). (This will kill off any "bad" bacterial cultures that may be in your milk.)

3   When the milk is heated, pour it into the aluminum bowl and cool to about 100–110°F (38–43°C). (This will allow the "good" bacterial cultures to live once you have added them.) Skim off any skin that has formed.

4   While you are waiting for the milk to cool, boil water and fill a hot water bottle.

5   Whisk the starter culture in a large bowl, to return it to a liquid state. If you've already gone through this process, you can use some of your last homemade batch as your starter culture. Gradually whisk in the cooled milk, mixing very well.

6   Pour into the mason jars, put lids on them and rings to screw the lids in place. Wrap each jar in a towel and set it in the cooler (or a draft-free place) and do the same with the other jar. Put the hot water bottle between the jars so they both stay equally cozy. Close the lid of the cooler. Sit back and wait. That is, go to bed and don't think about it. I leave it overnight so I am not tempted to open the cooler to see if it is thickening (it only happened to me once that it didn't set, and so of course I have been obsessed ever since—but I think it is reasonable to assume I forgot to add the starter culture). In the morning it will have thickened (unless you screwed up like I did, but don't think negatively, it affects the atmosphere and the yoghurt will pick up on the vibes) and is ready to be stored in the refrigerator. It will keep in the fridge for approximately two weeks. But probably won't last that long.

ADDITIONS

Simple way to get thicker yogurt; add 1 Tbsp (15 mL) of dried skim milk powder to the mixture before you heat it.

ALTERNATIVES

GREEK YOGHURT: Take 4 cups (950 mL) of fat-free plain yogurt and drain it in a cheesecloth-lined strainer. Put the strainer over a bowl and place in the refrigerator overnight.

Yoghurt with vanilla powder
PHOTO BY SUSAN MUSGRAVE

VANILLA YOGHURT: Add ⅓ cup (80 mL) sugar to the milk, before the scalding process. When it has scalded and cooled to 100–110°F (38–43°C) and you have added the starter culture, stir in 2 Tbsp (30 mL) vanilla extract. I also sprinkle in about 1 tsp (5 mL) vanilla powder. I like the way it looks—little tiny pinpoints of black throughout the white.

TIP

When it comes to starter culture, less is more, for both consistency and flavour. You will find the result thicker and less acidic than you would if using a more generous hand.

Keep in mind that if you are using a store-bought yoghurt for your starter, it must contain *live and active cultures* (you can find this on the label). If it doesn't, it's probably been heat-treated and may not work. If you are not sure try with a small amount of milk (4 cups (950 mL) instead of 8).

WILD BLUEBERRY AND YOGHURT PANCAKES

12–14 4-INCH (10 CM) PANCAKES

2 large eggs, separated	1¼ cups (310 mL) unbleached all-purpose flour*
1 cup (240 mL) plain, great big fat Greek-style yoghurt	2 Tbsp (30 mL) sugar
2–4 Tbsp (30–60 mL) milk	1 Tbsp + 1 tsp (20 mL) baking powder
¼ cup (60 mL) melted butter	½ tsp (2 mL) salt
1 tsp (5 mL) lemon zest (about 1 lemon)	1 cup (240 mL) wild blueberries, rinsed and dried†
1 tsp (5 mL) vanilla extract	

*   If you want an even more nutritious pancake use ½ cup (120 mL) whole wheat flour, ½ cup (120 mL) all-purpose flour and ¼ cup (60 mL) rye flour

†   If there are no wild ones available, the tame variety will do. And yes, you can even use frozen blueberries. Huckleberries make a wonderful substitute (and they won't turn your batter blue, even if you stir them in!)

WHAT YOU DO

1   Melt butter and allow to cool slightly before adding it to the wet ingredients.

2   Whisk egg yolks and yoghurt together in a bowl. Whisk in melted (cooled) butter, lemon zest and vanilla.

3   In a separate, small bowl, combine flour, sugar, baking powder and salt. Stir dry ingredients into wet ingredients only until dry ingredients are moistened. If there are a few remaining lumps, relax. No need to call 911. Lumps is fine.

4   Beat egg whites and gently fold into the batter.

5   Do NOT stir the blueberries into the batter. Your batter will turn blue the way mine did for years until I learned this trick. (See Step 8)

6   Preheat your oven to 175°F (80°C) and have a baking sheet ready (to keep pancakes warm). Heat your skillet to the low side of medium.

7   Melt a bit of butter in the bottom of the skillet and ladle onto it a scant ¼ cup (60 mL) of batter at a time, leaving a bit of space between each pancake.

8   Now you can scatter a small handful of wild blueberries onto the top of each pancake, or the larger, domesticated (tame) variety, very carefully, one at a time. The batter will be thick, so use a spatula to gently press down on the berries. When the pancakes are dry around the edges and you can see bubbles forming on the top, about 3 to 4 minutes, flip them and cook for another 3 minutes, until golden underneath.

9   Transfer pancakes to the baking sheet in the warm oven when they are done. Serve in a stack, with maple, or, for the more adventurous, Spruce Tip (see page 110) or Wild Rose Petal Syrup (see page 134). If there are leftovers, these are delicious eaten cold.

STEWED RHUBARB WITH BEET JUICE

2 CUPS (475 ML)

"Rhubarb may not be the most romantic looking edible on earth, but it's a welcome sight in early spring, when everyone's fancy turns to thoughts of pie."
—Unknown

For years, I have been stewing rhubarb and it never occurred to me that I might be doing it all wrong. My method was to pick the rhubarb, wash it, cut it into pieces, put it in a big pot, toss in some sugar, a little water, a bit of sweet cicely* and, my secret ingredient, beet juice, and let it boil, forget about it until it burned or I luckily remembered it was boiling at which point I'd turn it off, let it cool, and stick it in the fridge. It turned out differently each time (you can always try to disguise the burned flavour of anything by adding a bit of lemon juice) so then I decided to come up with a bona fide recipe. It turns out there are actual *methods* to stewing rhubarb, that it's not all madness. When it comes to the latter, I am with Hunter S. Thompson, who allegedly wrote, "I don't advocate sex, drugs, violence and insanity to anyone, but they've always worked for me."

The beet-juice tip is courtesy of Martijn Kajuiter of the Cliff House Hotel in Ardmore, County Waterford, Ireland. I have my own family ties to Ardmore: my great-grandfather's brother and his wife had a summer house on the cliff called Rock House, and no doubt they had a kitchen garden and grew rhubarb and beets† . . . but I digress. My great-grandmother-once-removed, would have her maid boil a cauldron of water every morning and carry it down the hundreds of steps to the beach. Bridie would empty the cauldron into the sea and my great-grandmother-once-removed would enter the sea to bathe.

Anyway, my point was—the addition of beet juice turns dull greenish-brown rhubarb into a beautiful full red; it will add a sweet earthy flavour as well.

THE TWO DON'TS

Rhubarb can be harvested from April onwards, and here's what you don't do. Don't cut it with a knife, but pull the stems with a twisting motion from the bottom to ensure the entire stalk comes away from the crown. Don't remove all the stalks from each crown—always leave three behind.

---

* Sweet cicely was once a widely cultivated culinary herb, but is now only occasionally grown in the herb garden. As a culinary herb it is a valuable sweetener, especially for diabetics and many others who are trying to reduce their sugar intake. The fern-like leaves smell of aniseed when crushed.

† We grew up calling beets "beet roots." I am told they are still referred to that way in Britain, as in "Her face turned beet root red." I suppose this is to distinguish them from beet greens. Beet greens are, of course, delicious, especially with lots of butter and salt.

Rhubarb compote PHOTO BY MICHELLE FURBACHER

LEFT: Archie Stocker Sr. picks his rhubarb. PHOTO BY LIZ STOCKER; RIGHT: Rhubarb PHOTO BY ARCHIE STOCKER SR.

STEWED RHUBARB WITH
BEET JUICE (CONT'D)

6 cups (1.4 L) or more rhubarb, cut into
½-inch (1 cm) pieces*

⅔ cup (160 mL) sugar, honey or maple
syrup—more or less, to taste

A sprinkling of dried or fresh sweet
cicely (optional)

2 Tbsp (30 mL) beet juice

WHAT YOU DO

4   Unless you have access to beet juice, you'll need some fresh beets and a juicer. I make a whole whack of juice, and then freeze it in small quantities so I won't have to go through the whole messy procedure next time I want to stew rhubarb.

5   Place the rhubarb, sugar and beet juice in a heavy-ish saucepan set over medium-high heat. (Higher than medium, but not *too* high.) Cook until the sugar is dissolved and the liquid begins to boil, about 5 minutes. Turn the heat to medium-low and continue cooking, stirring occasionally, until the rhubarb pieces are very soft and disintegrate easily, about 15 minutes. Make sure any of the larger chunks, or pieces that are on the outside of the pan, away from the centre of the heat, are spooned into the middle, because you want all your rhubarb to cook evenly. When you cook rhubarb this way it doesn't end up the consistency of applesauce. It still has chunks of recognizable rhubarb throughout.

---

*   To be honest, I never measure. I just use as much rhubarb as I have on hand and adjust the other ingredients accordingly. If the stalk is thick, cut it in half lengthwise.

Rhubarb

THE COLOUR of the rhubarb stick is determined not only by a plant's variety, but also by the rate at which it grows. In early spring the stick grows much slower than in summer so the colour is retained further along its length. In midsummer, at higher temperatures, the stick grows quickly and the colour is lost, the stalk becoming green.

Rhubarb leaves and roots are poisonous due to their high levels of oxalic acid and should not be eaten. They can be made, however, into an environmentally friendly liquid strong enough to kill a variety of garden bugs. I am not advocating killing bugs, as it hasn't always worked for me.

ADDITIONS

I sometimes add grated ginger or whole star anise. Remove the anise before serving. I also like to add blood orange zest. If blood oranges are not in season, you can use the common or garden variety. I just like the name "blood orange." So I use it (and them) as much as I can.

ASIDE: BLOOD ORANGES

Blood oranges took on a new layer of meaning when I went to Sicily a few years ago for a short working holiday with my brother, Robert. At our hotel in Catania, they served huge pitchers of blood orange juice with champagne for breakfast. I am dreaming that a Sicilian cookbook might be my next project.

I've included an excerpt from my essay, "Silent in its Shout: A Long Weekend in Sicilia," which won first prize in *Accenti* magazine's creative non-fiction contest in 2012. I am hoping this qualifies me as Italian-Canadian. Should help me land an Italian cookbook contract and a trip or two to visit the land of my adopted birth. I already have the title. *Blood Oranges*. This was also the astonishing title of an extraordinary novel by John Hawkes, but titles are not copyrightable and Jack (as we called him) is, alas, dead. But I know he would have approved of my title. I can hear him, sometimes at night when the cold wind blows, whispering, "*Blood Oranges*. You have to write a cookbook called *Blood Oranges*, Susie."

> *Over a "hair of the dog" champagne breakfast the next morning, we plan our itinerary. If we are to get out of Catania we will need a car: Robert has torn a coupon from an airline magazine with a special offer: 21 Euros a day with unlimited mileage. When he calls the company they advise him that the correct price is 80 Euros, the magazine*

offer probably "just a promotion". It doesn't take us long to figure out that pretty much everything in Sicily is negotiable.

I go online and book a car; we take a taxi back to the airport. The man at the Locauto desk looks up from his tabloid, taps on his keyboard, and indicates, in rapid Sicilian mixed with sign language, he has no cars for hire. I look over his shoulder to where rows of car keys hang on hooks. Probably just a promotion.

I check my watch: more than half our first day is shot. We spent thousands of dollars getting here and will probably spend our whole long weekend in Catania looking for things I have lost—my luggage, my car reservation, and after an hour of arguing in sign language with the man from Locauto, my mind. I am starting to think Locauto is just a money-laundering front. I am jet-lagged and hungover and in no mood to suffer La Cosa Nostra gladly. I take my brother's arm and head for the door.

"But what about your deposit?" my brother says. "You gave them your Visa number online."

In this moment I am the embodiment of the old Sicilian proverb: "Revenge is a dish which people of taste prefer to eat cold."

"We will kill them," I say. Icily.

The man from Locauto tosses aside his tabloid, signals "momento," and reaches for his telephone. He talks fast, taps on his keyboard and his printer springs to life, spitting out contracts. He is sweating, dodging the bullets he clearly sees spraying from my eyes. He shows me where to sign, plucks a set of keys off a hook, then leads us out into the parking lot under a blue, unappeasable sky.

WELSH GRIDDLE CAKES

MAKES 3–4 DOZEN, DEPENDING ON SIZE

"Thank you for making the best Welsh cakes I've had outside of my Gran's kitchen. You run a wonderful house and the welcome you give travelers can't be forced. My wife has endured two days of me talking about nothing else except Haida Gwaii and the people I met. She knows the islands pretty well but is now resigned to cancelling all our overseas trips indefinitely, so that we can concentrate on coming back to Haida Gwaii instead. Personally, I blame the Welsh cakes you made."

—John Davies, October 2011

I have been trying to find a way to connect Wales with Haida Gwaii, but I can't. I don't even have any Welsh ancestors. But the testament quoted above, from a guest at Copper Beech House, I feel allows me to include one of my favourite recipes in this book. I make these for breakfast, but also for afternoon tea.

Welsh cakes are so named because they are traditionally cooked on a bakestone or a cast iron griddle. They are flat like a thick pancake, as flaky and dense as a scone, and as toothsome as a cookie. The mothers and miners' wives of Wales used to make Welsh cakes—also known as bakestones, griddle cakes, Welsh tea cakes and Welsh miner cakes—for their children to lunch on at school and their husbands to take down into the mines.

I started making Welsh cakes when I moved to Port Clements in 1971. I had Bee Nilson's *The Penguin Cookery Book* and, well, it's what I had in those days. I still own the book, though it is missing both covers and everything after page 326, but this is where I learned to make Girdle Scones, "a traditional and popular fayre." I always suspected "girdle" was an allusion to the uncomfortable undergarment women wore in less liberated times. You cannot eat just one Girdle scone. Especially when they are so small. You probably eat six. And then your girdle gets tight. You can see where I am going with this.

Welsh griddle cakes have received attention in the media recently because Ann Romney, wife of Mitt Romney, the Republican nominee in the 2012 US presidential election is apparently a fan; Mrs. Romney's father hails from Wales. She has been serving Welsh cakes on her husband's campaign bus. Please do not let this stop you from trying these. Just close your eyes and—think of Wales. Not politics. Or girdles.

3 cups (700 mL) all-purpose flour	¼ tsp (1 mL) ground mace
1½ tsp (7 mL) baking powder	1 cup (240 mL) butter
½tsp (2 mL) baking soda	¾ cup (180 mL) currants
¼ tsp (1 mL) salt	¼ cup (60 mL) candied peel, finely chopped
1 scant cup (240 mL) sugar	2 eggs, beaten
1 tsp (5 mL) freshly ground nutmeg	6 Tbsp (90 mL) milk

WHAT YOU DO

1 Sift dry ingredients together.

2 Cut in butter until the texture of fine crumbs is formed.

3 Add currants, peel, eggs and milk; mix to a stiff dough.

4 Roll out to ¼ inch (6 mm) thickness—try to handle the dough as little as possible—and cut out in 2-inch (5 cm) rounds with a fluted cookie cutter. (The landlady at the MacKenzie House B&B in Fort Macleod made a batch of Welsh cakes for me when I arrived. She insisted the traditional shaped cookie-cutter was fluted, but I don't think anyone is going to hold it against you if you use any less traditional shape!)

5 Cook on low heat on a lightly greased preheated griddle, cast-iron frying pan or electric frying pan set at 250°F (120°C). Cook 4 minutes per side until golden brown.

6   Serve hot, by themselves, or with butter, jam or cheese. Serve them cold, cookie-style, after flavours have mellowed. Toast them, and then sprinkle with icing or berry sugar.

TIP: I have seen some recipes for Welsh cakes that use half lard/half butter. My grandmother used bacon fat in all her baking—rock cakes, scones, even in the loaves of white bread she baked every day. I think this is what made her baked goods so tender and flaky. They never tasted of bacon, either.

CHAPTER THREE: From the Forage of the Oven

WILD YEAST LEAVEN ("SOURDOUGH") BREAD

"It [sourdough] feeds the soul as much as it feeds the stomach."
—Richard Bertinet

My first experience with sourdough was in the Yukon many years ago, on a reading tour for National Book Week with the poet David McFadden. We had been plunked down at Mac's Fireweed Books in Whitehorse, in front of the sourdough starter (which the store offered as an additional enticement to customers, along with souvenirs of the North, such as the "legendary Alaska Ulu Knife") that was on sale. No one bought any of our books, but we sold a whole load of the starter.

Eventually we came up with the genius idea to change our nametags to Margaret Atwood and Pierre Berton. We sold even more sourdough starter after that.

Sourdough was the name given to the distinctive, pungent smelling bread baked in Northern California during the Klondike Gold Rush. Prospectors took either the bread or a bit of "starter" with them when they travelled further north. The scruffy miners, who frequently carried a pouch of starter around their neck or on a belt tied to their waist (or sometimes even slept with it in their beds) during the coldest months to keep it warm, were referred to as "sourdoughs" due to the smell that often emanated from their living quarters because of their fermenting concoctions.

There is more folklore, misinformation and anxiety surrounding sourdough starter than there is about making a baby. "Remember to breathe," might be the best advice a sourdough doula can give. Making a sourdough starter, and subsequently, bread, can be an anxiety producing experience, but it needn't be. People have been using sourdough for as long as the Haida have inhabited Haida Gwaii without much understanding of what sourdough is or how it works. It's a similar situation to having a baby—without much understanding of what a baby is or how it works. Most people just *do* it. And it usually all works out in the end.

THE STARTER
ALSO KNOWN AS THE MOTHER DOUGH, OR SIMPLY MOTHER

Making your own starter is fairly simple—but it does require a commitment. Be prepared to feed and care for your starter for up to three weeks before you even

The Mother PHOTO BY MICHELLE FURBACHER

begin to think about baking. I haven't included a recipe here for that initial process, but there are many helpful websites, such as Flourish (please see Further Reading, page 359) that will give you an illustrated step-by-step guide to making your own sourdough starter.

Personally I recommend cheating—obtaining your starter from a friend who, unlike you, has had three weeks to sit and watch his starter grow. I was given mine by the artist Michael Drebert who worked at Copper Beech House in the summer of 2011. I used his sourdough bread recipe for a year, kneading my loaves, until I discovered a preindustrial European slow-rise fermentation technique, and I stopped kneading and started "turning" instead . . . but I am jumping ahead of myself. That's what I tend to do when I am thinking about sourdough bread. I get excited and then I go off madly in all directions at once.

CARING FOR YOUR STARTER

A sourdough starter has a lot in common with a pet. Like a dog or cat, it needs food, water, a safe environment and oxygen. It is a living, breathing thing, with distinct moods and personality. Some cultures are delicate and require careful handling, others are almost bulletproof. Some require hours of therapy, others are well adjusted and easygoing. You get the picture. (When we were issued a tsunami warning after the 7.7 earthquake struck in October 2012, I am sorry to say I didn't take my cat, Boo, with me when we evacuated; I took my sourdough starter instead.)

Ever noticed how, when a friend gets tired of your company, or feels he might be outstaying his welcome, he (or she) will say, "I have to go home and check on my dog." What's to check, I always wonder (but don't ask)? Buddy is not likely to die of starvation or Owner Absentee Syndrome if his owner stays for another glass of beer. Too often these days, when I'm out visiting, I find myself saying, "I have to go home now and feed my starter." I have not gone so far as to give my starter a name, though I know one woman who christened hers Lance. Not long after that, her boyfriend moved out.

In a normal starter, mixed and allowed to stand at room temperature, a love story emerges between two types of microorganisms: yeast and bacteria. It's like two partners in a marriage. They're perfectly matched for each other, so any interlopers don't stand a chance. (Touch wood.)

Observation on Human Nature

How empty the white bowl
by the back door waiting to be
filled, lonely the cracked
rubber ball, sad the comforter
abandoned on the grass. Fetch,
death said, and they left to chase
the wind: three good dogs,
Bubba, Nike, and Slu'gu.

This poem was included in *Obituary of Light: the Sangan River Meditations,* published by Leaf Press. When I read it at the launch, at Trout House Restaurant on Tow Hill Road, a dog in the audience howled when I got to the last line. (Everyone and their dog's a critic.)

What I discovered, though, is that if you include the names of your friends' dogs in a book, they (the friends, not the dogs) will buy multiple copies. Imagine (she imagined, slyly) how many copies I could sell if I included *photographs* of dogs, not just names.

TOP: Brutus, Guy Kimola's owner PHOTO BY GUY KIMOLA;
BOTTOM: Banty, Chris and Elin's owner PHOTO BY ELIN PRICE

Left for a few days at room temperature, your starter will begin to ferment (I think this is where the love story analogy ends, though my friends who practise family law would say that is debatable.) As long as the starter dough is "fed" a small, fresh amount of flour and water daily in equal measure, the sourdough mixture can stay at room temperature indefinitely. It will continue to be healthy and usable. It can be refrigerated, but must be brought back to normal room temperature before using it to make bread.

HOW OFTEN TO FEED?

If your sourdough starter is at room temperature, feed it every day. Try to feed it at the same time. It will look forward to meal time and reward you with a wag of its tail (pet analogy—dog) or complete indifference (pet analogy—cat). The morning

works best for me because I usually think more clearly, especially after a cup of tea strong enough you wouldn't need faith to walk on it (as they'd say in Ireland.)

If your starter is refrigerated, you should still feed it once a week. But I sometimes go away for longer than a week and we have both survived the period of separation.

One year my youngest daughter was given a Talking Nano Baby for Christmas—a virtual pet she had to feed, put to sleep, wake up and otherwise care for. My daughter soon tired of the responsibility and stuffed the Nano pet under a cushion in the chesterfield where she hoped its batteries would expire quietly, but I still hear its plaintive voice growing weaker every day. "Feed me. I'm sick."

Your sourdough starter probably isn't going to speak to you (and if you think it is speaking to you, it may be time for you to get a dog, if you don't already have one). They are more used to suffering in silence, but if you don't feed it, a sinister blue-black or pinkish-purplish mold will eventually begin to appear on the surface. This means you have been a negligent parent and that your starter has likely kicked the bucket and should be given a decent burial. There's a lot of self-help out there when it comes to the death of a starter, books like *What To Do When Your Starter Dies*, and so on.

WHY REFRIGERATE?

There the starter will go dormant and stop growing.

Depending on how long your starter sits in the fridge, you may find a layer of nasty looking liquid on top of your starter (not to be confused with the blue-black-pinkish-purplish colour previously described). This is called the "hooch," (not to be confused with moonshine) and is a normal part of the sourdough's life. I simply swirl it in to mix it all up, then feed my starter once it has come to room temperature. Some people prefer to pour it off and feed the starter with slightly more water at the next feeding.

Ideally, a starter should be taken out and fed the night before it is used in baking.

HOW MUCH TO FEED?

My method for feeding is simple. Every morning I pour out just under half a cup of starter (3 Tbsp/45 mL to be precise) and keep it for another use; I give it to a friend, use it in other recipes (sourdough pizza crust or waffles) or (worst case scenario) mix it in with my compost and hope that any lurking rodents have gone gluten-free. Then I add 2 Tbsp (30 g) of flour and a scant 2 Tbsp (30 mL) of warm water, stir well, and loosely cover.

At first, having to throw out so much starter every day went against everything I believe in, which can be summed up by what my father said, frequently, as we refused to eat our cold porridge: "waste not, want not." I am not one to waste

LEFT: Sweetpea, Danny Escott's owner PHOTO BY EVELYN LAVRISA

RIGHT: Dark Star, Meredith Adams' owner PHOTO BY SUSAN MUSGRAVE

LEFT: Heidi, Randy Martin's owner
PHOTO BY PETER SLOAN

TOP RIGHT: Brokeback Boo,
The Author's owner PHOTO BY
KIMBERLEY FRENCH*

BOTTOM RIGHT: River Blue and
Willow Littlefoot, witnesses
at Tina and Jiro's wedding,
August 2013, North Beach
PHOTO BY MICHELLE FURBACHER

anything in the kitchen (my children call me the Leftover Queen)—I come from a long line of public-spirited Leftover Queens and Kings who went on rationing their food even after the world wars were over. My Great Aunt Polly made an onion last 27 days during wartime, and an ounce of tea for almost three weeks. She was gracious enough not to criticize me when I easily added two or three chopped onions to a stew, and fresh tea leaves to the pot every time I needed more of "the cup that cheers but does not inebriate."

Why discard so much of your starter at each feeding? Unless you do your starter will softly, calmly, take over your house, like "The Eggplant That Ate Chicago," only a gooier version. It's the stuff a horror movie could be made of. Keeping the volume down helps balance the pH and offers the wild yeast more to chew on every time you give it something to eat.

* Kimberley was a favourite guest at Copper Beech House and is famous for taking stills of film stars for major motion pictures. The poster you have probably seen promoting *Brokeback Mountain?* She shot that picture. This is why I have taken to calling my handsome boy Brokeback Boo. And also because he likes the lads.

If you believed everything you've heard or read you'd think that you'd need to nurture your starter for a hundred years to get a truly decent sourdough loaf. I don't know how many times I've heard people refer to their "100-year-old sourdough starter," but this, I think, is a case of sourdough starter one-upsmanship. The reality is, very old cultures are unlikely to have stayed unchanged.

Environmental conditions can radically change the blend of bacteria and yeast that live in a sourdough starter. So if you get some starter from a friend, feed it in the unique environment of your kitchen and bake with it regularly, it will incorporate the wild yeasts in your house and become entirely your own; it is no longer the same starter you got from your friend. If you took your sourdough culture and moved to Luxor (the Ancient Egyptian city of Thebes, not the Egyptian-themed hotel and casino in Las Vegas) and started baking there in the ambient temperatures, and tested the culture after a few months, you'd find something very different than what you started out with. I won't speculate on what sort of culture you'd end up with if you relocated your starter to an hotel in Vegas, but suffice it to say the taste fingerprint of each dough is unique to its home.

To summarize, a sourdough starter needs:

- **FOOD:** Sourdough is fed with flour. I use all-purpose white flour.

- **WATER:** I use my tap water, which is from a well. Heavily chlorinated water may kill a starter and should sit for 24 hours before being used. Bottled water is good, but not distilled water, which doesn't contain the necessary minerals.

- **ENVIRONMENT:** I house my starter in a glass quart jar, on the counter where I can keep an eye on it, being one of those helicopter mothers (when it comes to sourdough). Any plastic or glass container is fine. Avoid metal, which can affect the flavour.

- **OXYGEN:** When feeding my starter, I stir it vigorously to incorporate air. I cover my jar loosely with a lid (leaving a gap so the starter can breathe) to allow room for it to expand but to keep out dust.

- **EXERCISE:** A starter that is fed and used regularly will be more healthy and active than a starter that is abandoned in the fridge for long periods of time, but it is possible to neglect a starter and leave it refrigerated for several weeks (possibly even longer) and bring it back to a useful and fulfilling life.

Bread PHOTO BY MICHELLE FURBACHER

MAKING WILD YEAST LEAVEN BREAD

ENOUGH LEAVEN FOR 2 LOAVES

"In France I had fallen in love with the sweet, creamy flavour of bread fermented with wild yeast leaven that contradicts the widespread perception of 'sourdough.' I wanted anything but sour bread. I wanted a deep auburn crust to shatter between the teeth, giving way to tender, pearlescent crumb. I wanted my baker's signature, the score made with a blade on top, to rise and fissure, and the crust to be set with dangerous edges."
—*Tartine Bread* by Chad Robertson

Income earned by writers, composers, visual artists and sculptors from the sale of their works in Ireland is exempt from tax. The Irish BAR association tried to have the practice of law designated an "art" so that lawyers, too, could weasel out of paying income tax, but they didn't win their case.

Bread-making is an art, no question. But it can also be also an exacting science (no more "a cup or so of this," and "a pinch of that" the way Grannie used to bake, or a soupçon of this, a poignée of that, if your grand-mère was French). Close readers will observe that nowhere else in this book do I use grams and millilitres in such an obsessive-compulsive way as I do when I write about making bread; I prefer the old-fashioned teaspoons, cups and pecks. (Well, maybe not pecks.)

Most North Americans do not own scales, and for many home bakers measuring cups are fine (unless you are neurotic and a perfectionist like me.) Most baking professionals use weights exclusively, arguing that weighing ingredients is important to achieving consistency, which is desirable, of course, if you have customers lined upside your door before bakery opening time. Editors insist on including both volume and weight measurements in cookbooks,* but it is my opinion (one to which everyone else is entitled) that once you start weighing your flour you will never want to use any other method. The reason for this is that the type of flour, the humidity, room temperature, how the flour fluffs up and even the way it is scooped affects the volume. Weights are accurate. 1,000 grams of flour is never anything but 1,000 grams. I approach the task of bread-making the way I approach writing, with excruciating attention to detail, because the end result (in the case of the former) is a formidable loaf of bread and to do it any other way would be to disappoint the gazillion people who have claimed they will buy my book "just to have that sourdough bread recipe."

If you still have doubts about the merits of weights over measures, try this simple exercise. Measure 1 cup of flour at least seven times and weigh it each time on a digital scale set to grams (grams are much more precise than ounces, as there are approximately 30 grams in an ounce, 28.34 to be precise. Most of my generation

---

* Editor's Note: We insist for the benefit of all those people who don't own scales, Susan is correct that measuring by mass or weight is more accurate.

only learned metric in the '60s when we experimented with drugs which were, for some reason, sold in grams and "keys"). I guarantee you that you will get seven different results.

Jim Lahey, author of *My Bread: The Revolutionary No-Work, No-Knead Method*, doesn't think imprecision is any kind of a handicap. "I encourage a somewhat careless approach," he says, "and figure this may even be a disappointment to those who expect something more difficult. The proof is in the loaf." If you don't want to use weights, then don't. The bread will probably be just as delicious.

There are as many ways of making sourdough bread as there are ways of smoking salmon (See Debriefing Smoked Salmon, page 178) But I am hooked on this European bread-making technique, so much so that I have become a slave to it. I take my wet dough with me, for the four hours during its "first rise," when I go grocery shopping (I leave it in the car inside an insulated box with a hot water bottle) or when I volunteer at the Thrift Shop. I lug it to beach barbecues in the summer and potlucks in winter, or else I would have no social life. Making my wild yeast leaven bread has driven me, on more than one occasion, to the brink of (as John Lennon would say) "a nervous breadvan."

WHAT YOU WILL NEED

A digital scale* or measuring cups	A wooden spoon or spatula†
A small scoop for flour	A bench knife or dough scraper
A wide bowl for mixing; plus two wicker baskets (or bowls) where the loaves can do their final rise	A lame (pronounced "lahm")‡
	A Dutch oven.* I have two, so I can bake two loaves at the same time.

---

*   I weigh all my ingredients—even the water. I bought a digital scale the dimensions of an iPad, and bright purple (though they come in an array of tempting colours) and now I don't know how I lived without it. I use it every time I need to measure 1 ounce of cottage cheese—when I go back on a Weight Watchers regime because of eating too much of my own bread.

†   The Egyptians mixed their batches of dough with a hoe, according to Jim Lahey, author of *My Bread*.

‡   A double-sided blade used to slash or score the tops of loaves just before the bread is placed in the oven. Often the blade's cutting edge will be slightly concave-shaped, which allows bakers to score the loaves, or cut flaps considerably thinner than would be possible with a traditional straight razor. They are cheap to buy and well worth it. The first time I made this bread I used a kitchen knife to make my signature score. FAIL.

*   A thick-gauge, large pot with a heavy, relatively tight fitting lid. The idea is to create a steam oven inside the pan. The steam is what produces a nice crisp crust.

THE LEAVEN (STEP 1)

Once you have begged, borrowed, purchased or captured your own wild yeast and made a starter from scratch, you are ready to move on to the next step.

INGREDIENTS

½ cup + 5.5 Tbsp (200 mL) warm water

1 Tbsp (15 mL) mature starter

1 cup (100 g) Best for Bread* white flour

1 cup (100 g) Best for Bread multi-grain flour

WHAT YOU DO

1   The night before you plan to make the dough, measure warm water into a bowl and mix in the mature starter. Feed with white and multi-grain flour.

2   Cover with a kitchen towel, and let rest overnight. To test leaven's readiness, drop a spoonful into a bowl of room-temperature water. If it sinks, it is not ready and needs more time to ferment and ripen. (This is beginning to sound awfully like the Salem witch trials . . .)

*   Bread flour has more protein than all-purpose flour, so it's sturdier and helps produce rustic loaves with a good chew.

3 If your house is cold, you will have to wait longer before the float-test works. Sometimes I make my leaven around 8 p.m. but if the woodstove burns out during the night and the house cools down I have to wait until early afternoon the next day to begin my bread. It can take anywhere from 12 to 18 hours, depending on the temperature of your house.

CLASSIC SOURDOUGH BREAD MAKES 2 LOAVES

"The best thing since sliced bread."
—Guest at Copper Beech House

THE DOUGH (STEP 2)

NOTE: Conversions to volume measures, in some cases, are not precise, but have been rounded off for convenience.

3 cups (700 mL) + scant ¼ cup (50 mL) warm water, divided	1 cup (100 g) Best for Bread multi-grain flour
1 cup (200 g) leaven	4 tsp (20 g) salt
5 cups (900 g) Best for Bread white flour	Rice flour for dusting

WHAT YOU DO

1 Pour 3 cups (700 mL) warm water into a large glass bowl and add leaven. Stir to disperse. (What to do with your leftover starter? See "How Much To Feed" page 69. Same thing. Make pancakes, give it away or feed it to the ravens.)

2 Add flours and mix dough with your hands until no bits of dry flour remain. Let rest, covered, for 40 minutes.

3 Dissolve salt in remaining scant ¼ cup (50 mL) warm water, and massage into the dough with your hands until everything is well combined.

4 Cover with a kitchen towel, and let rest for 30 minutes.

BULK RISE (STEP 3)

The dough will now begin its first rise (called bulk fermentation or bulk rise) to develop flavour and strength.

5   In this bread-making method, you are going to forget about kneading your bread; the long, slow rise of a very wet dough does over hours what intensive kneading does in minutes. I know that kneading, punching it down, was in my mother's day one way a lot of women used to get rid of their seriously pent-up aggressions. My mother always claimed kneading was the perfect outlet for her frustration at being made to go out on the boat every weekend; she felt she was punching my father, presumably, though neither of my parents were given to domestic violence. I can't help but feel this kind of sublimated behaviour would have permeated the bread and transferred over to those who ate it, like me, for example. Mum made 12 loaves of bread every week.

TOP LEFT: Adding leaven to water PHOTO BY MICHELLE FURBACHER

TOP RIGHT: Adding flour to leaven and water PHOTO BY MICHELLE FURBACHER

BOTTOM LEFT: All the flour added PHOTO BY MICHELLE FURBACHER

BOTTOM RIGHT: Mixing the flour PHOTO BY MICHELLE FURBACHER

6   So no kneading, punching, or even having nasty thoughts about what you might like to do to the homogeneous blob of wet dough that resembles your partner's head. Instead you are going to allow the dough to develop by "turning" it, doing a stretch and fold, every half hour (I set a timer or else I'd never remember when 30 minutes was up) for 4 hours or until you see a 20 to 30 percent increase in volume. (I usually turn my bread for four hours but then let it sit for another hour or more until it reaches the top of my bowl. Something to remember: **It isn't the time or the room temperature that is critical. It is the percentage rise.)** This series of turns, I believe, is what gives you a chewy-textured bread full of big holes on the inside, what bakers refer to as an "open crumb."

7   To turn your dough, wet your hands so the dough won't stick to your fingers, reach down into the bottom of the bowl sliding your hands underneath the mass, and lift it, stretching it, folding it back over itself. For every turn, stretch and fold the dough two or three times. Do this turn technique, two or three times, every 30 minutes.

THE BENCH REST (STEP 4)

8   When the volume has increased and the bread holds its shape when you turn it, you are ready to move on to the next stage, which is called the bench rest. Tip the dough out of the container using your hands and a spatula to release any bits of dough still sticking to the sides of the bowl. Transfer to a large floured (I use rice flour) cutting board. Cut the dough in half using your bench knife, and shape each piece into a smooth and firm round.

9   Cover with a kitchen towel, and let rest on the work surface for 30 minutes.

FINAL SHAPING (STEP 5)

10 This sounds far more complicated than it is, like trying to explain to someone how to breathe. You are going to perform a series of folds, wrapping up on each loaf so that it holds its form and springs up when baked.

11 Work with one round at a time. Fold envelope-style, 4 times. Lift up the edge closest to you and fold it into the middle. Take the edge on the left, stretch it out, and then fold it down into the middle. Do the same with the right hand edge. Finally lift up the far edge of the round, the one farthest away from you,

and bring it down over the middle, then turn the dough over so the seam is underneath. This whole process should take less than a minute. Doing it is easier than describing it. The dough is fairly forgiving and seems to do what it is supposed to do even if you don't know what *you* are doing. I would go so far as to say my bread dough has a mind of its own, and yours will, too.

12 Line 2 medium baskets (or bowls) with clean kitchen towels; generously dust with rice flour. Transfer each round to the towel-lined basket and fold the towels over the bread so your loaves are covered.

THE FINAL RISE (STEP 6)

You can do one of two things: let the loaves rise at warm room temperature for 4 hours before baking, or "retard" the process by placing the loaves, wrapped snugly in their baskets, in the fridge overnight (up to 12 hours) and bake them first thing in the morning. The chilly environment delays the fermentation but doesn't stop it. I find the dough easier to handle when it is cold, and the end result seems to have developed a more pronounced flavour.

SCORING AND BAKING (STEP 7)

13 Twenty minutes before you are ready to bake the bread, preheat oven, with your Dutch oven inside (or any heavy ovenproof pot with a tight-fitting lid), to 500°F (260°C).

14 Lift a loaf out of its basket, still wrapped in towel, and then score the top of the loaf using your lame. A slash on the loaf's surface allows the dough to properly expand in the oven without tearing the crust. Proper scoring allows you to control exactly where the loaf will open or "bloom," and gives you a chance, after all your hard work, to be creative. **I cut a triangle on the top of my multi-grain loaves, a square on the white, and a deep X across loaves of my rye flour bread.** This way the loaves are instantly recognizable when I want to identify them in the freezer. Not that many loaves make it to the freezer. The smell of the bread as it springs up and out of the oven seems to lure visitors to my door, and who would *not* want to share a perfect loaf that took over 30 hours to make, from start to finish, while it is still warm?

15 Remove the Dutch oven from your oven (so you don't burn your hands trying to maneuver the loaf into it), lift the loaf from towel and drop it into the

TOP LEFT: Classic sourdough, multi-grain and rye breads scored PHOTO BY MICHELLE FURBACHER; TOP RIGHT: A chewy-textured bread full of big holes on the inside PHOTO BY MICHELLE FURBACHER; BOTTOM: Blood Orange Olive Oil with a good balsamic vinegar and carrot carving by Jiro Ooishi at the wedding feast he prepared for his bride, Tina, on North Beach PHOTO BY MICHELLE FURBACHER

Dutch oven. Cover with lid. Return to oven, and reduce temperature to 450°F (230°C). Bake for 20 minutes.

16 Carefully remove lid (a cloud of steam will be released). Bake until crust is deep golden brown, 20 minutes more.

17 Transfer loaf to a wire rack. It will feel light and sound hollow when tapped. Let cool. The most delightful part of this stage is listening to the bread pop, or "sing"—the hard, crisp crust contracting—as it cools.

18 To bake the second loaf, put the Dutch oven back in your oven and raise oven temperature back to 500°F (260°C). Repeat baking instructions.

SUBSTITUTIONS

Instead of tap water, use water in which potatoes have been boiled. It contains nutrients your starter will love, and adds even more flavour to your loaves.

TIP

If your loaf is hot out of the oven, or even still slightly warm, cut the loaf in half, lay the cut side down and then slice with a very sharp bread knife. If you don't cut the loaf in half it will "squish" down when you cut it.

TIP

I dip my bread in a puddle of Blood Orange Olive Oil with the best quality balsamic vinegar splashed in the middle. I also like Cara Cara Orange Vanilla White Balsamic Vinegar these days.

MULTI-GRAIN SOURDOUGH BREAD

MAKES 2 LOAVES

Since I began making sourdough bread I have experimented with many different kinds of flour. They say the most beautiful house in the world is the one you build yourself; I suspect the tastiest flour in the world is the kind you grind yourself in your personal flour mill. But that's somewhere down the road for me. Right now I dream of King Arthur (the flour many bakers recommend) but am loyal to Robin Hood, partly because I have a soft spot for outlaws, and also because their Best for Bread brands consistently makes loaves that behave the way I want them to. I brought a bag of Red Fife Wheat home with me to the Island, because so many people had recommended it, but found the loaves I baked were drier than what I am used to when I stick to flour milled exclusively for bread.

FOR THE DOUGH

3¼ cups (750 mL) + scant ¼ (50 mL) warm water, divided

5½ Cups (700 g) Best For Bread white flour

1 cup (200 g) leaven

4 tsp (20 g) salt

2½ cups (300 g) Best For Bread multi-grain flour*

Rice flour for dusting

WHAT YOU DO

1   The night before you plan to make your bread, prepare the leaven as directed in step 1 of the Classic Sourdough Bread (see page 76).

2   In the morning, pour the 3¼ cups (750 mL) warm water into a large mixing bowl. Add the leaven and stir to disperse. Add the multi-grain and the white flour. Use your hands to mix the dough thoroughly until no bits of dry flour are left in the bowl. Let the dough rest in the bowl for 40 minutes.

3   Dissolve salt in remaining scant ¼ cup (50 mL) warm water, and massage into the dough with your hands.

4   Follow STEP 3 (Bulk Rise) through STEP 7 (Scoring and Baking) on pages 77–81 for making and baking the loaves.

COUNTRY RYE MAKES 2 LOAVES

Rye flour absorbs more water than white or multi-grain or whole-wheat flour so it creates super sturdy loaves of bread. Many people use rye flour for their sourdough starter because it attracts more natural yeasts than many other flours.

FOR THE DOUGH

1 cup (200 g) leaven

6½ cups (830 g) Best for Bread white flour

3¼ cups (750 mL) + scant ¼ cup (50 mL) warm water, divided

4 tsp (20 g) salt

¾ cup (170 g) medium-fine whole-rye flour

*   You can use whole wheat flour instead, of course.

Gluten

BEFORE WE had commercial yeast, most bread was made in the "sourdough style," with its signature cavernous holes. Those holes develop during the process of fermentation; good bacteria breaks down the gluten proteins, thereby reducing or even eliminating the gluten content all together.

Italian food scientists found that gluten content was much lower in breads that were made in the traditional, old-world style. The difference was so stark that celiacs in their study were able to consume the sourdough with no ill effects. (Could this be why so many of my gluten-sensitive friends do fine on bread and cheese in France or love the pizza in Italy?)

WHAT YOU DO

1   The night before you make your bread, prepare the leaven as directed in step 1 of the Classic Sourdough Bread (see page 76).

2   In the morning, pour the 3¼ cups (750 mL) warm water into a large mixing bowl. Add the leaven and stir to disperse. Add the rye and the white flour. Use your hands to mix the dough thoroughly until no bits of dry flour are left in the bowl. Let the dough rest in the bowl for 40 minutes.

3   Dissolve the salt in remaining scant ¼ cup (50 mL) warm water, and massage into the dough with your hands.

4   Follow STEP 3 (Bulk Rise) through STEP 7 (Scoring and Baking) on pages 77–81 for making and baking the loaves.

FIG, ANISE, HAZELNUT AND GORGONZOLA SOURDOUGH BREAD

MAKES 2 LOAVES

I've adapted this toothsome recipe from Michele Genest's *The Boreal Gourmet: Adventures in Northern Cooking*. Michele uses 1 tsp (5 mL) yeast dissolved in 1½ cups (350 mL) warm water but I decided to rely on my sourdough starter alone, and use the no-knead method (for Classic Sourdough Bread) and it was a great success. I also left out the semolina flour. I didn't have anise seeds so went to a grocery store in Masset to buy a bottle, and when I got home checked the expiry date, which was cleverly hidden beneath a peel-back label: 2002. But even

10-year-old anise seed had flavour, at least a hint of one. I can only assume that fresh seeds would be 10-years-more intense.

1 cup (200 g) leaven	2 Tbsp (30 mL) anise seeds
3¼ cups (750 mL) + scant ¼ cup (50 mL) warm water	1½ cups (350 mL) dried figs, chopped
2½ cups (300 g) Best for Bread multi-grain flour	1 cup (240 mL) toasted hazelnuts*, chopped
5½ cups (700 g) Best for Bread white flour	4 tsp (20 g) salt
2 Tbsp (30 mL) olive oil	1 cup (240 mL) crumbled Gorgonzola

WHAT YOU DO

1   The night before you plan to make your bread, prepare the leaven as directed in step 1 (The Leaven) of the Classic Sourdough Bread (see page 76).

2   In the morning, pour the 3¼ cups (750 mL) warm water into a large mixing bowl. Add the leaven and stir to disperse. Add the flours, olive oil, anise seeds, dried figs and toasted hazelnuts. Use your hands to mix the dough thoroughly until no bits of dry flour are left in the bowl. Let the dough rest in the bowl for 40 minutes.

3   Dissolve the salt in remaining scant ¼ cup (50 mL) warm water, and massage into the dough with your hands.

4   Follow STEPS 3 (Bulk Rise) through 4 (Bench Rest) for Classic Sourdough Bread on pages 77 and 78.

5   As in STEP 3 of the Classic Sourdough Loaf you are now going to perform a series of folds, which will build tension inside each loaf so that it holds its form and springs up when baked (this dramatic rise is known to those in the bread-baking business as the "oven spring.")

---

*   TIP: To toast, place raw hazelnuts on a dry baking sheet and roast for about 8 to 10 minutes in a 325°F (160°C) oven until skins turn dark and begin to blister. Watch them carefully during the last 2 minutes—you don't want them to burn. Remove from oven, let cool for a few minutes, then remove skins by rubbing nuts together in a clean kitchen towel. Don't expect to have completely denuded nuts, but most of the skin will rub off if you keep at it.

6   Working with one loaf at a time, press the loaf into a flat circle with your fingertips. Sprinkle half of your crumbled Gorgonzola over the surface. Fold the near edge into the centre and tuck in the ends and turn the dough so the far edge is now the near edge, fold it into the centre, tuck in the ends and pinch the seams closed.

7   Place loaf in a floured tea towel in a medium-sized bowl. Cover with a tea towel. Repeat process with the second loaf.

8   Follow STEPS 6 (Final Rise) through 7 (Scoring and Baking) on page 79 for final rising, scoring and baking the loaves.

MOON OVER NAIKOON

In March 2010, in the middle of a southeast gale, I was making my Welsh Griddle Cakes (see recipe page 58) when Angie Long, a poet and long-time resident of Haida Gwaii, dropped by with a bottle of Tia Maria. She had been house sitting and polished off a bottle she'd found in her friends' cupboard, and had bought a replacement. Only theirs had been a quarter full, so Angie didn't feel the need to replace the whole amount. She suggested we break open the bottle and treat ourselves to a drop.

I can vouchsafe: griddle cakes and Tia Maria are a mighty combination in a gale. We had almost emptied the bottle to the replacement level (that is, we drank three-quarters of it) as the trees outside my windows bent over double and the

LEFT: Moon Over Naikoon Bakery before the fire PHOTO BY ARCHIE STOCKER SR.

RIGHT: Wendy Riley cooking at old Moon Over Naikoon Bakery PHOTO BY ARCHIE STOCKER SR.

rain blew past us sideways in sheets—when a fire truck, lights and sirens blazing, roared by. One thing about the volunteer fire department, they never fail to respond.

We found the top to the bottle, and sobered up. Angie lived "out the road," (how Islanders describe anyone who lives out of Masset, on Tow Hill Road) in the direction the fire truck was headed, where her husband Giuseppe and their cat Penelope would be hunkered down in The Spare Girl cabin (see "Paul Bower, Beachcomber" on page 256).

We piled into my truck and drove, and, just after the sign warning Fresh Bread Ahead, saw flames shooting through the trees. Our beloved off-the-grid bakery, with the Whale Museum inside, was well on its way to being burned to the ground. The trees all around were burning, too, and Giuseppe and Penelope had been evacuated from The Spare Girl, just over the hill.

The woodstove door, which had been left ajar by three young guests from the Kootenays, was deemed the culprit—though some blamed Paul Bower's ghost. Fire followed Paul everywhere. No lives were lost, but a lot of memorabilia—and Wendy Riley (whom Paul had invited to manage the bakery on the premises) with good-natured resilience relocated to another building on the property.

The new bakery, sometimes referred to as the New Moon Over Naikoon, continues to be open from the May long weekend to the day after Labour Day. This is the place you'll find tourists and residents alike, socializing and telling tales. "Come and sit with us," pleaded a group of locals to a visitor who wandered in on a rainy June afternoon. "We're sick of each other; we're dying to meet someone new."

Everything in this off-the-grid bakery is made from scratch. There is no menu per se, just whatever Wendy and her crew of devoted helpers feel in the mood to bake. Pizza, muffins, bread, delicious cookies and squares, and cinnamon buns, of course (see recipe page 88), tasting fresher than the air, served with tea or coffee, by candlelight, even when the sun shines. I asked Wendy what made their cinnamon buns different from so many others, "They are made by really, really happy people. We have so much fun making them!" she said.

The bakery is a huge success and in ways that have nothing to do with finances. (Wendy quit making her coveted Chocolate Chip Shortbread "because people kept buying it.") "You feel you're outside civilization, in a very ancient place," one guest commented. "Then you get to stop in a surreal little bakery right on the periphery of capitalism."

I tell visitors, "look for a sign nailed to a tree at the side of the road, saying 'Fresh Bread Ahead'"—though the "Fresh" has recently fallen off and been claimed by the moss, which happens to most things, eventually, on Haida Gwaii.

In the winter months, Wendy moves the bakery to The Bus, closer to Masset on the Tow Hill Road, so that locals and the odd visitor can have their cinnamon bun fix.

TOP LEFT: Not everything is reclaimed by the moss—like Fisher, aged three. PHOTO BY JANIE JOLLEY

TOP RIGHT: The Bus PHOTO BY KATHERINE HINKEL

BOTTOM LEFT: PHOTO BY MICHELLE FURBACHER

BOTTOM MIDDLE: PHOTO BY MICHELLE FURBACHER

BOTTOM RIGHT: Mossy whale-bones at Moon Over Naikoon PHOTO BY JANIE JOLLEY

MOON OVER NAIKOON CINNAMON BUNS

MAKES 1 DOZEN

Wendy Riley PHOTO BY PETER SLOAN

In the winter of 2014 I stayed at an upscale Tofino lodge where their breakfast buffet included, among other things, cinnamon buns. I watched as guest after guest salivated over the sticky buns oozing butter and sugar, but opted for a buttery croissant or calorie-laden lemon poppy seed muffin instead. It struck me that this is what sets Haida Gwaii apart from everywhere else. Here visitors line up for Wendy's cinnamon buns and are devastated if they don't get one. Here people relax enough to know a cinnamon bun a day comforts the body and feeds the soul.

Wendy doubles this recipe but if there is only one of you—or two at the most—one dozen happy cinnamon buns should do.

2 cups (475 mL) warm water	1 cup (240 mL) light brown sugar
2 Tbsp (30 mL) sugar	2 Tbsp (30 mL) ground cinnamon
2 Tbsp (30 mL) traditional, island-time (not fast-rising) yeast*	¾ cup (180 mL) raisins†
2 Tbsp vegetable oil	¼ cup (60 mL) butter
4–5 cups (1–1.25 L) unbleached flour	2 Tbsp (30 mL) whipping cream
¼ cup (60 mL) butter	1 tsp (5 mL) vanilla extract
	1¼ cups (310 mL) icing sugar

WHAT YOU DO

1 Dissolve sugar in the warm water (baby bath temperature).

2 Sprinkle yeast on water. Don't stir. Let sit, covered, for about 10 minutes or until bubbly.

---

*   We don't need to do anything fast around here. Island time is unhurried time. Here on Haida Gwaii you have time to sit and watch your bread dough rise.

†   If your raisins are dried up and hard, try soaking them in boiling water, or even in orange juice overnight. Drain, of course, before using.

"Randy"

When Bill gates made an incognito visit to Tow Hill Road to stay with my friend Gloria Roth, a.k.a. Chipper, (she introduced him as "Randy," and he blushed 10 shades of red so I knew he knew I was on to him) her internet was down so she brought him to the Moon Over Naikoon Bakery for coffee and a bite to eat. We remember it as "the summer Bill Gates picked the raisins out of Wendy's cinnamon buns."

3   Add vegetable oil.

4   Mix in flour. The first 2 cups can be stirred with a wooden spoon—the remainder must be kneaded in until dough sticks to itself, not to your hands.

5   Cover with a clean tea towel and let rise in a warm place until double in bulk, about 1 hour.

6   Punch dough down and roll dough out into a large rectangle.

7   Smooth butter in a layer over the dough. Cover evenly with brown sugar and sprinkle with cinnamon. Scatter the raisins over the dough.

8   Starting with a long side, roll the dough up, gently, into a log, jelly-roll style. Cut roll in half, then in quarters. Cut each quarter into three even slices—you should end up with a dozen same-sized pieces. Place on a parchment paper–lined baking sheet. Cover and let rise until double in bulk, about 45 minutes. (Let rise longer, if necessary. Don't rush it.)

9   Preheat the oven to 350°F (180°C). Bake the rolls until crusty and golden on top, about 20–25 minutes.*

10   Remove from oven, invert immediately onto rack and let cool for 10 minutes. Turn buns right side up.

11   Mix together the butter, cream, vanilla and icing-sugar over medium heat. **Don't let this mixture boil or it will dry hard.** Drizzle over warm cinnamon buns.

---

* One recipe I read reminded me to bake the buns uncovered, that is to remove the tea towel before putting the buns in the oven. I didn't think I would need to tell my readers to do this but when you think you are being clear, very often you aren't. I forget that there are still people like me who read instruction manuals and never even get past the first step of trying to figure out how to plug in the electrical cord.

CHOCOLATE CHIP SHORTBREAD

MAKES 35–40 COOKIES

What self-respecting cookbook doesn't include at least one cookie recipe? If I had my way I would live on cookies alone. Good vegetables go bad; meat, fish and chicken rot. But in my house, at least, there is no such thing as an inedible cookie.

Even though Wendy Riley doesn't make shortbread anymore because it was too popular, I decided I owed it to those who have never had the thrilling satisfaction of pressing one between their lips, to share in the ecstasy. Just spreading the love around. (Remember, joy is there, in everything, and even when we can't see it.)

This isn't her exact recipe, because I know she used part whole-wheat flour and, I think, cane sugar, in the interest of making these at least *pretend* to be healthy. But Wendy was the inspiration behind this recipe.

1¾ cups (410 mL) cake flour	½ cup (120 mL) icing sugar
1 cup (240 mL) semi-sweet mini chocolate chips	2 tsp (10 mL) cold water
¾ cup (180 mL) unsalted butter at room temperature	1 tsp (5 mL) vanilla extract
	Pinch of salt

WHAT YOU DO

1   Preheat oven to 325°F (160°C). Line two baking sheets with parchment paper.

2   In a small bowl, stir flour with chocolate chips.

3   In a large bowl, using an electric beater, beat butter until smooth, then gradually beat in sugar until fluffy, about 2–3 minutes. Beat in water, vanilla and salt.

4   Using a wooden spoon, gradually stir in the flour mixture.

5   Shape into 1–inch (2.5 cm) balls and place on baking sheets. Bake, a sheet at a time, until edges are light and golden, 15–20 minutes. Cool completely on a rack.

Chocolate Chip Shortbread PHOTO BY MICHELLE FURBACHER

CHAPTER FOUR: Food Gathering All Year Round

TOP: Tall grass in summer at Rose Spit PHOTO BY JANIE JOLLEY; BOTTOM: Trees in winter PHOTO BY JANIE JOLLEY

THE WILD
FOODS OF HAIDA GWAII

It is hard to define when seasons change on Haida Gwaii. It used to be that Islanders knew when summer had officially arrived because Serguis De Bucy would take the furry thing off the steering wheel of the airport limo, the old school bus that picked up passengers and drove them to the ferry at Alliford Bay, and then across to Skidegate. Now that Serguis has retired and prefers to be called Sergio, we don't have the same sense of certainty.

The Tlell Fall Fair takes place every "summer" on the first weekend in August. I've picked huckleberries in July, but some years they are even riper and juicier in mid-September. "Fall" can be anywhere from the first of August until the wild winds of November start to blow and the rain bounces back up off the road, and the northwesterlies hit and it starts feeling like . . . winter.

Because of the many overlaps (I pick sea asparagus and lambsquarters in spring and summer, for instance, and salmonberries, too. Salal berries can ripen in summer but go on being harvested when fall has officially begun) I have arranged the wild foods I gather in order of their appearance—from seaweed and elderflowers in the spring to chanterelles and other wild mushrooms in the fall, with one exception. For easier reference I have grouped the Berries of Haida Gwaii in one section, starting with salmonberries in spring and ending with cranberries in fall.

"It's important to remember stories and instructions from the elders when gathering food and medicine," says Margaret Edgars of Old Massett.* "Each plant has its time to be picked."

HAIDA TRADITIONAL
KNOWLEDGE
A YEAR OF HARVESTING THE SEA

The return of herring to the coast traditionally marked the start of food gathering for the Haida. By late February or early March people would leave their main villages and move to outlying areas to fish for spring salmon and halibut, to gather shellfish and pick seaweed while they waited for the herring to spawn. When

---

*   Interviewed in *Northword,* 2005, "Rural Foraging"

the spawn was deposited—usually on kelp—it was harvested—a Haida delicacy called *k'aaw*. Early spring, before the warmer weather, is the time to dig clams, and to fish for sockeye in the rivers.

In summer, the pink salmon and the Coho arrive. Halibut are fished year-round but come closer to shore during the summer months, and the weather is better for drying the fish, also. Sea urchins, chitons, sea cucumbers and octopus are gathered in the summer; people jig for rockfish and lingcod. Dungeness crabs are at their best in summer, which is also a good time for shrimp and prawns.

Chum and coho are the main species of salmon caught in the fall. Clams and cockles are plentiful in the cooler months. By late fall most of the salmon runs are over.

In winter, people would return to their main villages. Wild winter storms make fishing riskier, but the right conditions can result in "wash-up" where every kind of shellfish—scallops, clams, cockles—is tossed onto the beach.

PICKING SEAWEED AND STAYING AWAY FROM THE LAW

Jim Hart is Chief of the Stastas Eagle clan in Old Massett, and he is known the world over for his monumental carvings and his jewellery. He worked alongside Bill Reid on the cedar sculpture, "Raven and the First Men" at the Museum of Anthropology in Vancouver and in 1990 shaped a 30-foot-tall killer whale pole, which was then shipped to Sweden to be completed, and raised in the gardens of Sofiero Castle in Helsingborg. Most of the other sculptures in the King's garden were made of stone. "People over there like to burn wooden sculptures," Jim says, wryly.

I knew Jimmy back in the early '70s ("We were so much older then, we're younger than that now:" thanks, Mr. Dylan). He spent his misspent youth camping off by himself, facing his fear of bears, and "picking seaweed at Seven Mile and staying away from the law." This was the first time I heard anyone talk about picking seaweed (or staying away from the law, for that matter. The latter would change as the years passed and I grew younger, but that's a story for another book.)

LEFT: Jim Hart, 2013 PHOTO BY BYRON DAUNCEY

TOP RIGHT: Dried seaweed from Eagle's Feast PHOTO BY MICHELLE FURBACHER

BOTTOM RIGHT: Dolly Garza seaweed identification workshop PHOTO BY CHRIS ASHURST

"Thousands of edible seaweeds of various shapes and sizes occupy a wide array of ecological niches," writes Dolly Garza, author of *Common Edible Seaweeds in the Gulf of Alaska.*

The best black seaweed—genus *Porphyra abbottae* to scientists, common name black laver to English speakers, *nori* to the Japanese and *sgyuu* (in the Skidegate dialect) and *sGiw* (in the Masset dialect) in Haida—grows on rocks where there is plenty of tidal action. When dried it is a crinkly black delicacy packed with nutrients. Snipping it is simple, but first you have to find it, which may be more difficult if you don't know what you are looking for. (That would be me, for example.) Those who know what they are looking for, and where to look, can gather enough for a year in half an hour.

"*Porphyra* is very picky. It has a six-week growing season (in early spring), and if you miss it you've missed it for the whole year," says Garza, interviewed in *Northword* magazine. "If you're too early the seaweed will be short and hard to pick, and hard on your knuckles; if you are too late it may be encrusted with small snails and dying back, and it's not as tasty."

How to dry *Porphyra* after you have harvested it:

1   Do *not* rinse the delicate fronds of seaweed under the tap (i.e. in freshwater) or it will lose most of its flavour.

2   Spread your seaweed on a sheet in the sun when there is a breeze blowing.

3   Uncurl and turn each piece of seaweed every few hours until it is dried. This whole process can take anywhere from 12 to 48 hours.

4   Roast in an oven at 175°F (80°C) for 20 minutes.

5   When it comes to food gathering, preparation or cooking, nothing is definitive. Depending on the time of day, whether it rains or shines, whether the tide is in or out—whomever you talk to will give you a different take. It's what makes this process (writing about wild food) infinitely interesting and infinitely frustrating.

6   Marlene Liddle gathers seaweed anytime in April after the Easter weekend, up until the month of June. "Seaweed doesn't grow according to any calendar," she tells me, when we meet for coffee at her house in Masset.* "You need to pay attention, be in tune with the weather. If it's a warm spring the seaweed might be ready too, earlier in the season. Rain can wash the saltiness off, so some people prefer not to pick right after a rain."

LEFT: Marlene Liddle
PHOTO BY SOREN POULSEN

RIGHT: Seaweed hanging overnight PHOTO BY MARLENE LIDDLE

Marlene doesn't use scissors to pick seaweed, she says, but runs her fingers through the long strands ("it helps get any critters off") and pulls it from the rocks with her hands. The roots stay firmly planted so next year's crop can proliferate.

*   Another former Masset resident (now deceased) was more specific. "Now if you want good seaweed—*sGiw*—you've got to get it around April 20," said Stephen Brown (Tsinni Stephen). "The first ones that grow are the best. It's slow picking but it's sure dandy, though. We call that *sank sgiwee kusgat laa' guusdlang*—the early seaweed is good to get, it tastes the best."

She gathers her seaweed in small orange sacks (with tiny holes in them) from the cannery in Masset, but you can also use the mesh bags that onions come in, she says. In the old days people used flour sacks or pillowcases. She hangs her mesh bags overnight, and puts a chiton in with the seaweed, which sweetens it. (You can use the juice from other shellfish as well, and these days, she says, it is acceptable to use oyster sauce.)

One traditional way of preserving seaweed was to dry it in flat wooden boxes, about a foot square. First a layer of seaweed was laid in the box and sprinkled with the juices of fresh clams or chitons—obtained, traditionally, by chewing the clam or chiton and spitting out the saliva.*) The whole thing was pressed down tightly and covered over with a layer of thimbleberry leaves. Another layer of seaweed was placed on top of this, juice sprinkled over it, and again it was covered with a further layer of thimbleberry leaves. This process of alternating seaweed with leaves was repeated until the layers of seaweed filled the box. The layers were then weighted with rocks and the seaweed would begin the process of caking up firmly. It was afterwards put away in cedar bent boxes† for the winter.

Marlene knows better than to count on the sun to shine: she lays a white sheet over her dining room table, brings out her two dehydrators and starts a production line. After her bags of seaweed have spent the night draining, she spreads her crop out on the sheet to begin the drying process for a couple of hours. Next comes two hours at high heat in the dehydrator, and then, to really crisp it up, in her oven at the lowest heat (170°F/75°C) for a further two hours. Last spring she packed 140 large zip-lock bags full of dried seaweed in one day.

Marlene likes to crumble dried seaweed in her soups. Sometimes she grinds her seaweed into a fine powder. Another option ("it's almost like a salad") is to mix seaweed with fish eggs and a dollop of oolichan grease (See Oolichans and Grease, page 218) or a modern innovation is to serve creamed corn with seaweed.

Seaweed dried into a cake is the foundation of this recipe of Michael König's—an hors d'oeuvre he created spontaneously when I dropped by

Michael König in "The Diary of One who Disappeared" by Leoš Janáček, Opéra National de Paris PHOTO BY TILL GEIGER

---

* Nowadays, to extract juice, shuck clams then steam them briefly. The steaming water becomes a broth, which has a salty, sea flavour to it.

† Bentwood boxes were used to store food, clothing, household and ceremonial items. Some were painted and others were elaborately carved, but the majority were left undecorated. The sides were made from a single plank of cedar; it was bevelled or kerfed to allow the four sides to be bent into a box shape. After careful shaping of the plank, it was steamed, bent and sewn together using cedar roots or wooden pegs. The base was prepared so that the edges fitted snugly into the bottom, creating a watertight box. A lid was then added.

(spontaneously) one evening for supper. Michael is the world-famous Canadian-German tenor; when he is not abroad singing for Europe's major opera companies, he and his wife Sanne and their four daughters live on Sangan Drive, and when I am lucky I am invited for a spontaneous dinner.

SMOKED SALMON ON SEAWEED WITH AVOCADO

SERVES 4 AS AN APPETIZER

8 small cakes of dried seaweed*
(cut into bite-sized squares)

Light sesame oil (for frying)

¼–½ lb (110–250 g) smoked salmon

2 avocados, mashed

Black sesame seeds for garnish

WHAT YOU DO

1 Fry seaweed lightly in sesame oil—just to make it crisp, for about 30 seconds. This is a delicate operation—don't overdo it. Remove from frying pan and drain on paper towels.

2 Spoon a tablespoon of mashed avocado on top of the crisp seaweed.

3 Add a slice of smoked salmon.

4 Sprinkle black sesame seeds over the top.

SUBSTITUTE

You can try a scallop, lightly sautéed in butter, instead of the salmon.

People walk all over many other vitamin-and-mineral-packed types of seaweed in their race to harvest the prized black nori, Dolly Garza writes. She believes seaweed is undervalued, in general, simply because it is so common. Why do we value most what is rare and hard to find (truffles come to mind) instead of taking advantage of what is local and abundant and nourishing? Perhaps we spend our lifetime looking in the wrong places?

---

* If you don't have access to bags of Haida Gwaii seaweed, you can cheat and use roasted seaweed snack sheets.

In contrast (to the process of drying the black seaweed), big brown kelps can be harvested in very little time, hung out on a clothesline and forgotten about until they are dry. Bull kelp and popweed can be collected all year round, providing the "right wind" blows it up on the beach. On Haida Gwaii, it seems, we spend a lot of our time waiting for the right wind to blow.

Kelp and seaweed have been part of my life since the day I was plunked down in a tide pool next to the one where my mother washed my diapers. I was told not to put seaweed in my mouth; I think my mother must have considered it unclean. (She was, after all, washing my diapers in a tide pool that had seaweed and kelp in it.) Dad, when we were trolling, would take the Lord's name in vain if a piece of kelp floated by, or worse, if my mother steered us into a kelp patch, but it would not have occurred to anyone on board to slice off a few kelp blades and serve them up for dinner alongside the fish.

I was astonished when, in the early '70s, the writer Matt Cohen came to ruin my marriage on Haida Gwaii.* He had never seen kelp before (Matt hailed from Ontario) and was fascinated by something I had always taken for granted. Kelp was just there, the way sand and rocks and driftwood made up the landscape of the beach. Kelp and seaweed had always floated through the lines of my poetry—so much so that one English academic described me as having emerged from "the kelp school of poetry."

LEFT: Kelp rafts on beach PHOTO BY GUY KIMOLA

MIDDLE: Kelp and sea foam PHOTO BY JANIE JOLLEY

RIGHT: Giant and sugar kelp PHOTO BY ELIN PRICE

Cover of *Peach Melba*, ORIGINALLY PUBLISHED BY COACH HOUSE PRESS

---

*   Having just received the Matt Cohen Award: In Celebration of a Writing Life, I am free to divulge the details. Patsy Aldana, who spent many years married to Matt, and is the mother of his children, introduced me before I accepted the award, and told the audience that Matt's book, *Peach Melba*, was about our affair. I recommend the book. The cover is particularly beautiful.

LEFT: Dafne Romero and kelp
PHOTO BY MISTY BETHAM

RIGHT TOP: Kelp Bulb PHOTO BY
JANIE JOLLEY

RIGHT BOTTOM: Kelp fronds
PHOTO BY JANIE JOLLEY

Dafne Romero of Queen Charlotte started her own company, North Pacific Kelp Products. She hand-harvested giant kelp (*Macrocystis pyrifera*), one of the fastest-growing seaweeds in the world; she'd row out in her small boat with a pair of scissors to snip the blades (making sure to leave the small gas-filled bladders intact so the plant wouldn't sink.) She makes seaweed lasagne (using dried blades of giant kelp instead of noodles) and also sells seaweed to a company on Vancouver Island for use as seaweed wraps.

Bull kelp (*Nereocystis luetkeana*) is a separate species from giant kelp, but also edible. Nancy Turner, in her informative, thoroughly reliable *Plants of Haida Gwaii*, says the Haida used the dried and cured hollow bulbs of bull kelp as storage vessels for grease and fish oil.

Bull kelp blades (the leaf-like part of the algae), if harvested and dried in the spring, are said to have a mildly sweet buttery taste, but I can't vouch for this. (I tasted my first kelp blade in December 2013, on a beach in Metchosin near Victoria, BC A woman was gathering kelp, and we began a conversation about foraging, she tore off a piece and gave it to me. I ate it raw. I haven't told my mother.)

Romero has a license to harvest in Haida Gwaii waters that allows her to pick 20 percent of the kelp in the area, but she takes less than one percent of the giant kelp. With her license she could collect other kinds as well but she believes in keeping things small. "One kind is one world. It's big enough," she says, in *Northword*.

DAFNE ROMERO'S SEAWEED LASAGNE

SERVES 8

This recipe comes included with a package of Dafne's Giant Kelp Haida Gwaii Seaweed.

2 Tbsp (30 mL) grapeseed oil	Salt and pepper, to taste
½ cup (120 mL) chopped mushrooms	1 package (8 leaves) Seaweed Lasagne*
2 orange bell peppers, chopped	3 cups (700 mL) cottage cheese
3 large cloves garlic, minced	¼ cup (60 mL) Parmesan cheese, grated
5 cups (1.2 L) tomato sauce	1 cup (240 mL) shredded Mozzarella cheese, divided
1 Tbsp (30 mL) dried basil	½ lb (250 g) raw spinach
1 tsp (5 mL) dried oregano	

WHAT YOU DO

1   Preheat oven to 375°F (190°C)

2   In a large skillet, heat grapeseed oil and sauté mushrooms for 2 minutes. Add bell peppers, and garlic. Stir in tomato sauce, herbs, salt and pepper. Simmer for 5 minutes then remove from heat.

3   Coat a 9 ×13–inch (23 ×33 cm) pan with cooking oil and set aside.

4   Put the seaweed fronds in boiling water for 3 minutes or until colour changes. Drain and put aside.

5   In medium bowl mix the cottage cheese, Parmesan cheese and ¾ cup (180 mL) Mozzarella cheese together. Add raw spinach, season with pepper if desired.

6   Ladle about 1 cup (240 mL) of sauce into bottom of prepared baking dish. Top with one layer of Seaweed Lasagne noodles. Spread one-third of the cottage cheese mixture over noodles. Evenly spread another cup of sauce over that.

---

*   Romero's products can be ordered from www.northpacifickelp.com.

Repeat the process until all the noodles are used, ending with the last of the sauce. Sprinkle the remaining ¼ cup (60 mL) Mozzarella cheese over the top. Cover tightly with foil, Bake for 30 minutes. Uncover and continue to bake until cheese is browned.

ADDITIONS

This recipe can be changed for meat-eaters just by adding the meat of your choice. You can, of course, substitute plain lasagne noodles for the seaweed.

ELDERFLOWER
FROM THE PACIFIC RED ELDERBERRY

Elderflower PHOTO BY
PETER SLOAN

Though it often looks like a spindly tree, the elder is a shrub that grows like a weed along the sides of the roads. The elder's creamy white flowers start appearing in late April to early May on Haida Gwaii, but they can bloom in late March in other places, right through to September. The flowers later turn to bright red berries.

Many people believe the berries are toxic, but they aren't, not even if eaten raw, *not unless* you chew up the seeds. So don't do that. (You have been warned). Don't eat the roots, the stems, or the leaves, either, though I don't know why anyone would.

ELDERFLOWER CORDIAL
ABOUT 1 QUART (1 L) OF SYRUP

25 elderflower heads, stems removed
(about 2 cups (475 mL) flowers)

1 quart (1 L) water

4 cups (950 mL) sugar

2 lemons

1 tsp (5 mL) citric acid

WHAT YOU DO

1   Snip the flowers from the stalks into a bowl or bucket large enough to hold all your ingredients. Remove as much of the stems as you can; they are toxic. A few stray bits of stems will not hurt you, but you want to minimize it.

2   Zest the lemons and add zest to the bowl, then the citric acid and lemon juice.

(Always remember to zest citrus fruit *before* you juice it. It's a real pain to try and zest lemons and oranges once they have been juiced.)

Elderflower cordial PHOTO BY MICHELLE FURBACHER

3 Bring the water and sugar to a boil, stirring occasionally to dissolve. Let the syrup cool enough so that you can stick your finger in it without getting burned. (Obviously if you burn yourself, the syrup isn't cool enough. So I'd suggest sticking your finger in the sugar and water mixture later rather than sooner, or, perhaps more wisely, leaving it to cool to room temperature, and keep your fingers out of it altogether.) Pour the syrup over the flowers, lemons et al and stir to combine. Cover the bowl or bucket with a towel and leave it for 2–4 days.

4 When you are ready, strain the works through a fine-meshed sieve lined with cheesecloth or a paper towel into a clean jar. Seal the jar and store in the fridge.

5 To serve, pour 1–3 Tbsp (15–45 mL) of the syrup into a large glass and add water or seltzer. Or you can add a tablespoon to a glass of sparkling wine, or to a couple shots of vodka or gin.

NOTE: If you just want to make an elderflower simple syrup, which will ferment very fast if you don't keep it really cold, skip the lemon and citric acid. For a quart, boil 3 cups (700 mL) sugar and 3 cups (700 mL) water. Let it cool enough so you can stick your finger in it (or let come to room temperature if you're not a risk-taker) then pour it into a quart (1 L) jar full of elderflowers. Steep 1–2 days, then strain. Use within 3 weeks.

ELDERFLOWER GRANITA

SERVES 6 (½ CUP SERVINGS)

My first experience with granita was in the breakfast room at the Piazza San Domenico in Taormina, Sicily. Granita is a bit like a sorbet, but more slushy. And

LEFT: Dining room at Taormina PHOTO BY SUSAN MUSGRAVE; RIGHT: Dining room at Copper Beech House PHOTO BY RANDY MARTIN

ELDERFLOWER GRANITA
(CONT'D)

if you call it granita you don't have to feel guilty about eating dessert for breakfast. Plus it sounds so international-jet-setty, like saying *budino* instead of pudding, and Bellini instead of champagne cocktail. Granita is made from sugar, water and flavourings such as lemon juice, blood oranges, coffee, almonds, mint and when in season, wild strawberries.

3 cucumbers	1¼ cups (310 mL) elderflower cordial
3 limes	

WHAT YOU DO

1   Peel cucumbers and cut them into pieces. Blend to a pulp in a food processor.

2   Pour the pulp into a fine sieve set over a bowl. Use the back of a spoon to press out all the juice. You should end up with about 2 cups (475 mL). Discard the pulp.

3   Squeeze the limes, and then add their juice and the cordial to the cucumber liquid. Stir well. Taste a bit on a teaspoon. If it doesn't taste elderflowery enough, add a little more cordial.

4   Pour into a freezer-proof container, cover and freeze for 2 hours.

5   Remove the container from the freezer and scrape the partially frozen mixture with a fork to break up the ice crystals. Return to the freezer.

6   Every couple of hours remove the granita from the freezer and break up the crystals with a fork. You should do this about 4 times until the mixture should be pale lime green, with the texture of soft crushed ice-slush.

7   Once prepared, return the granita to the freezer until needed. Consume as soon as you can.

ELDERFLOWER LIQUEUR
MAKES ONE 26 OZ (750 ML) BOTTLE

You want to make this liqueur within an hour or two of picking the flowers to get the best effect.

Enough elderflowers to loosely fill a quart (1 L) jar, stems removed

1 26-oz (750 mL) bottle vodka,

100-proof or higher*

¼–½ cups (60–125 mL) sugar

WHAT YOU DO

1   In a large glass jar, cover the flowers with the alcohol and seal the jar. Make sure the flowers are completely submerged otherwise the top layer of flowers will oxidize from contact with air, and turn brown. This won't harm your liqueur; it just looks a bit sketchy. Weight the flowers down, if they insist on coming up for air.

2   Keep the jar in a cool, dark place for as long as you like, anywhere from a few days to a month. The longer you steep the flowers, the darker the liqueur will get.

3   Strain twice. First through a fine-meshed strainer to remove the flowers and debris, then strain it again through the same strainer, only with a piece of paper towel set inside it. This second straining removes very fine particulates, like the pollen. You can skip this second straining, but your liqueur will end up cloudy.

4   Add the sugar. Seal the jar again and shake well to combine.

---

*   The type of vodka you use is up to you. 80-proof vodka is fine, but I prefer 100-proof (and I've seen recipes that call for 151-plus). Why? The flavours and aromas of elderflowers are not all extractable by water. The higher the alcohol content, the cleaner and purer the elderflower flavor. WARNING: If you use the 151-plus proof, exercise caution in operating motor vehicles, etc. etc.

TOP LEFT: Frozen spruce tips PHOTO BY MICHELLE FURBACHER; MIDDLE LEFT: Spruce tips in a bucket PHOTO BY PETER SLOAN; TOP RIGHT: Susan picking spruce tips PHOTO BY PETER SLOAN; MIDDLE RIGHT: Spruce tip PHOTO BY PETER SLOAN; BOTTOM LEFT: Spruce tip PHOTO BY PETER SLOAN; BOTTOM RIGHT: Spruce tip PHOTO BY PETER SLOAN

5 Put the jar back in the cool, dark place, and shake it from time to time until the sugar has dissolved. When all the sugar is dissolved drink at room temperature or chilled in a cordial glass.

SPRUCE TIPS

The trick to harvesting spruce tips* is to catch them when the bright green tips are soft and bunched closely together (like the hairs of an artist's paintbrush before it is unwrapped) when they first begin to emerge from their brown papery husks. On Haida Gwaii this is usually around the middle of May. They will be ready to harvest at different times in different locations, depending on the warmth of the area, whether there is good exposure to the sun (or if indeed there *is* sun) and elevation. So you can go on picking them well into the month of June, if you are lucky.

At their prime, spruce tips are baby-tender and have a refreshing flavour that tastes lightly of resin with undertones of citrus. (The flavour should not overwhelm, but tease.) As spruce tips mature, the resinous aspect of their flavour becomes more intense. When the fragrant tips begin to harden, become tough and resinous, form actual needles, and lose their luminescent spring green color, they are past their prime, and no longer good to eat.

To harvest spruce tips, pop the tips off the ends of each branch, the way you would pluck a berry from a bush. Remove and discard the papery casings, and any hard stems that may have broken off with the tips.

As with many seasonal foods, I try to extend the spruce tip season by preserving them for later use. Where others pickle, can or dry their wild foods, I'm a great advocate of the freezer. Nearly everything I pick or catch or forage goes straight into the chest freezer, where it then becomes impossible to find. The day a salmon is filleted and laid to rest in my freezer, consider it six feet under. By the time I get round to thawing it, it has freezer burn, and only the ravens will eat it. The vegetables I lovingly freeze in baggies usually end up on the compost heap. (I hoard my compost too: I make loads of it and then go to the garden shop and buy bags of sea soil so that I don't have to "waste" the compost by using it.)

Nevertheless, I freeze my spruce tips so they can be used all year round. They freeze beautifully, and retain their intense colour. This versatile little tip (I wish I could find another word to use besides "tip") can be used to make Spruce Tip Vinegar, Spruce Tip Salt, Spruce Tip Sugar, Spruce Tip Syrup, Candied Spruce Tips,

---

*   Pine tips and fir tips are also edible, and could easily be substituted in spruce tip recipes if pine and fir are more readily available.

Spruce Tip Mayonnaise and Spruce Tip–Infused Olive Oil. You get the idea. You can pretty well use them in anything, including fish seasoning, spruce beer and salsa. I use them as a substitute for any herbs I might not have on hand, especially chives (they are more interesting, I think) and rosemary (which doesn't seem to thrive in my garden, probably because I have the opposite of a green thumb. I like plants that do well in poor soil, northern exposure and almost total shade. But that, too, is another book.)

SPRUCE TIP SYRUP MAKES 1 CUP (240 ML)

1 cup (240 mL) spruce tips	1 cup (240 mL) sugar
Scant ½ cup (115 mL) of water	Pinch of salt

WHAT YOU DO

1   Place spruce tips in the bowl of a food processor. Pulse until finely chopped, stopping to scrape down the sides of the bowl. Set aside.

2   Mix water, sugar and salt in a small saucepan over medium heat and whisk as mixture comes to a boil.

3   Boil, without stirring, for 1 minute, and then remove from heat. Stir in the spruce tips and let the syrup steep at room temperature for 2–3 hours.

4   Strain through a fine mesh strainer and discard solids.

5   Store in an airtight container in fridge for up to one month. (Or, of course, freeze.)

SPRUCE TIP VODKA MAKES ONE 26 OZ (750 ML) BOTTLE.

1 cup (240 mL) spruce tips	26 oz (750 mL) bottle inexpensive* vodka

*   You don't need a great vodka for infusions. Having said that, 100 proof vodka would be my first choice.

WHAT YOU DO

1   Place the spruce needles and one-third of the bottle of vodka in a blender. Blend at high speed for 2 minutes. Pour into a large clean jar.

2   Pour remaining vodka into blender and swirl it around to gather any green residue on the sides and bottom of the blender. Pour into the jar and stir to combine.

3   Cover and store in fridge for 1 week.

4   Strain the mixture through a fine-mesh strainer and discard the green puree. Strain again through a coffee filter. Pour the vodka into a clean bottle and store indefinitely in the freezer.

Spruce Tip Vodka PHOTO BY MICHELLE FURBACHER

DEVIL'S CLUB

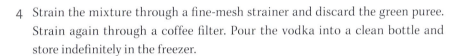

"This beautiful and powerful shrub, with its large maple-like prickly leaves and spiny stalks, has numerous medicinal applications for the Haida . . . there are many stories in which Devil's Club is portrayed as a supernatural power-giver."

—from *Plants of Haida Gwaii* by Nancy Turner

I've always known devil's club as a Haida medicinal plant, a physical and spiritual healer, one which can be toxic if improperly used by anyone who does not treat it with respect, and with strong ties to shamanism. To suggest using it as the principal ingredient in a stir fry or a chocolate sauce (read on) seems somewhat sacrilegious, like breaking into church to get blitzed on the Eucharist.

From the Alaska Herb Tea Company website: "Shamans may carry a power charm made with spruce twigs, devil's club roots and their animal tongue, acquired during their quests. During the spiritual quest . . . a novice goes into the woods for several weeks, eating nothing but devil's club. Nootka people on Vancouver purified themselves for whale hunting by drinking devil's club, bathing in devil's club and abstaining from sex. Devil's club is sometimes nailed to doors to keep out evil spirits or witches. Devil's club is also used to cure hangovers, as a

Devil's club bud PHOTO BY
LANGDON COOK

deodorant or perfume, as baby talc, to regulate menstrual flow and lactation, and as a powerful snuff."

An elder in Old Masset heard that my partner Stephen, on a two-week pass from the federal penitentiary, was afraid to go out to the woodshed on a night as black as the inside of a raven—because he was afraid of gogeets (see "Gogeet—Various Incarnations" page 113). The elder suggested Stephen wear a necklace of devil's club beads for protection, but Stephen returned to maximum security before I could find someone to make him the right charm.

Nancy Turner, in *Plants of Haida Gwaii,* cautions that devil's club can be extremely irritating if touched, that the spines can act as slivers, festering under the skin, and being difficult to remove. Its Latin name is *Oplopanax horridus—horridus,* I assume referring to the horrible pain inflicted upon you when you come in contact with its thorns. For this reason, perhaps, Langdon Cook (of *Fat of the Land*) advises harvesting the buds when they are no more than two to three inches long, "with nascent spines still soft—in stark contrast to the sharp, hardened spines on the stalk. I nabbed a scant two cups . . . with only a few flecks of blood on gloveless hands for my trouble."

Cook infuses cream and makes a chocolate sauce with devil's club buds. "Then I did the same thing with a Bordelaise sauce, which I poured over meat." But, he says, they are terrific simply sautéed in butter. What isn't?

DEVIL'S CLUB STIR FRY SERVES 2

3 cloves garlic, diced	1 small red pepper, cut into slivers
2 loose cups (500 mL) devil's club buds	1 Tbsp (15 mL) peanut oil
5 green onions, split lengthwise and cut into 3-inch (8 cm) sections	1 Tbsp (15 mL) chicken stock
	Salt, to taste

WHAT YOU DO

1 Heat oil in wok until hot but not smoking. Add garlic, stirring, careful not to overcook.

Gogeet—Various Incarnations

HAIDA: *gagitx* (Skidegate dialect) or *gagxiit* (Masset dialect)

MANY WHO live here, Haida and non-Haida alike, are genuinely afraid of the gogeet, regarding it as a bogeyman or bigfoot-of-the-woods.

"I have found as many descriptions of a gogeet as I have believers in them. One of the earliest is, 'person turned into an otter demon by river otters,'" wrote E. N. Anderson*. No other Haida belief has been so generally adopted by non-Haida residents.[†]

Henry White and Uncle Willis (Willis White) of Old Massett told me their version: a gogeet was someone who had become lost while fishing or hunting in the bush or on the remote west coast, and tried to find his way home, going mad in the process. When he finally found his village he was afraid to go home. He no longer belonged; he was so changed.

Gwaai Edenshaw is working on a screenplay about a gogeet. When we met for coffee at the Ground in Masset he told me this: that in order to restore a gogeet's humanity he must be cut all over with a knife and doused with urine.

Gogeet ILLUSTRATION BY GWAAI EDENSHAW

2   When garlic is fragrant and just starting to turn golden, tip wok back and forth a few times, spreading oil throughout. Add devil's club buds, green onions and red pepper, stirring vigorously.

3   Stir-fry together a few minutes, until green onions begin to darken. The wok will likely be dry. Add a splash of chicken stock, stir a few more times and remove to a serving dish. Sprinkle a few generous pinches of salt, to taste.

---

*   unpublished research; see Swanton 1905

†   *Ecologies of the Heart: Emotion, Belief, and the Environment,* by E. N. Anderson

THE BERRIES OF HAIDA GWAII

When I first lived on Haida Gwaii in the early '70s I was very keen to make jams and jellies out of every kind of berry that I found growing in wild abundance. Salmonberries, thimbleberries, salal berries, cloudberries, cranberries, huckleberries, blueberries: I admit I wasn't always pleased with the results, possibly because I'd been raised eating the blackberry jam and strawberry jam my mother made in copious amounts every summer. Perhaps my mistake was in not being able to think outside a jam jar. Traditionally, the Haida cooked, mashed and dried the juicier berries in cakes. The more acidic fruits like crabapples and cranberries, which ripened later in the year, they stored in bentwood cedar boxes lined with skunk cabbage leaves, topped with a layer of oolichan grease. The berries kept well and were a good source of vitamin C throughout the winter months. Salmonberries are the first berries to ripen in the spring. Next come thimbleberries. Huckleberries, blueberries and blackberries begin to ripen around the same time, anywhere from early July on, followed by cloudberries, red elderberries, salal berries. Then the bog cranberries and lingonberries in the fall.

There are many others, such as bunchberries (or frogberries) common juniper,

Salmonberry Jelly PHOTO BY SUSAN MUSGRAVE

Saskatoon berries (also known as serviceberries) that grow here, though I've never seen or picked Saskatoon berries on Haida Gwaii myself. Some berries I have not included in the edible category, such as crowberries, (also known as black twin berry or raven's berry) but were considered strong Haida medicine.

There is no point in me going on about berries that I don't pick because I don't want to poison my dinner guests, or berries I consider tasteless, or mild. So I intend only to provide recipes for those with which I have a healthy personal relationship.

SALMONBERRIES

We watch for the pink star-shaped blossoms (which I often toss in my salads) to appear, starting around the beginning of February, if the winter has been mild. The Haida traditionally picked the young shoots, which they peeled and ate raw. Salmonberry flowers mature into fruit between June (raw berry month) and August, depending on your latitude and your elevation.

Salmonberries are named for their similarity to a cluster of salmon eggs. (Some elders say if there are a lot of salmonberries, the salmon fishing will be good that year.) Florence Edenshaw Davidson, in Margaret Blackman's book *During My Time: Florence Edenshaw Davidson, A Haida Woman*, describes going with her mother to the Watun River, just south of Masset, to pick huckleberries. "She'd bring the berries home and cook them with salmon eggs for thickening. She boiled them till they were dry. She put them in a bentwood box with a cloth covering over them, then thimbleberry leaves and skunk cabbage leaves on top before she put the lid on."

Salmonberries range from golden yellow to orange in colour, and a deep dark red. The orange variety is tasty, but the darker reddish salmonberry tends not to be as flavourful and is generally avoided by all but a few unsuspecting hitchhikers stranded at the side of the road.

SALMONBERRY JELLY 6 CUPS (1.4 L)

4 cups (950 mL) salmonberries

1 cup (240 mL) water

½ cup (120 mL) lemon juice

7 cups (1.75 L) sugar

2 3 oz (90 mL) pouches liquid pectin

½ tsp (2 mL) butter

WHAT YOU DO

1   Combine the salmonberries and water in a saucepan; bring to a simmer, cover and simmer for 10 minutes. Crush the simmering berries from time to time to release the juice.

2   To separate the juice from the berries, pour the hot mixture into a jelly bag* or use layers of cheesecloth placed in a colander. Let the juice drip into a bowl. For clear juice, do not twist or press the berries while they drain. I froze the juice so I'd be able to make the jelly in the winter, when it isn't the busiest food-gathering time.

3   Sterilize pint (500 mL) or half-pint (250 mL) canning jars and lids.

LEFT: Thimbleberries PHOTO BY MARLENE LIDDLE

RIGHT: Haida Gwaii Homeland Security taking a break to pick thimbleberries. PHOTO BY MICHELLE FURBACHER

*   A bag made of cheesecloth or flannel through which the juices of berries used in the making for jelly are strained.

4 Pour salmonberry juice, lemon juice and sugar into a deep stainless steel pan. Add ½ tsp (2 mL) butter to reduce foaming.

5 Over high heat, bring the mixture to a full, rolling boil that cannot be stirred down. Stir constantly.

6 Add pouches of liquid pectin and boil hard for 1 minute. Remove from heat and quickly skim off foam. Immediately pour jelly into hot canning jars, leaving ¾ inch (2 cm) of space. Wipe jar rims clean, apply lids. Process for 5 minutes in a boiling water canner.

THIMBLEBERRIES

"Erect, unarmed shrub with palmately lobed leaves and raspberry like fruits," reads an entry for Thimbleberry from Meriwether Lewis's notes on the Lewis and Clark expedition in *Herbarium*. "A shrub of which the Natives eat the yung sprout without kooking. On the Columbia. Aprl. 15th 1805."

Thimbleberries have a taste that people often describe as "mild," and are somewhat hollow inside; if you turn one upside down, it looks like—surprise!—a thimble, which might fit on the tip of one of your fingers. The berries detach so easily when ripe that you can almost brush them off their stems. They are soft and delicate and easily squished when you're picking them.

Because they are hollow you need a lot of them if you are going to make a mild (i.e. slightly flavourless) jam, unlike a salmonberry, which is not hollow, but not enormously tasty, either, though many would disagree, due to the numbers of people I see harvesting out there, in the height of bug season, along the road. I pick salmonberries and huckleberries because they are there. And because it's an excuse to go outside, even in bug season. And so my neighbours don't pick them all first.

BLACKBERRIES

Blackberries have proliferated on the south end of Graham Island, in Queen Charlotte, and some have been found as far north as Port Clements, but I have never found any on the north end of the island. (I tried bringing blackberries from Vancouver Island and scattering them about my land on the Sangan River, with no luck. Then I found out why. The hard seeds of our native raspberries and blackberries need to be abraded in a bird's gizzard or eroded by digestive acids before water and air can enter the seed and germination can begin.)

BLACKBERRY LAVENDER NO-COOK FREEZER JAM 8 CUPS (1.9 L)

"Blackberries
Big as the ball of my thumb, and dumb as eyes
Ebon in the hedges, fat
With blue-red juices. These they squander on my fingers."
—Sylvia Plath, "Blackberrying"

One summer I brought lavender, *Lavandula angustifolia*, or English Lavender*, from Vancouver Island. This recipe doesn't call for much, so I had to find other ways to use my lavender hoard. Lavender shortbread, lavender ice cream, lavender roasted potatoes, lemon and lavender chicken. You can even include lavender in a rub for venison (or beef and lamb) or salmon. You can substitute lavender in any recipe calling for rosemary.

Blackberries conjure up surprisingly pleasant (for a change) childhood memories. Running up to Valdes Island† in my father's boat, rowing ashore at Shingle Point where Dad would don his oilskin raingear and charge into the middle of a blackberry patch. Mum lit a fire on the beach over which she placed a cauldron and made blackberry jelly while we gathered wood or floated out to sea on logs we pretended were Haida canoes. (I had seen one in a museum.)

I picked blackberries when I lived in Ireland, though never after the fall equinox. After that, so I was told, the Devil spits on them. I suspect the reality had more to do with worms invading the berries as the rains came in the fall and the berries began to mould on the vines. Irish adults devised the Devil spitting story to ensure their children avoided the blackberry patch. You never know.

---

*   French Lavender (Lavandula dentata) and Spanish Lavender (Lavandula stoechas) are both popular with gardeners these days, but their flowers are too strong and bitter with camphor-pine overtones to be used in cooking.

†   An island in the Southern Gulf Islands, across Porlier Pass from Galiano Island, between Vancouver Island and the British Columbia mainland.

4 cups (950 mL) blackberries, crushed	¼ cup (60 mL) lemon juice
1 tsp (5 mL) dried lavender flowers, minced	2 3-oz (90 mL) pouches liquid pectin*
8 cups (1.9 L) sugar	

WHAT YOU DO

1 In a large bowl, combine blackberries, lavender and sugar, and stir to mix. Mash with a potato masher until the blackberries just start to release juice but are still in chunks.

2 Let stand 10 minutes.

3 Add liquid pectin and lemon juice. Stir for 3 minutes.

4 Pour into clean jars or freezer containers, leaving ¾ inch (2 cm) of space at top to allow jam to expand in freezer. Cover and let sit at room temperature for 24 hours until set. Store refrigerated for up to 3 weeks or in freezer up to 1 year. Thaw in refrigerator when ready to use.

HUCKLEBERRIES AND BLUEBERRIES

Ever since I moved to the Islands people have argued about the berries we know as blueberries and huckleberries. Some say our blueberries are blue huckleberries, others say they are blueberries, and I have always said, up until this moment, "I'm not sure, but let's go and pick some." To further confuse the issue, if you look up "huckleberries" on the Internet, all the pictures are of blueberries. Or, if you like, blue huckleberries. The kind that don't grow on Haida Gwaii.

So whom to consult again but Nancy Turner. She has, in my mind, once and for all settled the argument:

---

* The first time I made this jam I used a recipe that called for 6 cups (1.5 L) of blackberries, 2 cups (500 mL) of sugar and 5 Tbsp (75 mL) "real-fruit instant pectin." I couldn't find the latter in Masset but liked the idea of cutting back on the sugar so tried using a product customers swore by at the "healthy store" (as my granddaughters call the health food store): a pectin extracted from citrus peel, whose gelling power is activated by calcium, not by sugar content. But my jam didn't set as well as I'd hoped it would (I guess I haven't learned to live with runny jam, even though it still tastes delicious). So have resorted to regular pectin and the scary amount of sugar, obeying the recipe for Blackberry Jam inside the package of pectin. It is usually 2 cups (500 mL) of sugar to 1 cup (240 mL) of berries. I only make freezer (no cook) jam or jelly these days; uncooked berries retain their berry-flavour so the blackberries taste like real blackberries, raspberries taste like real raspberries, and so on.) I assuage my guilt by eating less jam. (I can't believe how easy it is to lie when it comes to eating!)

Typical scattered shrubs are species of Vaccinium (red huckleberry V. parvifolium, Alaska blueberry V. alaskaense, oval-leaved blueberry V. ovalifolium).

UNHELPFUL TIDBIT #1: Blueberries and huckleberries are closely related. Unless you have a degree in botany, it's often difficult to tell the difference between the two, except by the seeds.

UNHELPFUL TIDBIT #2: Blueberries have a large number of very tiny and soft seeds, whereas huckleberries have 10 to 12 larger and harder seeds. This distinction is often lost, however, since in neither case are the seeds generally noticeable when eating the fruit.

My friend Lynda and I set off every August to drive up into the hills above Juskatla to pick the wild Alaska or oval-leaved blueberries. Lynda has her favourite spot where the bear scat around the blueberry bushes is the thickest. The first year we picked together I had a thorn in my eye (unbeknownst to me) and every few minutes would shriek as a stab of pain shot through my eyeball into my brain. Lynda always takes her rifle with her in case she sees something she wants to kill, and I am pretty sure she thought of dispatching me in the blueberry patch that day, though once she realized I was a harmless hypochondriac (albeit a very sick hypochondriac) she knew it would be more fun to watch me live.

I did go to the emergency room when we got home, and had a doctor try to remove the thorn with a needle. When that didn't work I was sent off-island to see

an eye specialist in Victoria. Removal of microscopic thorn-matter would require surgery, which I never had. Who has time for surgery, when there are more blueberries to pick?

While waiting to see the eye specialist in Victoria I was given an information form. I assume this helped the doctor determine how you might react when he stuck a needle in your eye.

"Personality Type

a) Easy Going

b) In the Middle

c) Perfectionist"

I crossed out "Perfectionist" and wrote "Extremely difficult—you try being me!"

NOTE: Often when I am using frozen blueberries in a recipe I reach into the bag and take out a handful, then, hours later, wonder how I came to have the strange blue-black bruises all over my hand.

TOP LEFT: Haida Gwaii black bear in search of blueberries PHOTO BY GUY KIMOLA

TOP MIDDLE: Lynda always takes her rifle with her PHOTO BY MARK BRISTOL

TOP RIGHT: Charley Jolley picking huckleberries PHOTO BY JANIE JOLLEY

BOTTOM LEFT: Washing the day's haul PHOTO BY JANIE JOLLEY

BOTTOM RIGHT: Huckleberries PHOTO BY FARHAD GHATAN

Berries

MANY TYPES of berries were traditionally stored for the winter in "bent" cedar boxes, sometimes lined with skunk cabbage leaves and smothered in oolichan grease. They were eaten with grease and sugar mixed with salmon roe.

There is a Haida expression for a person whose face is covered with bruises: *Hldaansgingaan 'la fang.iigeeng-gaangang* (literally "looks like blueberries.")

There is a Haida expression for a person whose face is covered with bruises: *Hldaansgingaan 'la fang.iigeenggaangang* (literally "looks like blueberries.")

Huckleberries are ubiquitous. Some of us use a berry scoop to rake berries from the bush in a simple sweeping motion that doesn't hurt the plant, and cuts down on the time you spend berry picking. Others, like Charley Jolley do it the old-fashioned way. That is, one berry at a time.

WILD STRAWBERRIES

Wild strawberries (also known as seaside strawberries) grow on the sand dunes along the beach from Masset to Rose Spit, particularly on Rose Spit where you can compete with the bears and the deer as you try to fill your bucket. They are tiny and hard to pick and gathering these pale, even whitish, berries is a labour of patient love. But there is more intense flavour in one tiny wild berry than you'll find in a handful of those giant imported hybrids.

CLOUDBERRIES

In the '70s I was much more of a romantic, and what could be more romantic than the word "cloudberry." I even wrote a poem called "Picking Cloudberries by Moonlight." This year, as I made my way through the bog picking in the dreamy August sunlight, I wondered—would it even be possible to *see* a cloudberry by moonlight?

At least the bugs wouldn't have been so bad after dark and I wouldn't have suffered the way this writer, Alice Ramirez, searching for cloudberries in Churchill, Manitoba, did. "The area's ferocious bugs had been plaguing me despite my protective armor. In their urgency to feed, mosquitoes and huge blackflies almost the size of olives had been throwing themselves at my face and bare hands. They were even crawling inside my clothes through the neckline . . . As I felt stingers injecting themselves into my veins and arteries, and horrid mandibles tearing chunks out of my legs, face, neck and scalp, I wanted only to get indoors."

Each cloudberry plant produces one flower and a single berry at the end of a stalk. This makes picking slow going; you can't just sit down in the muskeg and pick an ice-cream bucket full in one afternoon. When unripe, the berries are bright red or pale red, but they turn to yellow as they ripen. The plant is related to raspberries, but cloudberries taste nothing like raspberries. Some people say they taste like gooseberries, some describe a creamsicle taste. I even read one reference to a cloudberry as having a "tart, idiosyncratic flavour," whatever that means. The cloudberry is known as the bakeapple in Atlantic Canada, believed to be from the French, baie qu'appelle . . . meaning, "what is this berry called?" Florence Davidson refers to them as "maltberries."

P.S. I said I was much more of a romantic 40 years ago, but I think I lied. Recently I ordered a cookbook, simply because of the title: *Falling Cloudberries: A World of Family Recipes.* There turned out not to be a single cloudberry recipe in the book, though the cover is a tempting photograph of cranberry sorbet. The author, Tessa Kiros, had a Greek-Cypriot father and a Finnish (hence the cloudberry connection) mother: she, too, romances the cloudberry.

TOP LEFT: Wild strawberries PHOTO BY PETER SLOAN

TOP RIGHT: Wild strawberry PHOTO BY JAYNE MASON

BOTTOM LEFT: Cloudberry PHOTO BY BOB FRAUMENI

BOTTOM RIGHT: Picking cloudberries south of Masset in August PHOTO BY BOB FRAUMENI

Cloudberries

I N ALASKA, cloudberries are mixed with seal oil, reindeer or caribou fat (which is diced up and made fluffy with the seal oil) and sugar to make "Eskimo Ice Cream" or *agutak.* Recipes vary by region. Along the Yukon and Kuskokwim River areas, cloudberries are mixed with fat, sugar and either boiled with whitefish or mashed potatoes for "texture."

HANDS-FREE CLOUDBERRY JAM 5 CUPS (1.2 L)

Adapted from Nigella Lawson's easy to make and intensely fresh-flavoured raspberry jam recipe (from *How to be a Domestic Goddess*).

4 cups (950 mL) cloudberries

4 cups (950 mL) sugar

Juice of 1 lemon

WHAT YOU DO

1   Preheat oven to 350°F (180°C).

2   Mix the lemon juice with the cloudberries; place the cloudberries and the sugar in two separate pie plates (so the fruit will be spread out, and not be piled up) and put them both in the oven for 20–25 minutes, until they are really hot.

3   Take the two pie plates out of the oven, carefully, and add the piping hot sugar to the cloudberries. Nigella Lawson writes (of this process,) "As you do so you'll find the fruit turns into a molten, ruby-red river." If you are using cloudberries, the fruit turns into a molten river of gold.

4   Pour the jam into sterilized jars.

5   Put lids on and leave to cool.

6   Store in the fridge. Cloudberries contain so much benzoic acid that they can be stored in the fridge for long periods of time without bacterial or fungal spoilage. (If you prefer you can process the jars in a hot water bath. I find the jam gets eaten so quickly the spoilage has never been a problem.)

ILLUSTRATION BY DEJAHLEE BUSCH

SUBSTITUTIONS

What else? Raspberries.

Agutak

Here's how they make it in the Yukon. You place your fat (shortening or lard will work) in a large bowl and whip it with a bare hand, folding in lots of air, until it is light and fluffy. (I have never heard of whipping with a bare hand, but I guess this is what you must do if you live off-the-grid and don't have a working Kitchen Aid.) Add sugar and berries and whip away some more. Then add the cold boiled whitefish (or mashed potatoes), and continue whipping, until your concoction has a smooth, homogenous texture. The end result should appear, if not taste like, cake frosting. It can be eaten at room temperature, chilled, or frozen.

The fish or potatoes do not add a flavour to the dish, apparently, but are used to change the texture so the ice cream does not feel "slippery on the tongue." The key is in the whipping; lots of air must be whipped in for the dish to be light. Well-made *agutak* is said to be airy and flavourful and tasting of berries. I am determined never to find out. Short of lowering one's naked foot into the bottom of a slimy pond I cannot think of a more depressing experience.

Here is my version of *agutak,* Haida Gwaii–style.

CLOUDBERRY MOONLIGHT CREAM

(FOR OLD TIME'S SAKE) SERVES 4

1½ cups (350 mL) whipping cream

¼ cup (60 mL) sugar

2 teaspoons (10 mL) vanilla extract

½ cup (120 mL) freshly picked (by moonlight, for the authentic experience) cloudberries

WHAT YOU DO

1   With the aid of electric beaters, whip the cream with the sugar until it forms soft cloud-like peaks.

2   Add the vanilla extract (taking a good sniff of it first). (Whenever I made cookies at home this was one of our rituals: I would open the bottle of vanilla and let my daughters sniff it before adding a teaspoon or two to my recipe.)

3   Fold in the cloudberries.

4   Pour into your favourite serving dish. Decorate with more cloudberries.

Picking Cloudberries by Moonlight

under the powdery stars
and trudging home later
over frozen ground
with first light breaking
everything was easy.
Ice formed in our footsteps
as if where were coming from
was a thousand years ago.
Ice grew on my fingers around the glass,
on the berries inside
like blood clots barely pulsing.
With you wearing the old green

jacket that still holds your shape
even now long after you have
abandoned it; with you holding
your new knife and that weapon
I had suddenly grown curious of
everything seemed easy.
Often I have tried to remember
why you stopped, with me shivering
at the pond's edge, anxious to go on.
So often I have wanted to remember
the way we took, as if what we had been
hoping to find had little to do with the search.
Then the shining lake,
the insomniac moon.
Birds rose up out of the ice
(it seemed to take place over centuries);
frightened by my own awkwardness
you reached to draw me back.
Crouched down under a dead tree
for shelter we watched them, all
colours and music. It was ghostly;
you said *wait for me*. I never knew choice
until that moment.
Clutching my cold jar of berries
as it were fire to comfort us
or light to lead you
from whatever I felt unsure of
I walked away.
Yet waking alone in a strange world
even later, hearing you say *wait*
but not having had the courage,
everything is forgiven.
I do not remember the gun going off.
I have tried to forget this much.

Cloudberry PHOTO BY CHRIS ASHURST

SALAL BERRIES

In the old days Florence Davidson would walk from Old Massett to New Masset (mostly referred to as plain "Masset" these days) to pick salal berries. "There weren't any white people there then, just all kinds of berries.*" I think there are still more salal berries than there are white people in Masset, but I know what she meant.

The Haida used salal leaves between layers of dried spring salmon and sockeye, which helped preserve the fish. I had a neighbour on Tow Hill Road who used to mow his salal (it won, and he moved away). I've tasted salal berries raw, picked from the bushes surrounding my house, bushes that grow taller and more impenetrable every year so that I have to fight my way through them on my way to the compost; I've eaten salal berry jam, jelly, pies, wine, syrup and vinegar.

Salal berries are blue-black and slightly hairy tasting. If you have ever eaten one you will know what I mean.

SALAL BERRY JAM FOUR 1 CUP (240 ML) JARS

Though the berries are strained to extract the juice, this resembles jam more than jelly. The amount of sugar in the recipe is low (compared to what you would use for most jams and jellies) because salal berries are full of natural pectin, so sugar is not necessary for thickening. If you like a sweeter jam, add more sugar.

10 cups (2.4 L) of salal berries, rinsed and destemmed	½ cup (120 mL) sugar (or more if you want your jam sweeter)
¼ cup (60 mL) lemon juice	13 oz (90 mL) pouch liquid pectin
¼ cup (60 mL) of water	

WHAT YOU DO

1   Simmer the berries, lemon juice and water in a heavy saucepan on medium heat. When the berries are getting broken down and the juice is very purple, about 10–15 minutes, mash the mix with a potato masher until it is all a fine mess. At this point you'll want to strain it (the skins tend to be tough). You can do that by pressing it through a fine mesh sieve.

---

*   From *During My Time: Florence Edenshaw Davidson, A Haida Woman* by Margaret Blackman

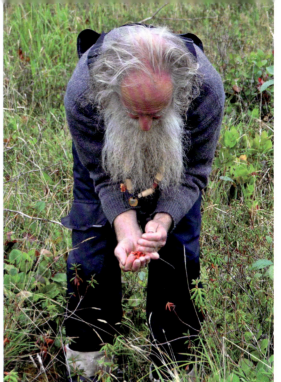

2 Return the salal berry mash to the saucepot and add the sugar and pectin, and bring to a simmer over medium heat. Remove from the heat and pour into your hot sterilized jars. Put your hot lids on with the rings and put in a hot water bath for 10 minutes.

CRANBERRIES

If you drive south from Masset in October you will see men and women bent over in the ditches, in what might appear to some as some kind of cultish ritual. Not at all. They are picking bog cranberries.

The first time I picked bog cranberries myself it took me an hour, in a cold wind and rain, to reap half a cup. I had to make sure my dinner guests heard about my efforts when I served my Pear, Cranberry and Vanilla Crumble (see recipe page 323). That year I hoarded them in the freezer, not wanting to use them because they were so hard to pick.

But once you get the hang of it, you will end up with more berries. One trick is to take three or four beginner-berry-pickers with you, who are more than likely to dump their berries in with yours when you are finished for the day. The next year you will have to find new uninitiated friends, though. Because once your first lot of beginner-berry-pickers has a taste of your crumble, or your Cranberry Relish Chutney, they will wish they hadn't given you their cranberries and in future years will be likely to hoard their own.

TOP LEFT: Bog cranberries PHOTO BY MICHELLE FURBACHER

BOTTOM LEFT: Cranberries PHOTO BY MICHELLE FURBACHER

RIGHT: Wilfred Penker picking cranberries near Masset PHOTO BY GUY KIMOLA

Simple Cranberry Sauce PHOTO BY MICHELLE FURBACHER

On Haida Gwaii, we have highbush cranberries, bog cranberries, and low-bush cranberries or lingonberries (also known as low cranberry, rock cranberry or moss cranberry) The highbush cranberry plant has largely disappeared over the last century, due in large part to introduced deer. In the old days high-ranking Haida matriarchs owned inherited patches of highbush cranberries, which were passed down, from generation to generation.

Bog cranberry differs from lingonberry in that its small vines lie on the ground in the muskeg (and in the ditches at the sides of the road), with one red berry on each thin stalk. Lingonberries grow in clusters—on short, upright stalks. Bog cranberry is often referred to as "the summer form" and lingonberry as "the winter form" but I have picked both types in the fall, growing alongside each other on the muskeg and in the boggy ditches.

SIMPLE CRANBERRY SAUCE 2 CUPS

Why anyone would buy canned cranberry sauce—also known as Splork, the sound this sauce makes as it slides out of the can—is beyond me. Proper presentation of the cran-o-log is to leave it whole, in the shape of the can and lying on its side preferably still bearing the indentations of the tin.

Making your own is simpler than struggling to open a can to begin with, and less energy consuming. The can openers I have seem to have minds of their own.

2 cups (475 mL) low bush cranberries   ¾ cups (190 mL) sugar

WHAT YOU DO

1   Combine berries and sugar in a heavy pot and cook over medium heat until the cranberries start to pop and the mixture thickens. This could take anywhere from 30–45 minutes.

2   How to tell when your sauce is cooked? Pour a little bit into a saucer, and then tilt the saucer to see if the sauce tries to run away. If it stays put, it's ready.

3   You can also double the recipe and squirrel your cranberry sauce away for the next occasion. The sauce will need to be poured into sterilized jars and processed in a boiling water bath. I prefer to freeze any amounts left over. Of course I freeze my cranberries as soon as I've picked them, so I always have fresh (well, fresh-frozen) cranberries on hand whenever I need to whip up a simple cranberry sauce.

SUBSTITUTION

You can use the domestic variety of cranberries, either fresh or frozen. It's just more fun to make your own, with berries you have suffered to pick, bending over in the ditch, being lashed by the elements. The large commercial variety of cranberries, which can be used here if you don't have access to a cranberry bog, tend to pop more wildly and enthusiastically than their tiny tight-lipped free-range counterparts.

CRANBERRY RELISH CHUTNEY 4 CUPS (950 ML)

For times when you want something slightly less simple, but still not all that hard to make.

½ cup (120 mL) water	½ cup (120 mL) figs, chopped
½ cup (120 mL) freshly squeezed orange juice	½ cup (120 mL) pecans, chopped
½ cup (120 mL) brown sugar	½ tsp (2 mL) cinnamon
1 ½ cups (350 mL) cranberries	½ tsp (2 mL) ground cardamom
1 cup (240 mL) dried apricots, diced	½ tsp (2 mL) freshly ground nutmeg
½ cup (120 mL) golden raisins	1 tsp (5 mL) fresh ginger, grated
	2 Tbsp (30 mL) brandy or dark rum

WHAT YOU DO

1   Bring sugar, water and orange juice to a gentle boil.

2   Add cranberries; cook over medium heat until they start to pop.

3   Add remaining ingredients. Cook 5–15 minutes, depending on how "cooked" you like your ingredients. I like not to be able to distinguish, say, a piece of cooked apricot from a cooked golden raisin.

4   Add brandy or rum. Cook for 3 minutes longer.

Cranberries

- There are several theories as to the origin of the name "cranberry." One is that the open flowers look like the head of a crane; another is that cranes like to eat these sour berries.
- Small pockets of air inside cause the cranberry to bounce, also to float in water.
- A common belief is that John says "I Buried Paul" at the end of Strawberry Fields Forever on the *Magical Mystery Tour* album. In fact, he actually says "Cranberry Sauce," not once, but twice.

Sandhill cranes PHOTO BY LISA FROESE PHOTOGRAPHY

WILD ROSES OR NOOTKA ROSES

I grew up calling wild roses briar roses. Briar Rose was the name of the princess in the Brothers Grimm's version of *Sleeping Beauty*, and a pseudonym used by Princess Aurora in the Walt Disney version. I had a china doll I romantically called Maureen Princess Aurora. At that time (my formative years) we lived in Honolulu and (so family lore goes) I buried Maureen Princess Aurora in the sands of Waikiki. My mother claims she knew, back then, she would be reading my name in the newspapers one day. I assume she meant in the Court Parade.

A rose by any other name. Whatever you call them—wild roses, briar roses, Nootka roses—the roses you want to gather while ye may (these can range in shade from whiter-shade-of-pale-pink to dark pink, warm red and even healthy-blood red) are the ones that grow where they choose to grow. Aside from being confident they will be organic, it is an experience—the sun, the sweet-smelling wind, the tender way the petals fall off into your hands—you will remember for the rest of your life. I have intoxicating memories of driving down to the Village of Old Massett on a fiercely windy but warm afternoon in June, and plucking wild rose petals, soft as the kisses of moths, while the bouldery clouds blew by overhead and ravens spoke in tongues from the trees.

WILD ROSE PETAL SYRUP

MAKES 4 CUPS (950 ML) OF SYRUP

If you want your syrup to be rich in colour, choose only the darkest pink wild rose petals for your syrup. Pick them first thing in the morning when the fragrance is strongest. (I found that on Haida Gwaii the time of day didn't make a lot of difference as to how strongly the roses smelled, but further south, it might.) Be careful not to pick the whole flower otherwise there will be no rosehip and therefore no rosehip tea. Bunch the fingers in one hand and tug gently on the petals, leaving the pistils and stamens behind.

The best-flavoured syrup comes from massaging the sugar into the petals and allowing both to sit overnight while the sugar draws the juices from the petals.

8 oz (225 g) wild rose petals	Juice of 1 large lemon, seeds included
7 cups (1.75 L) sugar, divided	3 cups (700 mL) water

WHAT YOU DO

1   Place the rose petals into a non-reactive bowl and toss with 2 cups (475 mL) of the sugar and rub gently with your fingertips, squeezing the petals gently to bruise slightly.

2   Cover with plastic film and let stand in a cool place overnight.

3   The following day, add the remaining 5 cups (1.2 L) of sugar, the water and lemon juice in a large pot. Bring to a boil and stir to dissolve the sugar, then add the rose petal–mixture including any liquid that might have formed, into the pot and bring to a boil once again.

4   Reduce heat to a soft boil and cook for about 30 minutes, or until a thermometer reads 220°F (105°C).

5   Remove from the heat and cool to room temperature.

6   Strain the syrup discarding the petals* and seeds. Dribble a little over yoghurt, or serve over vanilla ice cream. Store the syrup in the refrigerator, or freeze in sterilized jars.

SUBSTITUTIONS

The best roses to eat, other than wild roses, are those you grow yourself, as long as you haven't sprayed them or used systemic insecticides and fungicides. Try the old-fashioned heirloom roses that are low maintenance and don't require artificial-anything to encourage blooms.

Never use store-bought roses. Growing those long-stemmed—not to mention fragrance-less—dethorned-by-exploited-women-in-Colombia roses, takes a ton of chemicals and fertilizers—none of them safe to ingest, not even in the guise of ice cream.

If a rose smells good, then it should taste good, also. Many tea roses, as well as some of the endless-blooming roses, have no fragrance, and thus no flavour. Red roses, generally speaking, have little fragrance or flavour, but the pinks, yellows and occasionally the white bloomers often have both.

TOP LEFT: Wild rose petals
PHOTO BY SUSAN MUSGRAVE

TOP RIGHT: Dried rose petals
PHOTO BY MICHELLE FURBACHER

BOTTOM MIDDLE: Wild Rose Petal Syrup PHOTO BY MICHELLE FURBACHER

BOTTOM LEFT: Rose hips PHOTO BY MICHELLE FURBACHER

BOTTOM RIGHT: Yoghurt with Wild Rose Petal Syrup PHOTO BY MICHELLE FURBACHER

---

*   If you decide not to, see the recipe for Candied Rose Petals, page 136.

Briar Rose

- *Briar Rose*, a novel by Jane Yolen
- *Briar Rose*, a novella by Robert Coover
- *The Legend of Briar Rose*, a series of paintings by the Pre-Raphaelite artist Edward Burne-Jones
- *Briar Rose*, a traditional heavy metal band from Swansea, Massachusetts
- Briar Rose or *Rosa rubiginosa*, also known as sweet briar, a flowering plant

CANDIED ROSE PETALS

I can never bring myself to discard the intensely flavoured concoction of crushed rose petals and sugar from the Wild Rose Petal Syrup recipe. Besides, the petals take so long to pick I don't want to squander the results of my hard labour. I spread the mixture out on a baking tray lined with parchment paper and bake the sugary rose petals for 1 hour at 250°F (120°C). They are still a little moist when I remove them from the oven—moist but slightly crystallized—and they can probably baked longer, but I am impatient.

I don't share these with just *anyone*. Sometimes I add a few, along with the rose petal syrup, to a dish of vanilla ice cream. Or sprinkle them atop the mousse on my (Almost) Flourless Double Chocolate Torte (see page 290).

SEA ASPARAGUS

Sea asparagus growing PHOTO BY JOHANNE YOUNG

Sea asparagus, also known as beach asparagus, Salicornia tips, glasswort, pickleweed, samphire greens, sea beans, sea fennel, pousse-pied, crow's foot greens (in Nova Scotia) and my favourite—grass-land green skinny razor clams, and who-knows-what-someone-will-come-up-with-next, is an edible halophyte (new word to me, it means a plant tolerant of salt or salt water) that looks like a cross between small pieces of plump grass and midget (I mean really small) asparagus. It tastes salty—nothing like asparagus, either—and belongs to the *Salicornia* family, made up of 60 species that grow in salty waters, along beaches, sandy intertidal zones and salt marshes.

Sea asparagus is at its best in the spring, before it starts to flower, and in areas that are not heavily trafficked by boats, or where your neighbours walk their dogs! I pick (snip it off with scissors) my sea asparagus along the (tidal) Sangan River, and along the banks of the Tlell River where there is so much it is like walking over a green crunchy carpet.

Soak the sea asparagus in three parts fresh water to one part white vinegar (a white vinegar and water wash kills 98% of bacteria and will get rid of excess saltiness) for 20 minutes to half an hour before you cook it.

Sea asparagus can be eaten raw, pickled or cooked. It can be served on its own as a side dish—all you need is a frying pan and some butter or oil, and maybe some minced garlic. Cook it for just a few minutes so it keeps crunchy and serve over the top of rice, bulgur, chickpeas or any other bean or grain. I also toss handfuls in salads. It is pretty innocuous stuff, which means you can subject it to your will and it will roll over and do what you want!

One of the best parts is going down to the river to pick sea asparagus. Like all food gathering, it gets you out of the house, out of the kitchen, and you come home with a whole new appreciation for being outdoors—with a purpose!

PICKLED SEA ASPARAGUS

MAKES 8 HALF PINT (250 ML) JARS

"I am giving out tastes from my wee jar, to the chosen few I think worthy and as we stand by the fridge with our chopsticks and the jar, it's like a religious experience."
—Ilona Beiks, treasured guest and recipient of jarred Pickled Sea Asparagus from Copper Beech House, 2012

2 quarts (2 L) sea asparagus	A generous pinch of black peppercorns (for each jar)
3 cups (700 mL) apple cider vinegar	
3 cups (700 mL) water	2 red peppers (from which you cut 8 small heart-shaped pieces)
1 cup (240 mL) sugar	1 Tbsp (15 mL) mixed pickling spice (or use whole coriander seeds and whole yellow mustard seeds)
8 garlic cloves, peeled and sliced longways (one for each jar)	
8 bay leaves (one for each jar)	Sprinkling of dill seed

clipping them off at the base so more will grow back and I am not depleting the crop. As they get older, taller and tougher, I only take the tender tops. Collect plenty if you want to make a meal of it—the greens will shrink down—the same way spinach does—when boiled or steamed.

I blanch the leaves and then rinse them in ice water and store them in the freezer in one-pound bags. Lambsquarters contain oxalates, an acid also found in spinach, Swiss chard, potatoes and rhubarb, and freezing the leaves helps break down those acids.

A word of warning: lambsquarters is a "purifier herb" and in its fervour to cleanse the soil, it absorbs pollutants and concentrates them in its leaves. Foragers should be leery of waste ground where this plant grows in abundance—it could be an indication of soil pollution: it would be worth finding out what gets dumped in nearby fields or streams. Another abnormality to watch for is a reddish hue on the leaves, which indicates that spinach leaf miner larvae are squatting in the foliage.

CHAOS, QUINOA AND THE BUTTERFLY EFFECT

Confession. I have yet to harvest the seeds of our local lambsquarters even though it would help the Third World economy if we could find a closer-to-home alternative to our Bolivian connection. (Another of my million dollar ideas is to grow organic cocaine, but that idea is simpering on the back burner—for the time being.) Quinoa was once a staple crop, a peasant food of the Andes, but now, guess what? Farmers sell their crops to North American markets and prices have tripled, making quinoa unaffordable to many impoverished communities who are now able to afford a more varied diet, but have taken to supplementing their diets with cheaper processed foods. It's complicated, as they say on Facebook.

From Wikipedia (slightly simplified): In chaos theory, the **butterfly effect** is the *sensitive dependence on initial conditions* in which a small change at one place can result in large differences in a later state. The name of the effect, coined by Edward Lorenz, is derived from the theoretical example of a hurricane's formation being contingent on whether or not a distant butterfly had flapped its wings several weeks earlier.

Lambsquarters

LAMBSQUARTERS GREW in the Late Glacial- and the Post-Glacial–periods and was the accustomed diet of the Neolithic, Bronze Age and early Iron Age people. It contains more iron, protein and vitamin B$_2$ than spinach, and more calcium and vitamin B$_1$ than raw cabbage. It only fell out of favour after its relative, the nouveau spinach, was introduced to England from Southwest Asia in the 16th century.

Spurned by most gardeners today, lambsquarters was introduced to North America by settlers from Europe. Both have proliferated: by puberty the human female has about 300,000 eggs lying in wait to be fertilized, while a single lambsquarters plant can produce at least 75,000 seeds a season.

TIME, QUINOA AND THE SAPONIN EFFECT

My poor excuse for failing to pick lambsquarters seeds is that it would be too time-consuming. A less poor excuse is that quinoa is covered with a bitter substance called saponin, which birds and deer won't touch, and because of this coating, quinoa requires thorough rinsing before cooking—which is too time-consuming. (I am assuming that lambsquarters seeds would require the same treatment, and I know there is only one way to find out, but that would be— too time-consuming.)

There seem to be two ways of getting rid of the saponin covering your seeds.

METHOD #1: Put the grain in a blender with cool water at the lowest speed, changing the water until it is no longer soapy. It takes about five water changes to achieve the desired, non-frothy result.

METHOD #2: Tie the desired amount of quinoa in a stocking, a loose-weave muslin bag, or a pillowcase and run it through the cold-water cycle of an automatic washing machine.

Commercial quinoa, however, has had the saponin removed. No doubt seed by seed, by hand, by impoverished Third World workers high up in the Andes chewing coca leaves to stay awake. It becomes harder and harder to eat and have a social conscience at the same time.

Crab Apples

THERE ARE TWO thoughts about the origin of "crab" in "crab apples." The Scottish form is scrab or scrabbe, seemingly from a Norse source, as there is Swedish skrabba "fruit of the wild apple tree." This would suggest that crab and crabbe are aphetic forms of a much older word.

Another is the possibility is that it derives from "crabbed," which itself means, etymologically, "crooked or wayward gait of a crab" and the several figurative senses that follow from that (disagreeable, contrary, ill-tempered, or crooked). One of those senses might have been applied to the fruit of the crab apple: not right, not pleasant, ill-flavoured (because crab apples are very sour and astringent).

PACIFIC CRAB APPLE OR WILD CRAB APPLE

The crab apple, the wild apple, is source of all domestic apples grown today. Ovoid shaped and small (about 1 cm long) they grow in long-stemmed clusters; they are tart, but juicy, crisp and become sweeter after a frost or if you store them in a cool place. My mother and my grandmother used to make crab apple jelly every autumn; when I was in a contrary mood I remember being admonished: "Don't be such a crab apple."

When my father anchored *Froggie* in a desolate bay (which probably accounted for my contrary mood) and rowed us ashore to play on the beach in front of an abandoned village site, I remember orchards of twisted crab apple trees, and my father telling us that the people who lived there in years gone by had buried their dead with apple seeds in their mouths. I've never been able to find any proof of this—perhaps it was my parents' way of making sure we didn't try to climb the trees and pick and eat the crab apples—but I have always liked the idea of being buried with a crab apple seed inside my cheek. (Executors of my estate, take note.)

Crab apple trees were at one time plentiful, George M. Dawson noted, in his journal in 1878, that "many thickets of crab apple fringed the shores on the Masset "lakes." The Haida picked crab apples late in the fall, and boiled them and submerged them in water in bentwood cedar boxes until mid-winter, when fermentation transformed the hard, very sour crab apples into clusters of soft, sweet tangy effervescent deliciousness. The stems and stalks were removed and the crab apples were mixed with oolichan grease, "forming a delicious pabulum."

WILD MUSHROOMS

"When in doubt toss it out."
—Old mushroom hunter saying

"When in doubt, don't pick it."
—New age eco-sensitive mushroom hunter saying

ALERT: It's a pretty sure bet that any mushroom with *satanas* in its name should be avoided. Anything named after the devil is likely to have earned its reputation. Similarly, it would be tempting fate to pick and eat any mushroom whose name contains the word "death" or "deadly." Best to bone up on your Latin, too, before cooking up a mess of *Amanita phalloides* commonly known as the "death cap" and involved in the majority of human deaths from mushroom poisoning.

When I was growing up the only good mushroom was one found in a can of mushroom soup. Everything else could kill you if you even looked at it and then rubbed your eyes and (god forbid) touched your fingertips to your lips. Mushrooms were deadlier than the potato salad my mother insisted we eat while it was still refrigerated. We had to take turns standing in front of the fridge, waiting for our allotted forkful, while my father yelled, "For God's sake close the fridge door." If the salad was allowed to come to room temperature, my mother believed, we would catch botulism from something the eggs did to the mayonnaise while you had turned your back to put ketchup and mustard on your hot dog. (I exaggerate. We never ate hot dogs. We couldn't afford them.)

The first mushrooms I picked on Haida Gwaii were not the sort you would expect to read about in a serious cookbook. Or maybe you would? Certainly I have no recipes to include, other than "have one heavy blanket on hand with which to cover your face and head when the going gets rough." These types of mushrooms belong to the genus *Psilocybe* and cause hallucinations when ingested because they contain the psychotropic tryptamines psilocybin and psilocin. We called them psilocybin mushrooms but they are more commonly referred to as magic mushrooms, or shrooms.

My one experience with these hallucination-inducing mushrooms was in a trailer parked next to a swamp on the outskirts of Port Clements in 1972. There is possibly nothing more boring than a person describing a bad drug trip, so I'll spare you the details.

EDIBLE WILD MUSHROOMS OF HAIDA GWAII

The most commonly harvested mushroom on Haida Gwaii is the Pacific golden chanterelle. Many other edible species grow here, such as boletes, oyster mushrooms, blewits, shaggy manes, hedgehog mushrooms, blue and black chanterelles, chicken of the woods and puffballs. Pine mushrooms have been found, but rarely, from what I hear.

Boletes (*Boletus edulis*) are universally appreciated. The French refer to them affectionately as *cèpes*, the Germans glorify them as *Steinpilz*, and the Italians are wild about their *porcini*, meaning piglets (pigs compete for them). Here, *Boletus edulis* is often called "king bolete," and in my experience the worms compete for them. I have never found one that the worms haven't found first. Those early bird worm-gourmands, they get my king bolete.

The thing I like best about hedgehog mushrooms is their name. They grow profusely near the Masset cemetery so I feel a little creepy about eating them, as if it makes me a cannibal, by association. Talk about having a close relationship to your food.

Shaggy manes grow along the sides of the road, in the gravel, as if daring passersby to kick them over or run them down. All day they snort dust and fumes

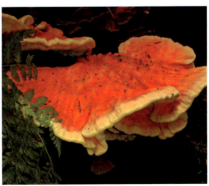

TOP LEFT: Hedgehog PHOTO BY CHRIS ASHURST

TOP RIGHT: *Bolete Incrediblus* PHOTO BY CHRIS ASHURST

MIDDLE (TOP) LEFT: Puffballs PHOTO BY CHRIS ASHURST

MIDDLE (TOP) RIGHT: Shaggy Manes PHOTO BY CHRIS ASHURST

MIDDLE (BOTTOM) LEFT: Full chanterelle PHOTO BY CHRIS ASHURST

MIDDLE (BOTTOM) RIGHT: Stump o' chicken PHOTO BY CHRIS ASHURST

BOTTOM LEFT: Blewit PHOTO BY CHRIS ASHURST

BOTTOM RIGHT: Close up of chicken of the woods PHOTO BY CHRIS ASHURST

from passing motorcars. I am hesitant to pick and eat them because they look like every stranger my mother warned me about. Why can't they grow in the clean, green woods like a self-respecting chanterelle?

Puffballs were poisonous, my parents said. You never saw a Campbell's Cream of Puffball Soup, did you? I looked them up. Puffballs are so named "because clouds of brown dust-like spores are emitted when the mature fruiting body bursts, or in response to impacts such as those of falling raindrops" or us as kids, squeezing them in each other's faces. "There are a number of false puffballs that look similar to the true ones." (Wikipedia) That's what I thought. My parents were right. Eschew them.

Chicken of the woods can make a decent chicken substitute as long as you make sure to fully cook the mushroom (same applies to chicken itself.) There is nothing more cheerful-making than seeing this bright orange fungi beckoning me from the tree it is slowly destabilizing by causing a reddish brown cubical heart-rot of wood and hollowing out the tree's centre. (As a friend of mine's mother said, after watching a violent programme on the Discovery Channel, "Don't you just hate nature?") Chicken of the woods should be harvested when they are young and tender, as the old ones tend to grow bitter and unpalatable. Be wary of chickens growing on conifers (in the Northeast) as they are a different species and can poison you. (I have no firsthand experience of this; it is just something I read and thought it prudent to pass along.)

My favourite chicken of the woods fact? "Historically, this fungus was known to damage the wooden ships of the British Naval Fleet." A mushroom after my own heart-rot, obviously.

If you find a chicken of the woods do not simply tear it from the tree and rush home and spread the pores in the bulwarks of your father's old boat. It would be tempting, but . . . if you tear it from the tree this will damage the mycelium and could kill the parent fungus and stop it from growing again next year. If you cut off a chunk close to the tree, you can have your mushrooms and eat them, too— next season there will be a bright new crop of wooden ship-destroyers. What I do is cut the outer edge (about 5 cm of the fungus) and return later in the season for a second helping.

I can't tell you anything about blewits, oyster mushrooms, pine mushrooms or blue and black chanterelles,[*] because I have never found any. It's probably just as well. I might not have anything positive to say about them. I seem to be in a monogamous relationship with the trumpet-shaped sweet-talking golden femme fatale, the chanterelle.

---

[*] How quickly things change! September 13, 2014 I went out on the most beautiful day of the year, to the place where I have always picked the most chanterelles. There were very few, after the dry hot summer. But I found a very large patch of—black chanterelles! I have marked the spot (they will grow back, I've read) even though it was in an obvious clearing and I have no idea why other mushroom pickers wouldn't have stumbled over it.

I rushed it over to Guy Kimola to have it photographed.

NOT KENTUCKY
FRIED CHICKEN OF THE WOODS

2 GENEROUS SERVINGS OR 4 SMALL SERVINGS

1 lb (450 g) chicken of the woods

A glug of olive oil or a daub of butter

2 cloves (or more, to taste) chopped garlic

Juice of one lemon

Salt and pepper, to taste

WHAT YOU DO

1   Trim fresh chicken of the woods, discarding any tough parts that are no longer "juicy." Tear strips along grain (or cut if you prefer).

2   In a shallow pan, heat a glug of olive oil or a daub of butter along with plenty of chopped garlic (amount depends on preference—I use lots).

3   Add mushroom strips and lightly sauté 1–2 min. Lower heat.

4   Add the juice of one lemon.

5   Cover to keep moist and cook another few minutes until tender but not dry.

6   Season with salt and pepper to taste.

CHANTERELLES

Chanterelles light up forests all over the world—from Zimbabwe to Haida Gwaii, Siberia to Costa Rica, Saskatchewan to New Orleans. They grow under the live oaks in California, and in Nova Scotia under the pines. Once you have gone out picking with someone you trust, someone who knows how not to get lost (you would be surprised how many people wander into the woods and never come out) and can help you find what you are looking for—once you have picked your first chanterelle you will find them easy to identify and will never have doubts about harvesting or eating chanterelles again.

The best thing about picking chanterelles, next to cooking and eating them of course, is traipsing into the forest to pick them. They grow in the knee-deep Day-Glo green moss, primarily around second growth hemlock and spruce, and sometimes in secret pockets of earth underneath the deadfalls. You seldom find worms or other insect entrance or exit holes in them; you don't have to compete with bears as you do when you're picking blueberries. I didn't even think the deer had acquired a taste for them, but my friend Lynda says she has heard several stories of hunters shooting deer and butchering them to find a stomach full of chewed-up chanterelles.

The best time to look for chanterelles is in the fall, a week or two after the rains begin. On Haida Gwaii I've picked well into October and sometimes in November. When you find one, you will find more; they draw you deeper and deeper into the forest, luring you with their come-hither look. You stoop to pick one, and another, a little deeper in the woods, catches your eye. They seem to shine, almost, an iridescent gold amongst all that green. It is all too easy to fall under their chanterelle-spell and pursue them out of earshot range of your fellow mushrooming friends.

LEFT: *Chanterelles* PHOTO BY MICHELLE FURBACHER

RIGHT: *Picking chanterelles* PHOTO BY MICHELLE FURBACHER

Chanterelles will reappear in the same places year after year if carefully harvested so as not to disturb the ground in which the delicate mycelium (the vegetative part of the mushroom) grows. Chanterelles spread by releasing millions of little spores, which is why it is a good idea to use a basket, not a bucket when you are harvesting them. Most mushroom pickers I've gone into the bush with have cut the chanterelles at the base and left the root, covering it with the surrounding duff and patting it down. This small but important act also helps conceal your spot from the barbarian hordes of other mushroom pickers who, if they spot your cut stems, might mark the location on their GPS and come back and clean you out next September.

CLEANING

It's wise to clean the mushrooms as well as you can as you pick—saves you a lot of time later. You can buy a mushroom knife that comes with a ¾-inch (2 cm) wild boar bristle brush on one end to clean off your mushrooms, but my friends on Haida Gwaii save money by taping a toothbrush, or a nylon pastry brush, to the handle of their knife—with the brush facing in the opposite direction of the blade.

Chanterelles keep well in a brown paper bag in the refrigerator until they are cleaned and preserved. Whisk away any remaining dirt, moss or spruce needles with your brush, but don't soak the mushrooms in water. Wash them if you must (I don't) but in general, the less water the better. Drain them on paper towels. Cleaned chanterelles may also be stored in the refrigerator for a few days. They should be loosely arranged in a bowl lined with cloth or paper towels and covered lightly with towels.

COOKING

When it comes to cooking, there is no mushroom more versatile. Chanterelles are meaty and chewy; their texture is tender when gently fried and their flavour compliments nearly everything with which they are paired. Connie Green, in *The Wild Table: Seasonal Foraged Food and Recipes*, writes, "The famous apricot aroma and pepper taste of the raw chanterelle become a faint base note after cooking."

Tear them into hunks of a generous size, so that the maximum amount of flavour can be appreciated. The technique I've found most effective is to "dry fry" them in a pan to allow the water to cook off—chanterelles seem to have a lot more water than most other mushrooms —before adding any other ingredients, including oil or butter. If you skip this step, you'll often end up with a bit of a rubbery texture. I recommend cooking them in a small cast-iron pan, but a non-stick pan will do.

I usually season with little more than shallots or garlic, plus butter, salt and pepper. But I always add the butter after a fair amount of water has been extracted from the mushrooms and cooked off. A little white wine and a bit of cream and/or chicken broth is a good addition. Chanterelles bake well and retain their flavour after long cooking. Eggs, chicken, pork and veal harmonize beautifully with them.

I like to keep it simple. You can't go wrong with chanterelle recipes that call for butter, onions, white wine and cream. These ingredients will bring out the flavour of the mushroom for a simple chicken and green pea pasta dish. If you want to avoid cream, mango juice is particularly effective to add both sweetness and complexity. Chanterelles are wonderful, as you can imagine, in risottos. Try adding butternut squash and pine nuts along with the chanterelles, and use a mild, flavourful chicken stock.

PRESERVING

Chanterelles are well suited for drying, and tend to maintain their aroma and consistency quite well though I find they become chewy. Dried chanterelles crush well and the powder can be used to season soups or sauces. If you are going to freeze them, fry them in a dry pan first. Cook until the liquid evaporates, then freeze them in ½ cup amounts in baggies. When defrosted, they will retain most of their flavour.

Chanterelle garnish on venison stew PHOTO BY MICHELLE FURBACHER

Mushroom picking PHOTO BY MICHELLE FURBACHER

Mushroom Facts

- While humans and most species are divided into only two sexes, mushrooms contain over 36,000 sexes.
- Based on popular usage, it is 1.224 times more common for Mushroom to be a girl's name than a boy's.
- Fungi recycle plants after they die and transform them into rich soil. If not for mushrooms and fungi, Earth would be buried in several feet of debris and life on the planet would soon disappear.
- Mushroom soup is the second most popular Campbell's soup. Tomato is number one.

BUYING CHANTERELLES

More and more golden chanterelles are appearing in grocery stores. They are expensive (certainly compared to picking them, free, in the woods) so only buy those in prime condition. Look for fragrant chanterelles with a golden or apricot colour, with no slime or dark, decaying parts, and no granular gills fragmenting off the fleshy portion of the mushrooms.

Buck and bog cotton PHOTO BY GUY KIMOLA

DEER

The original title of this section was "Venison" but as my friend and neighbour Chris Ashurst pointed out, on Haida Gwaii we don't say we are having "venison" for dinner; we say we are having "deer." "Venison," Chris says, "is the word they use in cookbooks." God forbid.

I invited Chris and Elin for dinner, hoping to ply them with wine and have them reveal a plethora of local food stories. Instead, Elin and I talked about evading polar bears and her time on Cambridge Bay in the Arctic cleaning up after the military, whilst Chris speed-read *The Beginner's Guide to Hunting Deer for Food*, a book I had ordered from the Vancouver Island Regional Library branch in Masset. I had no intention of going hunting myself, but figured if I was going to write about cooking deer, the subject of killing was likely to rear its antlered head.

Somewhere under a rainbow
PHOTO BY CHRIS ASHURST

Chris asked if he could borrow the book. He'd never shot a deer before and needed some tips. Two days later he returned it with the news that he had shot his first buck on Moresby Island somewhere under a rainbow. If only I had known I was going to contribute to its demise I would have had a copy of *Why Hunting and Eating Deer for Food is Cruel and Unnecessary* on my coffee table. That practically magnificent buck might still be rutting away in Gwaii Haanas National Park, having progeny galore to decimate the native wild flowers and create mossy dead zones in our forests. The deer's effect on the ecological integrity of Haida Gwaii has been ruinous.

So where *do* I stand? Same with most problems. I just wish they would go away.

Thirty-nine of these mainland upstarts (Sitka black-tailed deer or *Odocoileus hemionus sitkensis* as we refer to them around the dinner table) were introduced to Haida Gwaii in the late 1800s (today, there are somewhere between 150,000 and 200,000) possibly by hungry settlers looking for a source of protein, or by missionaries. These same missionaries also introduced the smallpox vaccine to those Haida in Skidegate and Masset who chopped down their totem poles and

CHILE CON CARNE DE VENADO SERVES 6
(CHILI WITH VENISON)

"Frank and Jesse James are said to have eaten a few bowls of 'red' before pulling many of their bank jobs. Their favourite chili joint was in McKinney, Texas, and the boys vowed never to rob the bank there because 'anyplace that has a chili joint like this just oughta' be treated better.'"
—Linda Stradley, "History of Chili, Chili Con Carne" from WhatsCookingAmerica.net

"Wish I had time for just one more bowl of chili."
—Kit Carson's dying words

"Chili today, hot tamale: Mexican weather report."
—My favourite childhood joke

When I was the size of a fire hydrant my mother would occasionally lower her standards and treat us to eat something that came in a tin called Chilly con Carney. At least that's how we pronounced it. (We also had macaroni and cheese when we were boating and Mum was too tired to cook (See "Aside: We Don't Eat That Kind of Food," page 164) It wasn't until I moved to Panama and took Spanish lessons in the Canal Zone that I learned (among useful phrases such as "*Mi esposa toca el piano muy bien*," ("My wife plays the piano very well,") and how to communicate with the maid: "*Esas ollas, que bonitos, como brilliant*," ("These pots, how pretty, how they shine") how to pronounce *chile* properly.

"Chee-lay cone carnay" is how it is pronounced, but most people just call it "chili." Every year tens of thousands participate in hundreds of chili cook-offs that raise millions of dollars for charities; most of these occur in Texas, where they also execute a distressing number of people on Death Row every year. But don't get me started on *that* subject. (Okay, well, yes I *have* written about it, a whole novel—*Cargo of Orchids*—and a number of essays on the subject of state-sanctioned murder, but for the moment I intend to keep politics out of the chili.)

Notable cook-offs (i.e. the ones that caught my attention because of their names) include the Chilympiad in San Marcos, Texas (for men only), and the Hell Hath No Fury Like a Woman Scorned cook-off in Luckenbach, Texas. I assume the latter feel scorned and are getting their own back because they weren't allowed to cook off with the men in San Marcos? Personally I would never attend a chili cook-off in Texas, where outside the Death Row facilities, shortly before midnight, the death penalty advocates fire up their barbecues and begin grilling greasy slabs of bacon. Too far to drive from Haida Gwaii for a chili cook-off. If they had scrambled egg cook-offs, however, I'd have to reconsider.

2–3 Tbsp (30–45 mL) chili powder

1½ tsp (7 mL) chipotle powder

1 tsp (5 mL) ground cumin

1 tsp (5 mL) ground coriander

1 tsp (5 mL) dried thyme or 1 Tbsp (15 mL) fresh, chopped

1 tsp (5 mL) dried oregano or 1 Tbsp (15 mL) fresh, chopped

¼–⅓ cup (60–80 mL) water

2 lb (1 kg) ground deer meat

2 medium onions, diced

Plenty of garlic (¾ of a bulb), chopped

½ red pepper, seeded and diced

½ yellow pepper, seeded and diced

½ green pepper, seeded and diced (optional)*

2 Tbsp (30 mL) olive oil

1 tsp (5 mL) red pepper flakes

2 Tbsp (30 mL) good balsamic vinegar or balsamic reduction (fig is my favourite!)

2 Tbsp (30 mL) maple syrup

1 cup (240 mL) red wine

Juice of 1 lime

Water, as needed (to thin sauce, if necessary)

One 14-oz can tomato sauce

One 14-oz can kidney beans

One 14-oz can corn niblets

Chopped cilantro for garnish (or the ubiquitous parsley)

WHAT YOU DO

1   In a small bowl mix the chili powder, chipotle powder, ground cumin, ground coriander, oregano and thyme. Mix in water so that chili forms a light paste. Set aside.

2   Sauté the chopped onions, garlic and peppers (yellow, red, and, if you are really determined to, the green) in olive oil over medium high until soft, 5–8 minutes. I use a 6-quart (6 L) thick-bottomed Dutch oven, or deep cast-iron frying pan. With a slotted spoon remove vegetables from pan and set aside. (At this

---

*   I don't like green peppers, so I never cook with them. This is my cookbook so I can do what I want. But if you are determined to use green peppers, this chili has enough going for it that no one will hold it against you.

point I'd recommend picking out any green peppers you may have incautiously used, and throwing them on the floor (what Julia Child claims to do with cilantro.)

3 Decrease heat to medium and sauté the ground deer meat with the red pepper flakes until lightly browned. If your pan is not big enough, I suggest cooking in two batches so you don't crowd the meat: crowding it will steam cook the meat instead of browning it.

4 Push meat to sides of pan, making a hole in the centre. Add balsamic vinegar and cook until syrupy.* Add spice paste and cook until fragrant.

5 Add wine, lime juice, maple syrup and tomato sauce. Mix well, bring to a boil, and adjust heat to low. (The maple syrup balances out the acidity of the tomatoes and lime juice.)

6 Simmer, uncovered, for about an hour and stir frequently, adding water as needed. Taste and adjust seasonings, adding more chili powder or chipotle chilies if you want more heat. If you have too much heat, there's little that can be done at this stage. (See Note page 163.)

7 Add beans, corn niblets and the vegetable you set aside and cook for another hour, continuing to stir. The chili is done whenever you think it's thick enough.

8 Garnish with chopped cilantro or a sprig of parsley.

VARIATIONS

There are as many ways to prepare chili as there are cooks who make chili. Ground beef versus chunks, pork versus beef, pinto versus kidney beans, beans versus no beans, red chili or green chili—the combinations, as the preferences for them, are endless.

If you don't have venison, you can use any other kind of meat. Bison, beef. Even chicken. Or a white fish, like halibut.

TIP: Do not use an expensive cut of beef, if you are going to substitute beef for venison. My first husband once brought home $32 worth of tenderloin, which I stewed for three hours to make Beef Bourguignon back in the day. It was inedible

---

* I suspect this is more likely to happen if you use a balsamic reduction. I really wanted it to turn syrupy, but it never did. Didn't matter. I don't think it made any difference to the finished dish. At least no one has ever said, "It tastes as if your balsamic vinegar didn't cook until it was syrupy." I have had people say, "This is the best chili I've ever eaten!," though.

The Pepper in Folklore

- Want to stop an elephant destroying your farm? Surround it with chile peppers.
- Chiles, not garlic, crosses or silver bullets, were often considered the best deterrent against vampires and werewolves. Hot peppers have been used in witchcraft both to excise demons and ill humors. East Indian Trinidadians wrap "seven red pepper pods with salt, onion skins and garlic skins in paper" and pass it seven times around a baby to "remove najar, the evil eye, which is believed to cause unnecessary crying."
- According to an African-American legend from the American south, in order for peppers to be hot, you must be angry when you plant them.
- Jethro Kloss, in his book *Back to Eden* writes that if someone is "thoroughly saturated" with cayenne and dies in the desert "the vultures will not touch the body on account of its being so impregnated with the capsicum."
- The Transcendental Capsaicinophilic Society's web site on "worshipping spicy food" includes the "Litany Against Pain," which is to be repeated silently when someone is tempted to complain of the burning derived from eating fiery foods and chiles.

and had to be fed to Georgie, the rebarbative dog. Use chuck roast—it holds up the best to long stewing. (Same thing for venison, don't use the backstrap; use flank, shoulder or shank meat.)

HEALTH TIP: Using deer meat instead of beef increases the health benefits of your chili. A 3.5 oz (100 g) serving of venison contains 3.3 g of fat, 66 mg of cholesterol and 159 calories, while a similar serving of beef has 9.8 g of fat, 92 mg of cholesterol and 214 calories.

NOTE: I found this on a site called Chow, and thought it worth sharing:
"Taking the Heat out of my too Spicy Chili," by foodrocks

"So last night I decided to make this great sounding chili recipe I got off of the Craigslist message board. It sounded great, but the fact that part of the directions read "throw all the shit in the pan and cook it" should have been the first sign that the person who posted it was not the most meticulous recipe writer. Despite my better judgment, I ended up following the recipe, and 1 jalapeño and 1/8 cup of cayenne powder later (I know, I know) . . . My question is, is there any way to take the heat out of chili when you accidentally put too much hot stuff in?"

TangledHeart responds: "I have stirred in a couple tablespoons of smooth peanut butter to cut the heat. Sounds strange, but it seems to work, and doesn't alter the taste (gives a little depth to the flavour). It also makes the chili a little creamier, if that makes sense."

ASIDE: "WE DON'T EAT THAT KIND OF FOOD"

Last year our children begged us to take them camping. Camping was cool. They'd seen it on TV. Besides, we'd be together all day, as a family, in the car, getting there. And, since Dad couldn't smoke in the car, he could use the opportunity to quit smoking, just like he'd been threatening to.

The first day was pretty standard, the kids fighting over who got to sit in the front seat, all of us fighting over whose turn it was to listen to Kurt Cobain, Raffi or Pavarotti. We ended up compromising on "Found a Peanut."

Despair didn't set in until we approached Hope. It had been close in the car but as soon as we hit the national park the first clouds rolled in over the mountains. As I rolled the sleeping bags out to air, the first raindrops began to settle the dust that was making my eldest daughter have asthma.

On either side of us, vacationers were pulling up in their RVs, setting up their satellite dishes, and microwaving dinner while I was still trying to find matches to get a pile of wet cedar burning into some kind of smudge fire to suffocate the mosquitoes, and my husband gave the children a lecture on the dying art of tent raising.

The kids, tired from fighting in the car all day, demanded Smurfaghetti. I never lower my standards just because I'm roughing it: on tonight's menu were freeze-dried "gourmet-style" beans. The word "style" should have been a tip-off: all you had to do, once you got the fire blazing, was add water. Of course the nearest tap was half a mile down the road, by the outhouse the kids wouldn't venture near because it smelled "different" from our conveniences at home.

But by now the rain was washing out the fire pit so I gave up trying to cook. We drove ten miles back down the road to eat at a family restaurant. I told my husband that if he said, "Are we having fun yet?" one more time, I was leaving him. It turned out I couldn't have left even if I'd wanted to because my husband had absentmindedly locked the keys in the car. I had to call the Canadian Automobile Association's 1-800 number and ask them to send someone capable of breaking into our car.

The next night we attended a lecture on bears. The ranger told us never to keep shampoo, deodorant or toothpaste in our tent because bears are attracted to the perfumed scent. Lock your toiletries in the trunk of the car, he cautioned us. If you wanted to discourage bears, the natural state of unwashed human flesh was the best deterrent.

By the end of the lecture I was considering locking *myself* in the car. But when we got back to the campsite my husband had absentmindedly locked the keys in the trunk of the car and, after calling the Automobile Association again—who

said they'd send a truck in the morning—I crawled into my sleeping bag along with our toiletries, with the vain hope a bear wouldn't be attracted to them if they were in the same bag as my unwashed feet. My husband stayed up late, making twig tea on the fire. He'd read that it helped curb nicotine cravings.

On the last day of our vacation my husband lost the car keys altogether. I accused him of absentmindedly losing his mind and called the CAA. "Don't tell me, let me guess," the dispatcher interrupted when I began to explain. "Your name is Susan Musgrave and you're locked out of your car again."

On our way home we decided not to camp but to drop in on some friends who had a cottage on Larvae Lake. We all needed baths—no human beings had come near us for days, let alone bears. I was too demoralized to cook so we stopped to pick up a can of Smurfaghetti for the kids and a package of Player's Light for Himself.

Our friends were throwing a barbecue. One of their guests had a child who demanded Smurfaghetti because my kids were having it. Her mother said, "No dear, we don't eat that kind of food." My husband was chain smoking on the balcony so I slunk into a corner with some escapist literature I'd brought with me for the camping trip. This was the first time on our holiday I'd had time to read a book.

Relaxing, I had just read, was a major cause of stress—when the mother (who must have felt guilty for sounding judgmental) tried to strike up a conversation. She asked me if I was reading *Pain and Possibility* for pleasure. I said "It depends," and she looked at me in a new way. "What's your last name?" she said.

I told her. After a stunned pause, she said, "Are you *the* Susan Musgrave."

For a terrible moment I thought—she must work for the CAA, she's the dispatcher I've spoken to every time I dialled that 1-800 number. Then she said, "I studied your poetry at university." And added, superfluously I thought, "You don't look anything like your poetry."

LEFT: Camper at Agate Beach
PHOTO BY ARCHIE STOCKER SR.

RIGHT: The author's glass outhouse PHOTO BY KATHLEEN HINKEL

Chile Con Carne

The first documented recipe for "chile con carne" is dated September 2, 1519. The ingredients were boiled tomatoes, salt, chiles and meat. Bernal Diaz del Castillo, one of Hernan Cortez's captains and the source of the recipe, states in his book that the Cholulan Indians, allied with the Aztecs, were so confident of victory in a battle against the Conquistadors that they had "already prepared cauldrons of tomatoes, salt and chiles" in anticipation of a victory feast. The one missing ingredient, the meat, was to be furnished by the Conquistadors themselves: their own flesh.

—(from *The Discovery and Conquest of Mexico* by Bernal Diaz del Castillo) cited on the website *Chilixx*.

Chile, Chili or Chilli

- Chile with an "e" at the end is the correct spelling in Spanish.
- Chili with an "i" at the end is the Americanized version.
- Chilli with a double "l" is the UK spelling.
- In Canada, we use all three spellings because we don't want to hurt anybody's feelings.

Before I could tell her that was because I'd been *relaxing* for two weeks, her husband, who had been eavesdropping, chimed in. He guessed I must be *the* Susan Musgrave married to *the* Jim Musgrave who had the Massey-Ferguson franchise up the road. In any case I'm sure their daughter now gets Smurfaghetti on demand.

ILLUSTRATION BY DEJAHLEE BUSCH

SALMON

The English poet Ted Hughes, who came often to northern British Columbia to fish for steelhead, had a theory (widely held, it turns out) that salmon are sexually attracted to female anglers. Because the biggest salmon are cock fish (old word for male Atlantic salmon—one I am *so* glad I have discovered!) they are naturally attracted to a woman's pheromones, which transmit themselves to the water when she smears them on her bait or lure in the process of handling her fishing tackle. Old Ted told me he frequently went fishing in Ireland with a friend who tied his salmon flies using his girlfriend's pubic hair.

Susan Musgrave and Ted Hughes in Victoria, BC, 1988 PHOTO BY DAVID ANDERSON

I've yet to find a fisherman friend who has begged me to rub his flies in my knickers (that sounds complicated) in order to give him an edge, but I experimented once by wiping a lure through my hair (public, not pubic) when Jim Fulton and I went to the place he called the Meat Hole on the Tlell River. He caught a whopping big Coho on his first cast; I don't know if it was my pheromones, or the Meat Hole living up to its fecund reputation.

SIR RICHARD MUSGRAVE'S TYEE

As a child my sole claim to glory was this big-ass fish, a '70 lb tyee, caught by my great-grandfather in Campbell River in 1896. A replica hung in the Royal Museum in Victoria; on field trips I lured my whole class to the glass case displaying the facsimile of the leviathan my great-grandfather played for three days (in our family it was legendary) alone in a boat at the mouth of (what I imagined to be) the deep dark green mysterious Campbell River all set about by cedar trees. A plaque acclaimed it to be the largest salmon ever taken on a simple rod and line, *by Sir Richard Musgrave.* Not only had my great-grandfather landed a fish heavier than me, plainly I came from royalty. How hard I fought to hook and hold on to that vainglorious notion, the stoop-shouldered child I was, standing erect for once, head slightly bowed, nose flattened against the glass we weren't supposed to touch, as the fish cast his cold eye on life, on death, and Mrs. Guest's combined

Grade One and Two classes. I envisioned my great-grandfather not stopping to eat or sleep for three days, intent on reeling in the mother of all tyees so that one day I might stand before it feeling as if—in a world that has never been my home—I was someone.

I have since discovered that Sir Richard was not my great-grandfather after all, but my great-grandfather's older brother (my lowlier ancestor raised sheep on Salt Spring Island.) Nor was Sir Musgrave alone, but in a dugout canoe paddled by native guides from Cape Mudge, the fish hooked and landed before lunch. So much for family mythology; no more high-ass Muckamuck.

FISHING WITH DAD

"There's a thing he doesn't know. He doesn't know that you can't catch the glory on a hook and hold on to it. That when you fish for glory you catch the darkness too. That if you hook twice the glory you hook twice the fear."
—from *The Double Hook* by Sheila Watson

When I was growing up, in the culinary dark ages of the 1950s, salmon was the pink fish that skinny people ordered at high-priced restaurants. It was also what we ate when we were poor, at the end of the month, in the week leading up to payday. Naturally enough, I equated salmon with boating (See Aside: All the Comforts of Home page 37) and poverty, neither of which I enjoyed.

Dad used to climb in the dinghy and row up Sansum Narrows between Salt Spring Island where my actual great-grandfather had settled at Musgrave Landing, and Vancouver Island, and catch a couple of grilse* for breakfast and fry them to a shade just past well-done, filling the cabin with an oily fishy smoke, which made it hard for me to choke down my Coco Puffs.

During the day Dad cruised along at about 7 knots in the *Froggie,* fishing off the stern using a bucktail fly. He was a true sports fisherman: the fly always rode about six inches above the surface of the water because he believed in giving the fish more than a sporting chance. Dad would call to the salmon the way he'd heard native fishermen in Cowichan Bay when he was a boy—"Cooooooome saaaaaaamon cooooooooome saaaaaaaamon." When the fish didn't bite (or possibly because they couldn't reach the fly flying above the water) Dad would climb

---

*   Grilse is the common word used in Ireland and the UK for non mature or small salmon. We used it on the west coast of Canada until the late '70s, prior to the influences of Americans and interlopers from the east. It is a beautiful word and it is unfortunate that it has gone out of style.

Little Known Facts About Fish

- They range from tiny creatures that would fit on a fingernail to monsters the size of cabin cruisers.

- They can sleep with their eyes open, and float without casting a shadow.

- Fishes' ability to taste is similarly well developed. Many species have taste buds not just on their tongues, but on their fins, face and tail area as well. They are capable of tasting food before they have it in their mouths.

back in the *Tadpole,* our dinghy, and row up the narrows; he'd come back before dusk with a rock cod he had jigged for our dinner.

I went fishing with him in the dinghy, once. I hooked something big, something glorious, which I wasn't strong enough to bring to the surface, and finally took the whole rod out of my hands, unfuriating dad. (I was sorry about the rod, but secretly glad the fish got away.) I didn't know anything about psychology then, but the idea of letting a line down into the unfathomable wet darkness and waiting for a bite struck me as, well, uncomfortably symbolic. (Did you know "trouser trout" was slang for penis? I didn't.)

I don't own a boat (surprise!) but I like to go fishing now that I have learned I can go out to Rennell Sound, or through the Gut (Skidegate Narrows) and spend the day on the water if I pretend to be interested in fishing, though I still pray the fish gets away. I hope none of the friends who take me fishing are reading this because it is probably bad luck to take a woman along, despite her salmon-luring pheromones, when she is down below praying the fish will spit out the hook and swim off.

LEFT: The Author, aged three, and her Dad PHOTO BY JUDITH MUSGRAVE

RIGHT: Wake, Rennell Sound PHOTO BY BOB FRAUMENI

KEEP IT COLD, KEEP IT CLEAN

Assuming you get it into the boat, bonk the fish on the head with a fish billy to keep it from thrashing and bruising the meat. Cut the gills of the fish to bleed it out and kill it. The heart will continue to pump blood out of the meat long after the fish has gone to the great hunting ground in the sky. If the blood is left in the fish, it could settle in the meat, which will then have a distinctly unpleasant taste.

Fish begin to spoil immediately after they are killed. Anytime you smell that "fishy" smell you are smelling fish that is starting to rot. To retard the process of decomposition in the muscle tissue, or spoilage, chill the meat as soon as you kill the fish and keep the meat clean.

After you've bled your fish, place it in an ice chest surrounded by crushed ice. Some fishermen like to chop the head off and gut their fish as soon as it's in the boat, which is a good idea—but again, get it on ice as soon as you can. You want to keep air off your meat as much possible, too, so when you get home cut it up quickly (into fillets or steaks, with the sharpest knife you have) and then do what most people do—vacuum-seal your fish in FoodSaver bags, making sure the seal is 100 percent dry before sealing, wiping the area to be sealed with a dry paper towel.

The best way to store your fish is to glaze it after it is frozen. Meat that is quick-frozen with a super-cold commercial process (i.e. frozen at sea) is the best-kept meat, but most of us don't own fish boats with walk-in freezers on board.

At this point, becoming a committed vegetarian is starting to feel like the best option. When you kill and cook a carrot, there isn't—on the surface—so much to have to remember and stress about.

COOKING YOUR FISH

I spent many years not eating salmon for one simple reason (and it's the same reason so many people claim to not like fish): I had never had it cooked properly. And I often suspected it wasn't fresh. (If people found out how good fresh-caught seafood of *any* kind really was they would never set foot in most so-called seafood restaurants.) I have to concede that it wasn't the *salmon* that was to blame, but rather the person doing the cooking. Properly cooked salmon has brown, crisp,

crackling skin with no greasy fat underneath, a thin layer of ever-so-slightly flaky meat followed by an expanse of tender, juicy, not-the-least-bit-chalky or stringy flesh, and a central core with a creamy, buttery texture bordering on the sashimi-esque. How are these heights of salmon-bliss achieved?

Just like all meats, the texture of salmon flesh alters as a direct result of the temperature is it raised to:

- **At 110°F (43°C) and below** your salmon flesh is essentially raw. Translucent and deep orange or red, it has the soft, fleshy texture of good sashimi.

- **At 110 to 125°F (43 to 52°C)** your salmon is medium rare. The connective tissue between layers of flesh has begun to weaken and if you insert a toothpick into the filet, it should slide in and out with no resistance. The meat is relatively opaque, but still juicy and moist.

- **Try to keep your salmon around the 125°F (52°C) mark while it is cooking.**

- **At 125°F to 140° (52 to 60°C)** you are beginning to enter medium to well-done territory. Flakiness will increase, and a chalky texture will start to develop. If unattractive white clumps of gunk (polite term: albumen) ooze up out of the layers of salmon flesh, it's a pretty good bet that your salmon is crab bait. In the early stages of this clumping, your salmon is still rescuable (just stop cooking it *immediately* and have a bottle of wine.)

- **At 140°F (60°C) and above,** your salmon is overdone like dinner in the '50s. This is what happens to salmon that sits in the steam table at the buffet, and another credible reason why so many people say they don't like fish.

For the specifics of pan-frying or grilling salmon, please see page 278.

34 Words for Salmon in the Haida Language*

Salmon	Meaning
ts'iing.aa	any old white salmon in a stream
ga taa k'aay	dog or chum salmon—nickname from Mr. Raven
sk'aak'uu	female salmon spawned out
tsiin tluwaa	an unidentified variety of salmon with a big head and a long thin body
táay.yii táay.yiigaay	coho salmon
sGwaagan sGwaagang swaaGan	salmon (the common name in the Massett dialect)
sk'aagii	dog or chum salmon
daagaaysdll	dried dog or chum salmon, laid alongside each other
daa kaajiiaaw	dried dog or chum salmon, hanging down with heads apart
chaaga	female salmon
Gayda daahlging Gayda daahlgyang	the last run of coho salmon in November, found in Skidegate Inlet between Alliford Bay and South Bay and the Sandspit Bar, also seen in Slatechuck Creek in early December—the literal meaning is needle fish found in the belly of coho salmon

* Skidegate dialect unless otherwise stated, from the Skidegate Haida language—X̲aayda Kíl website.

hlaay.ya	male salmon
ts'iit'an *ts'iit'aan*	pink salmon
k'iing k'ii	prepared dog or chum salmon head cartilage that has been brought down to low tide, covered with kelp that pops, covered with rocks, left awhile and then rinsed in fresh water and eaten
taaGun Gaw sGid	red spring salmon
chiina k'aayging	school of dog or chum salmon
hlGaahlkundal	school of pink salmon moving
hlGaahl k'aayging	school of pink salmon or herring that looks black and is not moving
taaxid	sockeye salmon
taaxid *taaxaayd*	sockeye salmon (in Copper Bay-Church Creek-Guudal dialect)
taaGun	spring salmon
ts'ing k'iiga *ts'ing k'iida*	three-year-old coho salmon caught in January or February
taaGun Gaw Gaada	white spring salmon
maaluu	salmon and trout fry

OTHER SPECIES
OF SALMON

TOP LEFT: Nets across Yakoun River PHOTO BY ARCHIE STOCKER SR.

MIDDLE LEFT: Cleaning sockeye PHOTO BY ARCHIE STOCKER SR.

BOTTOM LEFT: Salmon drying at Christian White's Yahgulaanas totem pole raising, Old Massett. PHOTO BY ARCHIE STOCKER SR.

RIGHT: Dried salmon and halibut PHOTO BY MICHELLE FURBACHER

FARMED OR GENETICALLY ENGINEERED SALMON: We don't have salmon farms on Haida Gwaii, but to give you a taste, here's what goes on south of the Islands at the Boundary of the World.

ASIDE: WILD SALMON DON'T DO OXYTETRACYCLINE

"Super. Natural. While supplies last."

—Susan Musgrave, on being commissioned to write a new slogan for Tourism British Columbia

Cedar and salmon were our lifeblood once. Now, in British Columbia, we have a wilderness of stumps, and sea pens full of diseased carnivores on drugs.

Once the salmon was monarch of the sea, a creature whose life cycle, a perfect circle, we studied in school. We watched scratchy filmstrips of the salmon

Sockeye

- *Swagan* (Massett dialect) *SGwaagang* (Skidegate dialect)
- Sockeye fisheries in the rivers are important for many Haida people starting in the month of May. Skidegate Haidas travel to K'aasda (Copper Bay) to fish for a unique type of sockeye known as *taaxid*.

- By late May or early June, the sockeye salmon are running up the Yakoun River. Haida families from Old Massett head to the camps and cabins on the river for days at a time, fishing, smoking and then canning the catch.
- When sockeye is dried it is called *ts'iljii*.

being born in pure mountain streams, narrated with deep male authority. We followed the salmon as it swam out to sea where it performed a vital function, eating the slower swimmers. Then some Higher Fish Power guided the salmon back to the very place where it had begun; it spawned, (this was where we started paying attention, though fish-sex looked as lonely to me as when humans attempted it) and died. Before the ravens had chowed down on its eyes, a thousand tiny offspring were shooting back down to the sea.

These days the circle of life begins when a guy in gumboots mixes a whack of milt and a whack of roe in a five-gallon Chevron bucket, according to Andrew Struthers in his book *The Green Shadow*, about (among other things) doing time in a Tofino fish plant. The minute they are deemed tough enough to survive the saltchuk, the smolt are dosed with oxytetracycline and herded into giant open mesh net-cages suspended from anchored metal cage frames.

Now these sea pens full of fledglings have to be protected from predators. Fish farmers admit to shooting thousands of seals and sea lions each year because they rip the pen walls apart hoping for a free lunch. Hundreds of crows—seagulls, too—get dispatched for trying to hone in on the feed the fish get seeded to them from a sack labelled NOT FOR HUMAN CONSUMPTION.

Why, then, is this fishy food full of antibiotics suitable for humans labelled NOT FOR HUMAN CONSUMPTION? It could have to do with the fact the feed has to be laced with orange pigment, there being no krill in captivity, which is what wild salmon eat and what makes them deliciously orange. Struthers says there are two kinds of feed on the market. One is considered safe in America but toxic in Japan, the other okey-dokey in Japan but deadly in America. They have one thing in common, however. They are both orange.

And then there are the drugs. When a wild salmon gets stressed (and believe me they do, especially these days, what with all the lawsuits being waged over them—BC accusing Ottawa of treason, Ottawa suing BC for cancelling the US lease at Nanoose Bay to crank up fish talks; BC countersuing Ottawa, BC suing the US for stealing our fish) it often gets a kidney disease, and goes belly-up. The kidneys of feedlot fish, packed at 10 kilograms per cubic metre in their underwater Auschwitzes (imagine you in your bathtub with two 10-pound sockeyes leaping over you—that's how crowded it gets) are chopped liver, so to speak. That's why they get doped to the gills with (and we have a rule around our house: never eat anything you can't pronounce) Trimethoprim-sulfadiazine, Ormethoprim-sulfadimethoxine, Enrofloxacin, Erythomycin, Florfenicol, and of course more Oxytetracycline (this also means sewage into pristine BC coves equal to a city of 500,000 each day) so they'll live.

At least until the farmer decides it's time for them to die, and cuts off their food supply to trim them up for harvesting. After two weeks of starvation it's a fish-eat-fish—or pencil stubs, beer caps, folded up tally sheets—world. Struthers has found any number of unfortunate objects inside the bellies of the beasts he has gutted, cleaned, scrubbed and shipped to Vancouver to be eaten by skinny people in upscale restaurants.

MORE THAN ONE WAY TO CATCH A SALMON

It had been an exceptionally good fishing year, he'd been catching fish all week, and Randy Martin was confident that he'd be able to catch his contribution to the annual potluck Thanksgiving dinner held in the Tow Hill community. He trekked two kilometers up the ▉▉▉ ▉▉▉ (name redacted to protect the sanctity of the spot) river, through the ancient rainforest where the trees looked otherworldly, dripping magical strands of moss. He waded, the sun in his eyes, through the knee-deep green moss that carpeted the forest floor, to his secret fishing hole—the one he had told no one about, ever—and cast his lucky lure, and waited.

Not a single fish rising. He wasn't worried—he had half a dozen more pools he could count on so after a while he moved downstream to his next secret spot. Once again no sign of the coho, which, a week earlier, had been so thick you could walk across the river on their backs. He moved on and struck out at two more pools and now he was starting to feel concerned: how could he turn up for the annual Thanksgiving potluck empty-handed? Susan Musgrave would strike him from her ever-diminishing list of "friends who follow-through" and he would spend the next Thanksgivings in a state of Single Cussedness (as Butch Cassidy put it) with a lonely can of turkey noodle soup.

With only one secret pool left to go, he could feel his anxiety rising. The giant trees creaked overhead like planks, pushy, ill-tempered spruce with needles that felt as friendly as barbed wire. He hacked his way through the foreboding underbrush, the branches of the dying hemlocks weirdly bearded with cloying strands of moss, tearing at his face.

He stumbled, sinking to his knees in the wet, bug-infested moss until, as he puts it, "he popped out at the last pool" only to see four otters splashing around, giving him the stink-eye as if to say, "Ha ha, we beat you to it. All the fish are gone."

Randy was deflated. "Nnnnnnnooooooo," he said to himself, and out loud to the otters, who looked him over, evilly. He cast his eyes across the river to the other side where he saw a fifth otter taking a bite out of the largest salmon he had seen all day. He knew what had to be done.

He crossed the river on a log (because there were no fish left upon whose backs he could walk) and shooed the otter away. He checked the fish over, wondering if the otter had caught it because it was old and sick, but no, it was still healthy, though dead. Recently dead, too, with blood still running down its neck and spilling down its sides.

Randy thought to himself, "It wouldn't be right to take it all, but maybe I can take half," and he got out his lucky knife and filleted that fish right there on the spot. Then he made his way home through the ancient rainforest that seemed mysterious once again, over the gentle carpet of moss, to Susan's house, where, after a quick pan fry, Thanksgiving dinner was on the table, which was lucky because Susan had forgotten to take the turkey out of the freezer the night before and it was still sitting frozen in the sink.

RANDY'S SECRET SALMON

Randy Martin PHOTO BY PETER SLOAN

Prepare the fish (i.e. trim off the teeth marks). Coat fillet in secret seasoning mix (i.e. salt and pepper) dip it in next secret ingredient (beaten egg) then roll it in third secret ingredient (bread crumbs). Prepare the pan. Don't tell anyone what temperature to cook it at (high). Fry the fish. Don't tell anyone what you fried it in (olive oil and/or butter) or for how long to cook it (one minute on each side). It's a secret. His and the salmon's. Remember how the song goes? *"Two can keep a secret if one of them is dead."*

SMOKED SALMON

"You don't have to cook fancy or complicated masterpieces—just good food from fresh ingredients."
—Julia Child

At Eagle's Feast House PHOTO BY MICHELLE FURBACHER

You will find tidbits of smoked salmon throughout this book. I use it as a garnish in my chowder, serve it with chèvre and spruce tip spread. I make omelettes with chanterelles and crab, or substitute smoked salmon if anyone's in the mood. But you won't find recipes here for smoked salmon with beetroot and vodka crème fraîche or smoked salmon canapé with green olive grapefruit tapenade. Canapés, the fiddly idea of them, have always annoyed me (how is it you can eat a ton of them and then leave the party hungry and go out for a five-course meal?) and besides I never remember how to pronounce them. Is the last "e" accented as in "canopy," only with an "a" at the end, or is it "ca-nap?" I avoid the problem by not serving them. Enough said.

Life strikes me as being too short to learn German (a line I overheard once at my favourite Vancouver Island restaurant, Deep Cove Chalet—hello Bev and Pierre!) or make smoked salmon ravioli, or smoked salmon *gâteau* or smoked salmon and lemon risotto. I admit I like my smoked salmon *au natural*, as it comes from the sea. If you've never caught your own smoked salmon before, don't worry. I'm about to tell you how to take the unsmoked salmon you caught, and smoke it yourself, at home. (No, I haven't been smoking anything. I'm just on a roll.)

DEBRIEFING SMOKED SALMON

You'd think I'd be an expert on smoked salmon. When I got pregnant in 1981 my second husband, a gentleman of spirit (as my father referred to my those who had fallen afoul of the law) decided there might be more sensible ways to make ends meet, and went into partnership with a con artist (who shall remain nameless to protect the guilty and since he could very well be moonlighting in the cook-book-author leg breaking business these days) and bought an out-of-service ferry in Alaska, sailed it to Seattle, and converted it into a fish processing plant. There the spirited two smoked boatloads of salmon, and numerous samples found their way north to be sequestered in my small chest freezer.

The con artist, who had escaped from Auschwitz when he was a boy and wandered across Europe surviving on leaves and twigs, spoke English with a thick Polish accent. Many telephone calls were made to our home on Vancouver Island from his home in the Washington State Penitentiary.

One assumes my husband's business partner's phone was tapped, as was our home phone, my husband still being, at the time, "a person of interest." When, driving the Volvo he'd bought for me so our baby would have a safe vehicle for cross-border smuggling, he was arrested in Seattle with the $90,000 US cash he was going to use to purchase fish to smoke; the vehicle was seized as proceeds of crime. In order to get my car back I agreed to be deposed by the DEA who had gone over hours of incriminating wire tap information and hoped I might help them in their investigation.

I read the transcripts.

The con artist, to my husband, in thick Polish accent: *I got a connection down south they (inaudible) . . . you (inaudible) more product (inaudible), the smoke, the good stuff? The Gold? Three ton (inaudible) delivery (inaudible) eighteenth (inaudible) millions (inaudible . . .*

What the DEA heard: *The Colombians will deliver three tons of Acapulco Gold for eighteen million dollars.*

The con artist, decoded by me: *A customer in California is interested in buying three tons of cold smoked salmon to be delivered on the 18th. Price around half a million dollars.*

I told the DEA agents I could see how they might think that "smoke" referred to marijuana—even *I* thought it did as I listened to the tapes—but that it was, literally, smoked salmon. I gave them a heartfelt lecture on the difference between cold and hot smoked salmon: they must have believed me or else they were keenly disinterested in the subject, because they offered to let me buy back my car, for $1,500, the cost of the "storage fees."

Smoked Salmon refers to any salmon that is smoked, regardless of the specific process involved. My friend and renowned fisherman, Bob Fraumeni, who owns the fine shops, Finest at Sea* and FAS Seafood in Victoria and Vancouver, says

---

* If you are in Victoria or Vancouver you should go to Finest at Sea and buy their smoked salmon. It is the best, not just the finest (in case anyone wants to debate which is better: best or finest.) On the other hand, if you want to have fun, and if you have patience and time, you can try home-smoking your own, as many Haida Gwaiilanders do. I smoked salmon with Chipper Roth and Peter Fleming, who live "out the road" as we say about anyone who lives on Tow Hill Road. The results were—varied: the white spring (chinook) was moister than the regular spring, but that could have just been an accident. It's not an exact science. When you try anything at home, results will vary.

Smoked salmon in jars PHOTO BY MICHELLE FURBACHER

there are as many ways to smoke salmon as there are to make bread. Bob is smart that way; he knows I speak the Language of Bread, though I am not at all fluent in Smoked Salmon-ese, and by comparing salmon smoking to bread making he knew I'd be able the comprehend the nuances of the operation. It's easy for some of us (who are not experts, and have untrained eyes) to confuse cold smoked with hot smoked salmon. The merchants who sell smoked salmon often don't distinguish between cold or hot smoked in any way that is helpful to the consumer (i.e. with identifying labels to tell us how the fish was smoked) and while hot smoked tastes yumsome (yes, I think I invented a word) it's quite a different kettle of smoked fish from the cold smoked stuff.

Although there are many types of hot and cold salmon produced around the world, I am not going to talk about them here. I mean, why would I write about Scottish Smoked Salmon, or Danish Smoked Salmon (which tends to be sweeter than the Scottish because more sugar is used in the seasoning mix) or Norwegian Smoked Salmon or, closer to home, Nova Scotia Smoked Salmon: I live on Haida Gwaii, and what we have here is Haida Gwaii Smoked Salmon. And depending on who smoked it (and what, if anything, they were smoking at the time), how they cured it, and whether they froze it, dried it or canned it—results will vary.

NOTE: I do not preface the word "salmon" with the word "wild" because wild salmon is a given. I would never, never, never eat a farmed salmon, after reading Andrew Struthers *The Green Shadow* where he describes working in a farmed-fish processing plant in Tofino. You don't want to eat farmed salmon, ever, ever, ever. It is, Struthers says, like eating an 80-year-old cancer patient.

To make **hot-smoked salmon,** the salmon is filleted and then brined. Hot smoking "cooks" the salmon—most do-it-yourself "fish smokers," such as The Luhr Jensen Big Chief and Little Chief smokers that operate at around 160°F (71°C), are perfect for this operation—making the product less moist, and firmer, with a less delicate taste. When smoked, the flesh is somewhat-to-fully-opaque and it flakes, like regular cooked salmon.

Candy salmon—thin strips of salmon that have been cured in a salt-sugar brine before being hot-smoked until they become jerky-like—is a form of hot-smoked salmon that is popular both on Haida Gwaii and abroad.

To make **cold-smoked salmon,** the salmon is filleted and then brined. The cold smoking does not cook the fish; the interior texture remains translucent. Technically, the fish is raw, but cured.

The best home-smoker on the market (I've asked around) seems to be the Bradley Smoker, which *can* cold smoke, but tends to run too hot unless steps are taken to keep the temperature lower. The smoke temperature must be below 70°F (21°C).

Cold smoking is best done in winter when the temperature is cold and the air is dry. If you live on Haida Gwaii, of course, cold smoking can be done all year round.

Lox, sometimes called "regular" or "belly lox," is traditionally made by brining in a solution of water or oil, salt, sugars and spices. Usually served thinly sliced—less than 5 mm (0.2 in) in thickness—and, typically (in North America), with cream cheese, onions and capers. Lox is a Yiddish word for salmon, and is derived from the Swedish *lax,* Danish/Norwegian *laks,* German *Lachs* and Old English *læx.* Yiddish is not commonly spoken on Haida Gwaii, but you hear the word "lox" bandied about quite a bit.

Cold-Smoked Salmon PHOTO BY MICHELLE FURBACHER

BRINING AND HOME-SMOKING SALMON

A typical Haida Gwaii late summer evening: Peter comes home from a fishing trip with more salmon than we know what to do with. Chipper and I leave him to clean the fish while we go for a walk on the beach to collect agates.

By the time we fill our pockets and make it home, Peter has the salmon filleted, deboned, and cut into 2-inch (5 cm) wide chunks: the smaller pieces will brine and smoke more quickly because more surface area of each piece is exposed. (He left the skin on, which is what you are supposed to do, to hold everything together.)

The next step is to make a brine. Brining is crucial in smoking because it keeps you from getting sick or possibly even dying, which is important in the short run, though inevitable in the long haul, if you think about it. Brining, according to *The Joy of Cooking,* will "draw the natural sugars and moistures from foods, thus protecting them against spoilage bacteria." I have to assume they know what they are talking about, because, honestly, I don't. So, brine's the word. Otherwise you could find yourself living on Haida Gwaii as a permanent resident under an Afro of moss.

OUR FIRST ATTEMPT:
HOT-SMOKED SALMON FOR 2 LB (1 KG) OF SALMON

1¼ cups (310 mL) coarse (non-iodine) or kosher salt*

1 ¾ cups (410 mL) brown sugar

¼ cup (60 mL) maple syrup

2 cloves of garlic, crushed

2 Tbsp (30 mL) cracked peppercorns

1 gallon (4 L) water

2 lb (1 kg) of salmon fillets

ADDITIONS

You may add any flavour you want to the wet brine. More garlic, soy sauce, lemon, coriander seeds; there are no rules for flavour.

* Table salt (iodized salt) should not be used in any of these methods, as the iodine can impart a dark colour and bitter aftertaste to the fish.

1   Combine all the ingredients but the salmon in a large pan and heat to a boil.

2   Simmer for 5 minutes, cover the pan and then cool to room temperature. One way to tell if you have used enough salt is to float an (uncracked) egg in the mixture. If it floats then you have enough, but if the egg sinks, mix in another ¼ cup (60 mL) of salt. Test again with the egg. Repeat until the egg floats.

3   Refrigerate the brine until it is 40°F (4°C) or less before adding the salmon.

4   WARNING: The brine must be 35–40°F (2–4°C). Too cold and it slows the brining reactions, and if too warm it could allow bacteria to grow . . . over 40°F (4°C) is getting into the Unsafe Food Danger Zone.

5   The salmon now goes into the brine. Lay the filleted chunks flesh side down in a stainless steel or glass pan, in one layer. The brine should completely drown the fish. That is, cover it, from one tip of your fillet to the other. (I would usually say from head to toe, but heads and toes are removed from the salmon during the process of it being filleted.)

6   Refrigerate for at least 8 hours, or overnight. (The brining time is variable due to a couple of factors . . . thickness, and whether your salmon was previously frozen. The thicker the fillets are, the longer they'll need to brine. If previously frozen, decrease the brining time.)

7   When your fish is brined, here are your next instructions. (Are you having fun yet? How many days have you invested in this operation so far?)

8   The salmon needs to be rinsed to remove the excess salt. Remove the salmon from the brine and rinse away. (If you were me you would freeze the brine for a future occasion, but this is highly unrecommended for at least two reasons: one, it will take up too much room in your freezer and two, why would you even bother?)

9   After the brining comes the drying stage. Pat your fish dry with paper towels then lay it skin side down on your racks and let it rest in the fridge, uncovered, for 12 hours. As the salmon cures, the remaining salt in the flesh evenly redistributes. The proteins start to bind together, and the salmon dehydrates a bit, too; both need to happen before it hits the smoker. This is also when the pellicle forms—a hard, semi-glossy, clear coating on the fish, which should feel

slightly tacky to the touch. The pellicle keeps contaminants out and prevents large amounts of liquid from oozing out of the salmon as it smokes, which would create whitish curds on the surface . . . unattractive, but harmless.

10 Once the pellicle is formed (it can take anywhere from 1–3 hours) the salmon is ready for your smoker. Leave plenty of space around each piece of salmon on the rack so the air and the smoke can circulate. Put the racks in the smoker, and—Bob Fraumeni's your uncle!

RECIPE FOR OUR NEXT ATTEMPT: COLD-SMOKED SALMON

MAKES ENOUGH FOR SIX FILLETS OR MORE DEPENDING ON SIZE

This involves even more time and patience than the last procedure. These instructions are for an average sized fish of 10–12 lb (4.5–5.4 kg) (before being filleted). This process is for cold smoking salmon, preferably with a Bradley Smoker, unless you have your own homemade smokehouse. If using the latter, makes sure the heating element (auxiliary burner) IS OFF, or better yet unplug it from the smoke generator.

DRY BRINE INGREDIENTS

5 lb (2.3 kg) coarse (non-iodine) or kosher salt

2 lb (1 kg) brown sugar

WHAT YOU DO

1 Fillet your salmon, removing all the tiny bones that could stick in your throat and cause you to choke and land up being a permanent resident you-know-where.

2 Mix salt and sugar well, using your hands to break up the chunks of brown sugar. This will be used for dry brining the fish. Any leftover can be sealed in a container or a zip-lock bag. It will keep for a long time until you need it again.

3 Use a small (stainless steel or glass) container that is just wide and long enough in which to lay your whole fillets flat; spread an even ½-inch (1 cm) layer of the dry-brine mix on the bottom.

4   Lay the first layer of fillets skin side down on the dry mix. Now cover fillets with more dry mix (½ inch/1 cm).

5   Place next layer of fillets on top with skin side up (meat to meat). Cover with ½-inch (1 cm) dry mix. Make sure fish is completely covered in the mix (that's why the size of your container is important so you don't waste excess mix). Continue to layer the fish. This process will remove excess moisture from the fish and really firm it up.

6   Place fish in the refrigerator for 7–8 hours.

7   **WARNING:** If you forget this part of the process and dry brine for too long, you will ruin your fish. Set a timer so you don't forget.

8   After the 7–8 hours have passed you will see a considerable amount of syrupy liquid, the moisture from the fish, in the bottom of the container. Take it out of the refrigerator and remove one fillet at a time and cut in half. Rinse the mixture off the fish; the fish will seem hard, firm and a lot smaller than when you started. Discard the syrupy liquid from the dry brine process. Note to self: do not freeze and reuse.

9   Put fillets in your smoker.

If you wish you can wet brine (see recipe page 186) your fish instead of dry brining it. You'll get quite a different effect each way, as you'll find when you have time to try out both methods.

WET BRINE INGREDIENTS

3.5 gal. (14 L) water

6 cups (1.4 L) coarse (non-iodine)
or kosher salt

3 cups (700 mL) brown sugar

1–2 cups (250–500 mL) maple syrup

¼ cup (60 mL) whole black peppercorns

2 cloves garlic

Chopped fresh dill, to taste

WHAT YOU DO

1   In a 5 gallon (20 L) food bucket (or non-metal container large enough to hold your fish and brine), mix all ingredients well, making sure that all the salt and sugar is completely dissolved. (See previous instructions re: salinity check and the floating (or undesirably sinking) egg in Hot-Smoked Salmon recipe page 182.)

2   Submerge fillets in the wet brine. Brine for at least 8 hours, or overnight.

3   Remove the fillets from the brine and rinse in fresh water. Discard brine and rinse out your bucket. Now put the fillets back in the bucket and fill with clean water. Let the water run into the bucket (do not use too much pressure or you will damage the fish) for 30 minutes, stirring the fish gently with your hand every 10 minutes.

4   You can now taste a small piece of the fish. If still too salty, rinse for another 10 minutes, but no longer or the fish will begin to get waterlogged. Rinse for 30 minutes and you should have consistently excellent results.

5   After brining, wet or dry, dry fillets for approximately 8 hours to achieve a firm pellicle. You may smoke from 1–3 days, depending on your taste, and the amount of smoke or density of smoke, applied. Buy or make hardwood chips— apple, alder, oak, hickory, cherry—whatever flavour you like. Soak wood chips in water to prevent them from burning rather than smouldering during the smoking process.

6   Watch your temperature carefully: if it goes above 70°F (21°C) your fish can be ruined. Well, not ruined. It will be hot smoked salmon, not cold smoked. Still tasty, only ruinously so.

7 Recommended: a barbeque thermometer with a remote pager. The probe hangs through the top vent and the pager notifies you if the temperature gets to 70°F (21°C).

8 Alternately (and this is Haida Gwaii–style), once you have smoked enough salmon, you will know by instinct—or by the smell—when your fish is done. The finished color is almost red (if it's coho you are smoking) due to the caramel in the brown sugar coloring the fish during the dry brine process. The final texture is like velvet and slices really well.

9 If you don't have a vacuum food sealer, borrow or buy one. Vacuum storage is the ideal way to pack cold smoked salmon. After sealing your smoked salmon, refrigerate it for short term storage, or freeze it to gorge on all year.

HALIBUT

"A fisher will talk respectfully to the halibut, referring to it as k'aagaay, or elder, while asking it to bite his hook."
—from *Just Fish 2000* by Chief Nang Jingwas (Russ Jones) and gid7ahl-gudsllaay lalaxaaygans (Terri-Lynn Williams-Davidson)

The first fish I hooked on Haida Gwaii, at the mouth of Masset Sound, was a halibut. Reeling it in was like trying to bring up a refrigerator door from the bottom of the sea. (It weighed in at 70 lb on the scales at the Masset dock.)

When my friend Farhad brought the halibut alongside the boat, he harpooned it before bringing it on board. (Another method I've heard suggested is that instead of using a harpoon, squirt some whiskey, vodka, or other alcohol into their gills. Ten seconds later, they are dead. "At least they die happy.") However you decide to send a halibut into the afterlife, the idea is to do it

Masset dock PHOTO BY CHARLOTTE MUSGRAVE

before you bring it on board where it will demonstrate, violently, its desire to live. I've heard too many stories about fishermen being found dead under the bodies of halibut—and now when there's one on the line, I stay well out of the way.

It's a Fish-Eat-Rocks World

- Several weeks before the big Alaska earthquake in 1964, fishermen reported that the stomachs of the halibut they were catching were filled with rocks. A *Scientific American* article theorized that the fish had felt the tremors long before we felt them on land, and had swallowed the stones to give them ballast when the big earthquake hit.

- Stomach contents of a halibut cleaned by fishers on the *F/V Provider* off Alaska: two crabs, three rocks, one spiny rockfish and a 5-pound pork roast.

DEATH BY HALIBUT

The Tsimshian tribe of the Northwest Coast has a tale of a monster halibut that ate a whole canoe, carrying a prince and two princesses. A two-man team paddled out to get revenge, and they were consumed, also; they lived long enough to gut the fish from the inside, which resulted in the halibut dying, too.

Snake Charmer advertisemnt ILLUSTRATION FROM H.KOON, INC.

Alaskan fisherman Joseph T. Cash, 67, was killed by a 150 lb halibut in 1973. He was alone on his boat when he caught the fish near Kupreanof Island and succeeded in hauling it aboard. In the process, though, the flailing fish broke the fisherman's leg, severing a femoral artery and sending Cash crashing to the deck, where he cracked three ribs. Mortally injured, he managed to lash himself to the boat's winch to avoid being washed overboard and becoming (his greatest fear) crab bait. His boat was found days later, drifting, his body still tied to the winch, the halibut at his feet.

In Washington waters a firearm can be used to dispatch halibut. Some use a .38 Special pistol, while others swear by a .410 bore shotgun. One Internet site suggests, The "Snake Charmer" is a "nice little shotgun for this." Note to our American friends: Do not even *consider* trying to bring a firearm into Canada.

MORE THAN ONE WAY
TO CATCH A HALIBUT

Barrett, who works as a kayak-tour guide during the summers in Gwaii Haanas, tells this story:

> *"We were headed towards Rose Harbour on the mother ship, the* Island Bay, *for dinner at Susan Cohen's. I was jigging from the side of the boat and hooked a small halibut—whacked it on the head, cut its gills and tail and hung it by the gills on the stern deck of the boat.*
>
> *"The guests, who had all changed for dinner, were about to climb in the skiff to go ashore, when one of them suggested I give the fish another good smack to make sure it was dead (I'd been in a bit of a rush earlier). My somewhat timid knock set it to shaking, splattering slime all over me and the deck and spewing up a small octopus that slid across the deck and in through the door to the cabin."*

When his job was over and he was home on North Beach,* Barrett didn't have access to a kayak or a motorboat or even a rowboat with oars, and he missed having freshly caught halibut for his dinner every night. He did, however, own a surfboard.

Barrett and his good friend Nate squeezed into their wet suits, made a small offering to the ocean, and launched their longboards from the long sandy beach in front of Nate and Charley's house. Catching any fish from a surfboard would be a ride in itself; it takes skill and chutzpah to try and land a big, flat halibut—one with large teeth and a high IQ—while keeping your balance. If you let a halibut stick the tiniest bit of its nose out of the water before you've netted it, it will flick off your lure and be gone, so (in Barrett's words again) "most folks will 'gaff' the hali and pull it on board their boat. In our situation we had to adapt to being in the water."

The two paddled to where the halibut hang out, a little outside the break, and dropped a line over the side.

The best way to catch a halibut is to jig your line up and down across the ocean bottom; the halibut, a bottom-feeder, will dart upward, attracted by the motion, and take the lure. I've heard it described as the halibut inhaling the lure, the way it would a small fish, and the moment the fisherman feels that slight inhalation

---

* "North Beach is the local name given to the great stretch of sand beach fringing the shoreline from Rose Spit to Masset. It is the home of the famous razor clams."—Kathleen Dalzell, The *Queen Charlotte Islands Vol. 2: Of Places and Names.* I include this information because some of the newer residents of the area have taken to calling a portion of North Beach "South Beach." This, of course, irks me. "South Beach" is, if anything, west of North Beach. I suspect there are people who like the word "south" because it conjures up hot sandy beaches covered with humans sipping drinks with little umbrellas sticking out of them, and working on their melanomas. The antithesis of North Beach. May it always be so.

LEFT: Fishing for halibut PHOTO BY NATE; TOP RIGHT: Hali and equipment PHOTO BY NATE; BOTTOM RIGHT: Barret and Hali and board PHOTO BY NATE

he has to give a sharp pull to get the fish firmly on the hook. Before you could say, "What's for dinner?" Barrett felt that light tug on his line:

> *We lay on our surfboards with our heads under the water to watch the halibut as we pulled him in. When he was close enough I put a second hook, a shark hook, as gently as I could into his open mouth and forced it back though his cheek. Now on two lines (one being the fishing line that we jigged him up on, the other being a thick braided rope attached to the shark hook) the 40 lb fish took off for the deep. On its way down— running—it shook loose the shark hook and was only hooked on the original line again.*
>
> *When we brought it back up again, we did the same thing, but this time I forced the shark hook directly into the fish's head. I jumped off my board into the water and pulled him in close (like a hug) to stop him wriggling as much as I could, and then forced the shark hook the rest of the way through his head. I held on to the barbed end, also, to make sure not to lose the fish.*
>
> *Nate paddled over and cut its tail on the top side, and then sliced its gills as I held on tight. When we saw the blood in the water all around us, turning the ocean red, we decided that might have been a mistake. We emptied our huge dry bag backpack,* and slid the hali in, tail first. It hardly fit into the bag, but we bent it enough to get the bag clipped [closed]. Even though it wasn't sealed properly we knew now that we had it for sure. Then we tidied our hand lines, Nate put the backpack on and we paddled back to shore.*

OTHER FISH IN THE SEA

"If people concentrated on the really important things in life, there'd be a shortage of fishing poles."
—Doug Larson

Salmon and halibut are the two fish I have concentrated on in this book (in terms of recipes) because that's mostly what we've caught whenever I've gone out fishing. It isn't unusual, though, to find other species of fish on your line when you

---

*   Waterproof backpack.

100-year old cod helmet at Copper Beech House PHOTO BY WILLIAM GIBSON

are waiting for something bigger to bite. A variety of rockfish and ling cod are often caught when you are fishing for halibut and your line is down deep. If you head out into open water (25 km/16 miles or more off the West Coast) you might catch an albacore tuna. Black cod (or sablefish) are fished commercially using a bottom longline baited with hooks and anchored to the ocean floor. A longline can be from 1.6 to 5 km (1 to 3 miles) long and have up to 2000 hooks.

The yellow eye rockfish (commonly referred to as "red snapper" and often marketed as such) is especially beautiful, as it flashes towards you through black water, a brilliant golden red. But bringing a rockfish to the surface can be traumatizing for those on *either* end of the line. A rockfish experiences severe barotrauma ("baro" means pressure, and I am confident that "trauma" is universally understood) when he is "out of his depth." Rockfish have a swim bladder—a gas bladder in their gut cavity, and the gas is under pressure. If you bring these fish up from 60 m, or even 30 m, (200 or 100 feet) the gas expands and, well, think of it as having a balloon inside your body.

The condition isn't fatal, though it usually means a death sentence if you throw the fish back because he is too small or you've already caught your limit. If you release him he has no way to make it back down to depth, so he floats on the surface—for about a minute before an eagle or some eagle-eyed seabird scoops him up.

The good rockfish news is that devices are made by which these fish can be lowered back down to the depths from which they came, and with fishing stories to tell about being the one who got away. (Many don't make it, despite our attempts to resuscitate. If you start catching rockfish and don't want to—fish somewhere else. Move away from pinnacles and kelp beds, where they hang out, to avoid them.)

FRESHWATER FISHING

"There are two things I like to see in my water; one's fish, the other's whisky."
—Old ghillie*saying

---

*   (In Scotland) a ghillie is a man or boy who attends someone on a hunting or fishing expedition.

I can't not mention the fresh water fishing, and fly-fishing in the rivers here—Dolly Varden, cutthroat and rainbow trout, stickleback, and steelhead. (Steelhead are catch-and-release only.)

Fly-fishing is an art. One legendary Scottish angling instructor, Hugh Falkus, would advise his students to practice casting with a glass of whisky on their head. When they were able to cast out without spilling a drop, they would know they had mastered the art of fly-casting.

Bob Fraumeni and cutthroat trout
PHOTO BY SUSAN MUSGRAVE

CLAMS

"Paralytic Shellfish Poisoning (PSP, or red tide) is a life-threatening syndrome. Symptoms include tingling, numbness, and burning of the perioral region, ataxia, giddiness, drowsiness, fever, rash, and staggering. The most severe cases result in respiratory arrest within 24 hours of consumption of the toxic shellfish. If the patient is not breathing or if a pulse is not detected, artificial respiration and CPR may be needed as first aid. There is no antidote, supportive therapy is the rule and survivors recover fully."
—The Harmful Algae Page

"Old people used to say you quit eating [butter clams] when the ravens quit eating them. When the ravens start eating clams again, it's time to go after them."
—Claude Jones, Old Massett resident

ILLUSTRATION BY DEJAHLEE BUSCH

RAZOR CLAMS

You don't want to eat clams (or mussels, cockles or scallops) if there is a red tide warning. You won't get medical help quickly enough on Haida Gwaii. (There used to be a skeleton in the old Masset hospital holding a sign. It said, "We'll be with you shortly." It's been removed, out of politically correct respect for the bones.)

People on Haida Gwaii go to the beach in late fall and winter for butter clams and cockles, but the real prize is razor clams. The largest and oldest razor clams found in British Columbia live and breathe under the surf-swept North Beach at the north end of Graham Island. At one time North Beach was called Clam Beach; a razor clam cannery was built on the old Hiellen village site* just east of Tow Hill and operated between 1923 and 1930. The clams were dug every time the tide went out, and hauled off the beach by horse and wagon. Now when the clam-digging season starts in the spring, the village of Old Massett empties, as truckloads of razor clam diggers head out to Tow Hill. Whole families go to the beach for the day, clamming and picnicking together.

Razor clams are dug at very low tides. (Their shells look like something you might shave your legs with if you were marooned on North Beach without your toiletries; broken shells are razor sharp and can leave you gashed and bleeding.) You can tell where one is at home because of the hollow (about the size of a quarter) it leaves on the sand's surface as the clam withdraws its neck. Some of my clam digger friends recommend stomping or dancing on the sand between the hollow and the water. (Others say, "Why bother?") When you do this the clam thinks the tide is coming in and his siphon goes up. (Do not ask me how anyone knows what a clam thinks. You have to, as they say, "be here.")

Diggers use special narrow-bladed shovels and dig down quickly, trying to avoid breakage. After the first scoop or two, reach down into the hole, grab hold of the foot and pull it out. Clams can be difficult to wrench from their hole when the foot is "anchored," which is why you often see clam diggers a full arm's length into the sand, playing tug of war with a clam. This also explains the expletives you hear when the clam wins.

If you miss getting hold of it, give up. Do not try, try again. The clam will be long gone and you will exhaust yourself as you dig through the sand, digging your way towards China. ("If you dig far enough you'll end up in China," my parents used to say, leaving us on a sandy beach with our plastic shovels and plastic buckets and hoping to keep us occupied for the afternoon.) I myself have never

---

* An ancient village site that the Haida occupied for millennia fronting on the Hiellen River and Tow Hill beach and present-day site of Hiellen Longhouse Village.

managed to "catch" one. That's okay. As I once overheard a young woman from the southern United States say (in Crete, watching locals in the vineyards picking grapes), "I *love* to watch people work!"

If you are lucky enough to get your clam up onto the beach, put it in a sealed container immediately. It's safe to say that razor clams can get away faster than most getaway drivers my husband has partnered up with before making some of his less successful unauthorized withdrawals from banks. If you drop one on wet sand and turn your back, its powerful foot will start digging with movements so swift your eye will hardly believe what it hasn't seen. A razor clam can flip itself upright and disappear beneath the surface, digging as fast as one inch per second with a clammer in hot pursuit.

TOP LEFT: North Beach from Tow Hill PHOTO BY ARCHIE STOCKER SR.

TOP RIGHT: Dom PHOTO BY CHRIS ASHURST

BOTTOM LEFT: Razor clamming PHOTO BY KATHLEEN HINKEL

BOTTOM RIGHT: Ian, Hand Digger PHOTO BY CHRIS ASHURST

TOP LEFT: Sandy razor clams PHOTO BY KATHLEEN HINKEL; MIDDLE LEFT: Razor clams sandy PHOTO BY ARCHIE STOCKER SR.; BOTTOM LEFT: Razor clams washed, shells removed and cleaned PHOTO BY ARCHIE STOCKER SR.; TOP RIGHT: Razor clams PHOTO BY ARCHIE STOCKER SR.; MIDDLE RIGHT: Razor clams in tote PHOTO BY FARHAD GHATAN.; BOTTOM RIGHT: Razor clams ready for freezer PHOTO BY FARHAD GHATAN

The Razor Clam By Hilbert Gren

In the north beach sands lives the Razor Clam
A retiring little critter that don't give a damn.
He faces the world with his posterior
While the surging tide cools his interior.
He is like a ship without a rudder
Where his head should be he wears an udder
This brings to me a thoughtful frown
He is like most of those guys in Masset town.

RAZOR CLAM LINGUINE SERVES A GOODLY CROWD

"Nothing is ever the same twice."

—Bob Fraumeni, fisherman

I don't know how many times I have followed Bob around his summer kitchen by candlelight, a glass of Krim Crawford (what we call Kim Crawford, the New Zealand Sauvignon Blanc, after a few bottles) taking note of all the steps involved in making his sublime Razor Clam Pasta. I thought I had it down pat (I even ran it by him during his Birth Week Festivities in January 2014) but every time he makes the dish he sends me another version of his recipe! Since I do not in any way wish to incur the Wrath of Bob, I am going to quote him, verbatim. Of course this summer it will be updated again, but—too late to change. Book off to printer. Recipe immortalized, in Bob's name.

Linguine. Or pasta of choice. A whole whack of it. Approximately 2 oz (55 g) per person	Two 3 lb (1–1.5 kg) razor clams.[†]
1 small acorn squash, cut in 1-inch (2.5 cm) cubes (or less)	2 bunches asparagus or broccolini
1 onion, diced	Small and spicy peppers and/or banana peppers
2 plants of garlic[*]	2 large lemons, juiced
	INGREDIENTS CONTINUED . . .

---

[*]   I would have said "heads" but Bob wrote "plants" and it isn't my recipe, right?

[†]   Bob prefers fresh but frozen works, too, and I have canned razor clams from Choc Edenshaw and Randy Russ, which I use if I can't get fresh ones.

Olive oil

Black pepper

A whole bunch of green onions chopped
in 1 inch (2.5 cm) long pieces

FOR THE SAUCE

Half litre cream

Gorgonzola, or a similar cheese—blue,
Asiago or combination—a bunch, until
desired flavour

2 plants of garlic*

One large bunch fresh parsley,
chopped fine

Freshly ground black pepper

Olive oil

WHAT YOU DO

1   Start by cleaning up, peeling and slicing the two garlic plants [sic]. All cloves
    peeled; three crushed and chopped.

2   Peel and slice onion. Remove the skin from the squash and cut in 1-inch cubes
    (or less).

3   Break off the asparagus tips (this is all you will be using so save the rest for
    stock to make asparagus soup) or, if you are using broccolini, cut into bite-
    sized pieces.

4   Fry the clams in batches, in olive oil. Not too many, as a lot of liquid comes off.
    Add some of the onion slices then the crushed garlic.

5   Grind some pepper into the mixture. As the moisture comes out of the clams,
    spoon it into a bowl. Then the clams can sizzle a bit and get sort of glazed, not
    really browned, but almost.

6   As you are frying the clams in batches, enlist a friend/partner/sweetie to make
    the sauce. This is done by heavy coercion.

7   Put all the whole peeled garlic cloves in a sizzling saucepan of olive oil, then
    roll them around until browned and roasted looking.

---

*   I would have said "heads"—oh yes, I already said that!

RAZOR CLAMS LINGUINI (I LIKE FRESH CLAMS
BUT FROZEN OR THE
JARRED ONE'S SUSAN
GAVE ME ARE FINE
- ..3 POUNDS of RAZOR CLAMS.
- 2 PLANTS of GARLIC.
- 1 ONION
- 1 SQUASH - ACORN
- 2 BUNCHES of ASPARAGUS OR BROCCOLINI
- PEPPERS (BELL SPACE SMALL) AND DR BANANA -- NO REGULAR BELL PEPPER (WRONG FLAVOR)
- BLACK PEPPER
- OLIVE OIL
- LINGUINI OR PASTA of CHOICE
- A WHOLE BUNCH of GREEN ONIONS CHOPPED IN ONE INCH LONG PIECES
- HALF LITRE CREAM
- GORGONZOLA OR SIMILAR CHEESE, BLUE, ASIAGO OR COMBINATION (A BUNCH, UNTIL DESIRED FLAVOR.
- 2 PLANTS of GARLIC.
- OLIVE OIL

START BY CLEANING UP, PEELING AND SLICING, THE TWO GARLIC PLANTS - ALL CLOVES JUST BARED BUT THREE CRUSHED ONION PEELED + SLICED, SQUASH SKINNED AND CUT IN CUBES 1" OR LESS, ASPARAGUS, CUT TO JUST TIPS OR BROCCOLINI CLEANED AND READY TO COOK. AND SLICE THE START BY FRYING THE CLAMS (IN BATCHES) IN OLIVE OIL, FIRST PUT SOME OF THE

8 Pour in all the cream, whisking continuously. Add all the cheese, crumbled, and keep stirring until thickened. Add more cheese until you have the desired consistency.

9 After the batches of clams are cooked, put them in another bowl to keep warm. Add any onion that is left, and garlic, to the wok. Oh, did I tell you to use a large wok to cook all this in and a large gas blaster, on the edge of a beach? Well now you know!

10 Add the chunks of squash to the wok—nice, orange acorn is my favourite— looks beautiful. Stir these around until all the edges are brown. Every time you are cooking a new batch of something you are using olive oil. If you can't use olive oil, don't make this recipe! Oh, and I forgot to tell you should have a large pot of salted water boiling, ready for the pasta.

11 When the squash is brown and glazed, add slices of spicy peppers, and finally your greens, your asparagus tips or your broccolini.* Roll these ingredients around in the wok for half a minute or so. Meanwhile you have had the pasta in the boiling water for the last **four minutes** ONLY!

12 Tong the noodles out of the water into the wok—as many noodles as looks right. In other words, you don't have to necessarily use *all* the noodles. Keep the pot of water close by.

LEFT: A Wok on the Beach
PHOTO BY GUY KIMOLA[†]

RIGHT: Bob's handwritten recipe PHOTO BY SUSAN MUSGRAVE

---

* Bob waved these in a micro for a few minutes, but you can also blanch them if you are like me and don't have a micro-wave.

† I love Guy's photo of "A Wok on the Beach," but I resist puns with vigour. I tried retitling this to read, "A Wok in the Kelp," but the result was, more or less, the same.

13 Combine all ingredients in the wok at this stage, including the sauce. Add the clams last—sweet, tender razor clams must be cooked quickly: if cooked too long, they will be tough! Add the clam nectar you spooned out in the beginning (Step 5) when you were frying the clams. Toss everything together and add the juice of two lemons.

14 Now you are finishing cooking your pasta in the juices of everything—the pasta absorbs all the flavours. Yum! Add half a cup of the pasta water you have close by, or however much it takes to thicken the whole dish/wok-full.

15 Add the green onions just before you are done. Now!

GEODUCKS

Richard Hardy with geoduck
PHOTO BY DANIEL RABU

Geoducks (pronounced gooey-ducks) have nothing to do with ducks; they are the largest burrowing clams in the world. Geoducks hunker down under a meter of sand and gravel with their necks (siphons) breaking the sea floor to sift microscopic plankton for food. Fishermen have been known to gut halibut and find caches of geoduck necks in their stomachs.

Geoducks live long lives of quiet desperation (I am projecting here, since that is how I would feel if I were to lie deeply buried beneath the narrow strip of shore that only comes above water during the lowest tides of the year); the oldest known in BC was taken from Tasu Sound, on Haida Gwaii's west coast, and aged at over 160 years.

The lowest autumn tide will occur approximately two days after the full of the Mad Moon[*] in late October or early November. In the strip of shore where geoducks are found, the lowest of the tides will come in the middle of the night. Hunt the geoduck at midnight, two days after the Mad Moon is full, and you might get lucky.

[*] From Euell Gibbons's *Stalking the Blue-Eyed Scallop:* "Along in late October or early November, there comes the full of what some tribes of Indians call the Mad Moon. . . . It sounds like a psychotic sorcerer's formula to say the Geoduck must be sought at midnight, just two days after the full of the Mad Moon, but it happens to be a sober fact."

MUSSELS

I had always been nervous of shellfish. I remembered the warnings, how one bite of a contaminated bivalve could kill you before you had time to spit it out.

"How do you know they're safe?" I asked.

"You worry too much," he said, shaking his head and laughing at me.

"Worry's going to kill a person quicker than anything you pick off the beach."

—from *Given* by Susan Musgrave

My first food gathering experience on Haida Gwaii was in the early '70s: Benita Saunders and her husband Borje drove us out to Rennell Sound and we spent an afternoon in the rain clambering over beds of blue-violet mussels, picking them from the black rocks at the far end of a sandy beach, a short walk through the bush from the access road. It must have been in the fall, because when we got back to their house in Queen Charlotte, Benita sent us to her garden to pick snow peas and Borje steamed them and added them to a wok with the fiery orange mussels he had sautéed with garlic and a breath of white wine. It could have been because we were wet and tired after a long day of heavy west coast air and the rain, but nothing I had eaten before, and nothing I've eaten since, has imprinted itself with such ferocity on every one of my senses. (Yes, I can still hear the faraway roar of the sea that day, even as I write this 40 years later.)

Mussels PHOTO BY MARLENE LIDDLE

I've been back to Rennell Sound many times since but have never been able to find the beach, or the black rocks and the mussel beds. There might be some experiences you are only meant to have once in a lifetime. Might that just not be enough?

MUSSELS TRUDEAU   SERVES 4

In the mid '70s Pierre and Maggie Trudeau came to Haida Gwaii for a holiday. David Phillips organized their visit; he fixed up an old homestead farmhouse for them to stay in, leaving a copy of my slim volume, *The Impstone*, on a table beside their bed, along with the journals he'd written during his respites at Riverview mental hospital.

David cooked for the Trudeaus and I had wondered if this recipe for mussels, gathered on their visit to Lepas Bay on the northwest coast of Graham Island,

LEFT: Jenny's Mussels Trudeau in cursive PHOTO BY SUSAN MUSGRAVE; RIGHT: David with Pierre Trudeau PHOTO BY PROJECT KIUSTA

MUSSELS TRUDEAU
(CONT'D)

was his recipe, though I found it reproduced by Jenny Nelson in the G. M. Dawson High School's *A Cookbook with a Difference*. No book, and certainly no cookbook, is written by one person alone: Jenny, when asked about the origin of the recipe, passed on a list of people who could have been responsible for the dish. She believes it originated in a magazine called *All Alone Stone*, and credits Huckleberry (a.k.a. Thom Henley, who started the wilderness-heritage cultural Rediscovery Programme on Haida Gwaii in 1978). I have decided to credit Jenny.

½ cup (120 mL) mustard

¼ cup (60 mL) butter, melted

2 Tbsp (30 mL) lemon juice

Half a bucket full of bladderwrack (fresh, gathered from the rocks at low tide)

2 lb (1 kg) mussels, or however many you can pick

WHAT YOU DO

1 Mix mustard, butter and lemon juice and heat until the butter has melted. Set aside.

2 Make a bed of bladderwrack in a large pot or Dutch oven.

3 Fill your pot with mussels and cover with more seaweed. "Bladderwrack makes the steam and it's good eatin'!'" Jenny says, in the G. M. Dawson cookbook.

4 Serve the mussels HOT with the mustard sauce.

5   Mussels, of course, are also delicious steamed in white wine with a little garlic
    sautéed in butter first, and finished with a bit of cream.

DUNGENESS CRAB

TRUE FACT #1: Scottish immigrants settled in a small village on the coast of Washington State and named the resident crab "Dungeness" after their former home on the northeast coast of Scotland. (Isn't it true that most immigrants named things after themselves, or someone back at home? Douglas fir, the Straits of Juan de Fuca, the Queen Charlotte Islands?)

TRUE FACT #2: Those almost intact replicas of crabs you find washed up on the beach? They are not dead crabs. Crabs molt, shedding their hard outer shell and then growing a new, larger one.

TRUE FACT #3: The male Dungeness crab mates with a female in the hours following her molt. The act lasts about half an hour but the male crab often carries the female around with him for several days to make sure no other male attempts to have his way with her. (Why does this sound familiar?)

TRUE FACT #4: A male Dungeness crab can weigh up to about 2 kg (4.4 lb), and can live up to 10 years, unless of course you interrupt his life by eating him.

TRUE FACT #5: It is illegal to keep female crabs. You can identify females by the wider shell on their abdomen (the flap of shell that points toward the crab's eyes when you hold it upside down). If in doubt, ask someone who looks as if they know what they are doing. (It is also illegal to keep under-sized crabs.)

TRUE FACT #6: Dungeness crabs eat clams, mussels and other crustaceans. (Unverified True Fact: My friend Chris Taylor, a.k.a. Big Foot, says the reason the crabs from North Beach are so tasty is that they eat the tops of the siphons of razor clams. The clams die, but the crabs taste good!) When moving along the sea bottom, they find and capture prey by probing the sand with their legs or claws. Dungeness crabs can move in any direction (more quickly than I can, in most cases.) Crabs are bottom feeders—they'll eat anything that ends up on the ocean floor, and that includes you.

Best Answer

Truck with crab pots PHOTO BY JANIE JOLLEY

Found on YAHOO Answers: "im really curious, i heard some people talking about it. like if someone just tossed a dead body into the crab traps, would the crabs devour everything without leaving any traces behind?"

Best answer (Voter's choice) "The f- do you want to know? im calling the cops."

Many Islanders set out crab traps, baiting them more traditionally with old fish carcasses, canned cat food or canned tuna. (You poke holes in the can and wire it to the pot/ring or dump the contents of the can into a bait jar.) Raw poultry is said to be an adequate substitute.

COITUS INTERRUPTUS

You can catch Dungeness crabs on North Beach in the summer months (June through August). A minus tide* is best, but a low tide will do and some say it doesn't matter, just go to the beach with your dip net and take your chances. A net is a good idea, though I know of two women who, after staying up all night at their campfire, drinking, took off their clothes at low tide in the morning, walked naked into the sea and caught three Dungeness crabs with their bare hands. (Not recommended. Staying up all night and drinking has possible side effects.)

I say North Beach because it is 10 minutes from my house. There are other beaches, at the south end of the island where people go crabbing, but everyone from my end of the island says ours are tastier. (I wouldn't know, as you will learn if you read my far from definitive guide to killing and cooking crab on page 206.)

---

* Minus tides refer to low tides that drop below the "Mean Low Water" level. This generally occurs around the full and new moons when the tidal changes are greatest. It's especially important to clammers and crabbers because it means that seabed that is usually underwater is exposed during these very low tides.

TOP LEFT: To the crabs! PHOTO BY MICHELLE FURBACHER; TOP RIGHT: Julia with crab PHOTO BY BOB FRAUMENI; MIDDLE LEFT: Susan crabbing PHOTO BY BOB FRAUMENI; MIDDLE CENTRE: Julia with crab PHOTO BY BOB FRAUMENI; MIDDLE RIGHT: Crab PHOTO BY LYNDA OSBORNE; BOTTOM (TOP) LEFT: Julia and Randy crabbing PHOTO BY PETER SLOAN; BOTTOM LEFT: Crab in bucket PHOTO BY MICHELLE FURBACHER; BOTTOM RIGHT: Crabtime! PHOTO BY MICHELLE FURBACHER

PTSD

Traumatic events that can lead to PTSD include:

- War
- Natural disasters
- Car or plane crashes
- Terrorist attacks
- Sudden death of a loved one
- Rape
- Kidnapping
- Assault
- Sexual or physical abuse
- Childhood neglect
- Or any shattering event that leaves you stuck and feeling helpless and hopeless, i.e. cooking crab

Crab or Crabs?

Q: What is the plural of crab? Would you say **crab** or **crabs**? Please explain your reasoning.

A: "Crab," because "crabs" in English refers to crab lice.

There's a widely held belief that crustaceans cannot feel "pain" as they are lowered into boiling water. I don't believe this belief is held by the crabs, though, and recent tests (on crabs, of course) suggest that they suffer a prolonged excruciating death as they try to cling to the pot's sides and hook their claws over the rim whilst you try to push them back in, wielding the large pepper grinder. Even if you put a lid on the pot you can still hear the lid rattling as the crabs try to push it off in a last futile escape attempt. Or their claws scraping the sides of the pot, at which point I flee from the kitchen until the whole terrible process is over.

"What's wrong? You're not eating any crab!" my guests exclaim as I sit feeling detached and emotionally numb, with no interest in life in general and a strong sense of a limited future, symptoms of my impending PTSD. I try to brush it off by saying crabs are bottom feeders and that I can't forgive them for eating choice bits of a friend's body parts when he fell off the Port Clements dock at a graduation party in 1971. And then I tell them about Bill Reid, how he wanted his mortal remains taken by boat to Naden Harbour—where the crabs are mighty and plentiful—and tossed over the side. A few days later he wanted these same friends to catch a whole boatload of crabs and cook and eat them on the beach. I always find guests appreciate stories with local flavour.

Researching the least cruel way to kill Dungeness crabs, I came across this humdinger on Chowhounds from a letter writer called Motosport: "When I make crab and linguine with red sauce I literally clean the crabs by tearing them apart, tossing the large claws and the cleaned legless bodies into the bubbling red sauce. I know it's not humane but it does not really bother me. I am spiritual in many other ways."

Killing Mr. Crab (it's never Missus—if you catch a female you must throw her back) before cooking him is definitely the more spiritual path but does require vivisection and a lot of people (like me) are too sentimental to take a cleaver and chop a fellow being in half. However, you can usually find someone to do your dirty work for you, if you offer enough booze.

Helpful Hint: If you opt to drop the crabs into boiling water, put them in the boiling water upside down; the crab will fold its legs against its shell. So they say.

NEVER OVERCOOK AN OCTOPUS

"Free-diving is a recreational activity, celebrated as a relaxing, liberating, and unique experience."
—Wikipedia

Octopus is another one of those things that I don't eat on a daily basis. More like probably never. Along with squirrel, raccoon and sea lions. It turns out I have a conservative palate, and am often disappointed in myself. I could live on bread and jam alone. And of course cookies.

Heather and her husband Tom came to stay at Copper Beech House and told me a great octopus story, after which I felt octopus definitely had a place in this book, given their, um, attitude.

Ricardo Toledo was free-diving off BC Tel Point* near Queen Charlotte. Free-diving, I learned, means the diver doesn't use scuba gear or other external breathing apparatuses. He (or she—the champion record holder is a woman) stays underwater until their lungs run out of air.

Ricardo free-dives for food—rock scallops, mussels and urchins. He takes a breath, goes down as far as 80 to 100 feet, has a look around, and then comes back up again. (I'm sure it's more complicated than that, but Ricardo makes it sound simple, like all you have to do is be vaguely physically fit and know how to hold your breath . . .)

---

* Local name is "BC Tel Point," but marine charts call it "Haida Point."

Bread with jam and marmalade
PHOTO BY MICHELLE FURBACHER

The day of the Octopus Incident he had only gone down 25 feet and was sticking fairly close to shore. He didn't have a knife with him because he was "just poking around" and not in serious food-gathering mode. He poked under slabs in a rock face, and then, thinking he saw movement, explored further, seeing telltale signs of an octopus at home tending her garden—a pile of debris on the ocean floor. After a minute and a half he went back up for air, then dove down again: he knew that an octopus will usually have an escape hatch, a back door to her den, and was trying to figure out where this might be when he saw an arm, and he made a grab and tried to pull the octopus out. She was quicker: she wrapped one of her arms around one of his arms, and wouldn't let go.

He flipped one way, flipped the other, trying to shake her off. He created so much friction rubbing the octopus's limb against the rocky ledge that he sawed it completely off. With the arm still attached to his wet suit he jetted for the surface where his next job was to peel the suction cups off his own arm and bicep.

Ricardo took the arm home and cooked it—"fresher and bigger than any octopus I'd tasted before." He didn't, he said, stop to think about his circumstances—until later.

I particularly like this story because the octopus doesn't die. He merely loses an appendage, even if, somewhere in the depths off BC Tel Point there is a very

Ricardo's Appendage of Octopus: "It is like a 'saltado' or stir fry, typical of coastal Peru." PHOTO BY RICARDO TOLEDO

angry septopus. Which would you choose—your arm or your life? I used to ponder this question every time my kids brought home one of those life insurance packages from school every year, "Loss of life: $500. Loss of one eye $500,000. Loss of one arm $500,000,000." Personally, I would have suffered more of a loss if my daughters had lost their lives, and not just their arms. God forbid. I never bought the insurance.

Divers beware: The giant Pacific octopus found in the waters of Haida Gwaii is the largest octopus species in the world. People tell stories here of catching octopus that weigh anywhere from 96 to 232 kilograms (212 to 511 pounds).

Octopus

THE NAME "octopus" derives from Greek and means "eight legs." So what we call "arms" today was "legs" to the ancient Greeks. Many people today still call "arms" "legs," even in the 21st century. And they wouldn't be incorrect.

Ask anyone how many arms an octopus has, and the answer will most likely be eight. But aquatic experts in Europe now say that the octopus's front six limbs have the function of arms, for feeding and exploring, and that the back two take over the function of legs, for propelling the octopus across the sea bed.

Originally the study was designed to see if the octopus has a preferred arm. When they were given a Rubik's Cube to explore, marine biologists found that octopuses are ambidextrous. The giant Pacific octopus, the largest species in the world, has the ability to manipulate sections of the Rubik's Cube, if not to solve the puzzle.

A further misconception is that octopuses have tentacles. They do not, though their arms and legs are covered with up to 280 suckers that contain thousands of chemical receptors. Tentacles are longer than arms and usually have suckers at their tips only. Squid and cuttlefish have eight arms like octopuses, and also two tentacles, which is one good way to distinguish them from octopuses.

Whatever you call these octopus parts—legs, arms, tentacles, or suckers—you do not want one of them wrapped around any part of your anatomy. Especially if you are underwater, without oxygen, without a weapon or a Rubik's Cube to use as a diversionary tactic.

Octopus with Rubik's cube PHOTO BY TOM WREN COURTESY OF THE BOURNEMOUTH NEWS

APPENDAGE OF OCTOPUS RICARDO TOLEDO

Ricardo, whose family is from Peru, says he doesn't prepare his octopus the way other people do. He says most people tenderize it using a variety of different tricks of the octopus-cooking trade. Greeks like to beat the octopus against a rock in time to the theme song from *Zorba the Greek*, whilst knocking back copious amounts of ouzo. Italians simmer it with the corks from two bottles of Valpolicella, an Italian red wine. Irish chefs recommend boiling the octopus with half a chopped potato. David Phillips used to marinate octopus in Coca-Cola when he prepared it at Copper Beech House.

I tell Ricardo, from what I've read, no matter which way you are determined to prepare the octopus, it must be boiled first.

I could hear him shaking his head over the telephone. "You wash it, peel off the membrane, pan fry it with a little garlic and butter. Like most food that comes from the sea, you don't want to cook it to death."

HAIDA GWAII BRIDAL CAKE

"Genius is not a gift. It is the way one invents in desperate situations."
—Jean Paul Sartre

Greg Martin baked this bridal cake in the fall of 1970 for his friend Nancy's wedding. Nancy, along with Greg and his girlfriend Molly, had traveled to Haida Gwaii from Illinois that summer. He sent me the story:

> *Through the kindness of Dorothy and Francis Richardson, I was appointed caretaker of the Nelson Brothers' Lodge on Beitush Road in Tlell. Nancy fell in love with Stan, a Calgarian whom I found to be rather 'grasping,' and perhaps not the best match for my friend, but Stan moved in with Molly, Nancy and me for the winter.*
>
> *It was a spontaneous and unplanned pregnancy that rang the wedding bells, and baking the wedding cake fell to me. Nancy suggested a dark fruitcake from her Fanny Farmer cookbook, saying that it had been the custom in early 20th century New England.*
>
> *So there I was in the Nelson Lodge mixing up the cake, but I got stuck on the "1 cup of candied fruit," as there had been none at Chapman's General Store (as it was known in the '70s*) in Port Clements. The Nelson family owned Nelson Bros. Fisheries, and had stocked the pantry with a variety of canned foods, including crab, salmon and even octopus. So I sliced up the octopus and separated it off into 4 different bowls, each with a different food colouring and substituted it for the candied fruit. I'm not known as a good cook[†], so everyone took great pains to praise the cake. Frankly, I thought it was pretty tasty!*

---

[*] Now Bayview Market

[†] Carol Kulesha, long-time mayor of Queen Charlotte, and pictured in the above photograph, described one of Greg's specialities: sardines and Velveeta cheese on pasta. Greg could not be reached to confirm or deny this accusation.

Some of the wedding party at the Nelson Place, 1970. PHOTO BY GREG MARTIN

I didn't mention this substitution until well after the wedding celebration, but after I got to know Stan better, the substitution seemed very appropriate. He was aggressive in his dealings, and the home that he designed and had built in Queen Charlotte became known as "The Cash Register," partly because it physically resembles one. (It is still standing, on Relax Road.)

So feel free to use/rewrite any of this. Don't worry about liability, as Stan moved away a long time ago and died.

WASH. BIOL. SURV.

A guest at Copper Beech House asked me if we shot and ate ravens on Haida Gwaii. Definitely not. Nor do we eat crow, unless we have made a serious error and need to acknowledge it humbly.* A friend and Tow Hill Road neighbour, Peter Rempel, sent me this morsel (October 2012):

Earthquake aftershocks, tsunami nightmares, and life delayed me sending you the WASH. BIOL. SURV. story.

I put it to the Internet (Snopes) and found the . . ."Wash. Biol. Surv." tale started out as a joke at least as far back as the 1940s, one which played on the stereotype of the backwards, rural farmer as too unsophisticated to recognize the significance of a banded bird, too unschooled to interpret the designation on its band as anything but cooking instructions, and too poor to let something he'd killed go to waste by not eating it.

---

* When you have made a serious error and wish to take responsibility for your actions, it is highly probable that the expression you use to describe the process will have something to do with food. "I will have to eat crow;" "she ate humble pie;" "he ate his hat and swallowed the buckle whole;" "eat your heart out." What this says about erring and eating, I don't know. There is so much to know about everything, which makes it hard to write about any subject with any kind of authority, and provides a great excuse for not meeting deadlines.

In Washington, a government survey was ordered to study the migratory habits of birds. Thousands of all species were released with metal strips attached reading, "Notify Fish and Wild Life Division. Wash. Biol. Surv." The abbreviation was changed abruptly following receipt of this penciled note from a vexed Alberta agriculturist: "Gents: I shot one of your crows last week and followed instructions attached to it. I washed it, bioled it, and surved it. It was awful. You should stop trying to fool the public with things like this."

TRADITIONAL FOODS

"In the old days there wasn't such thing as a dollar bill. The most important thing that ever existed was the food."
—John Yeltatzie, Gaawaas Eagle Clan, 1996

K'AAW

As told by Kii'iljus (Barbara Wilson) in *Staying the Course, Staying Alive*:

> *As salmonberries are the first berries to ripen in the spring, the herring was the first from the ocean to be harvested. Our women would go in their boats to harvest the k'aaw [herring roe] and celebrate another cycle of life.*
>
> *In season, herring will spawn on anything in the water they can find, bicycles and old boots included, but kelp is the plant we prefer for getting our k'aaw on. If that is not possible we have other forms*

of sea-grass (t'aanuu) *that is used. If all else fails we use the hemlock [branches are set so that they will just be submerged at low tide].*

K'aaw can be eaten dried, raw, cooked or frozen to be consumed later in the year. To cook it, cut the fronds into small squares and fry for 1 to 2 minutes with butter until the eggs turn from translucent to white.

RED SEA URCHIN

Lardo (Italian cured pork fat) + sea urchin + Iberico ham on bread = "a sex bagel."
—Tom Sietsema via Twitter

Sea urchins, close relatives of starfish, use their spines as stilts to move across the bottom of the ocean (I love that image!) and it is these spines that gave the creature its common name, "urchin," an old English name for the spiny hedgehog. They graze on seaweed, kelp and algae; on the underside of a sea urchin there are five teeth which they use to break down and devour their food. These teeth continue to grow throughout their life; the sea urchin uses them for grinding.

Washington Post food critic Tom Sietsema describes sea urchins as "the foie gras of the ocean" having an "achingly voluptuous taste filling your mouth with the pure soul of the sea." Sea urchin roe—egg and sperm sacs—is a traditional food of the Haida.

LEFT: *K'aaw,* herring roe on kelp
PHOTO BY ARCHIE STOCKER SR.

RIGHT: *K'aaw* on hemlock branches PHOTO BY MICHELLE FURBACHER

An Urchin by Another Name

URCHIN IS an old name for the round spiny hedge hogs that sea urchins resemble: *riccio* in Italian; *erizo* in Spanish; in the eastern US (State of Maine) sea urchins are known as whore's eggs—who knows why?

In the Orkney Islands of Scotland (home of night-less summers and 'simmer dim'*) urchin was once used instead of butter.

When the sea otters were wiped out in the mid-1800s, shellfish went forth and—unchecked by their natural predators—multiplied. Red urchins ate all the kelp in their path creating a phenomenon called "urchin barrens," where red urchins carpeted the ocean floor, in some places (such as Cape Knox) extending for hundreds of meters offshore.

Sea urchins are one of the few remaining delicacies that must be harvested from the wild and cannot, for most purposes, be frozen. Ricardo Toledo (of octopus-tentacle fame, see page 211) describes being with a guide in Gwaii Haanas who cracked open a sea urchin where he found it, in a tide pool. "Sushi right there in front of us, on the beach."

TOP AND BOTTOM LEFT: Purple sea urchins PHOTOS BY JANIE JOLLEY

RIGHT: Starfish PHOTO BY GUY KIMOLA

---

* During Midsummer in the Shetland Islands, the sun sets around 10:30 in the evening, and rises again about 3:30 a.m. The five hours in between are a time of prolonged dusk, known as the simmer dim. If the sky is clear then, it remains light enough to read outside for the entire night.

THE NORTHERN ABALONE

When Henry White was a boy at school, his mother Lavina invited a South African teacher home to have a traditional Haida meal with the family. He tried a little bit of everything, but when it came to the abalone (this was before 1990 when the abalone fishery was closed due to a threatened abalone population) he pushed it aside. When Henry asked his teacher why he wasn't going to try this delicacy, he replied, "It took her so long to kill it." He had watched Lavina in the kitchen pounding the abalone with a wooden mallet, not knowing that a thorough pounding is what makes the difference between a tough, barely edible abalone, and a tenderized utterly edible one.

The Northern Abalone is the smallest abalone found along the West Coast. It lives further north than any other species. Harvesting peaked at 425 tonnes in the late 1970s when markets to Japan opened up; the slow growing species never recovered even when the harvest ban was imposed. (Locals remember almost a million pounds being taken from Cumshewa Inlet alone.)

CHITON

I collected shells when I was a child. I didn't realize then that what I called "butterfly shells" were part of the body of a chiton. I loved their turquoise blue "wings" and never knew the individual shells I collected were part of something bigger. (It turns out I was not alone. Euell Gibbons, in *Stalking the Blue-Eyed Scallop*, says children call the middle shells Butterfly Shells, and the two rounded end shells, which look something like upper dental plates, False-Teeth Shells.)

Of local interest: the name Skidegate is an English version of the Haida word *Sgiidagids* which means *child of red chiton.*

Each chiton yields one small, thin steak. One way of preparing the meat is to cut the fleshy foot into bite-size pieces and eat it raw, right on the spot, within a few minutes of catching it. It doesn't take a lot of energy to "catch" a chiton, unlike a razor clam. Chitons are light-sensitive and cling darkly to the under sides of rocks, in tide pools where they are trapped when the tide goes out. At night they venture out from under their rocks to feed on algae. Chiton steaks must be fresher than fresh. Keep them packed in ice if you pick them and don't want to eat them immediately.

From Mary Swanson, Haida elder from Old Massett:

Put chitons in boiling water. When the skin begins to peel, test the shell on the back. If the skin comes off easily, remove the chitons and place in cold water. Peel the shells and the black skin off. They are okay to eat even if the black skin doesn't come off.

Nowadays people grind the chitons and then fry them with chopped onions. People also make chiton burgers—they don't just 'boil and eat' like in the old days.

OOLICHANS AND GREASE

Oolichans, or ooligans, hooligans or eulachons, (a kind of smelt)—also known as candlefish because they are so oily you can leave one in the sun for a few days, insert a wick down its throat and it will burn like a candle—at one time ran by the millions to spawn up mainland rivers, but not in recent history on Haida Gwaii. The Haida tell a story: oolichan once spawned here, but they were taken away as a lesson to the people for having fished irresponsibly, i.e. they burned their candle-fish at both ends. The Haida traded cakes of seaweed for oolichan grease, which they used to preserve other foods such as berries, with the Tsimshian people along the Nass and the Skeena Rivers.

Reverend William H. Collison of Masset, who visited Skidegate in 1876 with Albert Edward Edenshaw and his son George Cowhoe, describes a feast given in his honour as quoted by the Canadian Museum of History:

The first food offered us was dried salmon and eulachon grease . . . The next dish was boiling dulse, which, when gathered, is made up into square cakes about twelve inches by twelve and about one and a half inches in thickness, and dried in the sun. Before boiling, this is chopped fine, and it is also mixed with eulachon grease before being served out.

After this dish we were served with dried halibut and grease, and then with boiled herring spawn. During this repast I had remarked upon two young men, stripped to the waist, beating up in tubs dried berries with water until it became a frothy substance, not unlike ice cream in appearance. This was served up last as dessert." [This would have been soapberries, not found on Haida Gwaii, either, but also traded with people from the mainland.]

In the last decade, oolichan stocks have begun to crash, river by river, from the Fraser River near Vancouver to the Skeena near Prince Rupert though for reasons unknown, they still return to the Nass. This spring I saw a notice in the Co-Op in Masset, "Grease for sale." The latest news is that the oolichan fishery in northwest BC is rebounding after a few dismal years.

LEFT: Oolichan grease PHOTO BY MICHELLE FURBACHER

RIGHT: Oolichans PHOTO BY MICHELLE FURBACHER

CHAPTER SIX: Wash-Up

TOP: "Will You Marry Me?" PHOTO BY PETER SLOAN; BOTTOM: Banty and Chris with Glass Ball PHOTO BY ELIN PRICE

BEACHCOMBING

Over the years we've had our share of the bounty swept overboard from cargo ships hit, mid-ocean, by imperfect storms or rogue waves. Thousands of Tommy Pickles cartoon heads, dozens of sports-themed fly swatters, rubber ducks, 3 million Lego pieces (who will ever forget the day Masa Takei came home from East Beach with an eight-foot-tall, one-hundred-pound Ego Leonard Lego man with the message "No Real Than You Are" printed on his torso?) hockey gloves, and of course 60,000 Nike cross-trainers that have been, since 1990, circling the globe like a convoy of waterlogged canoes. (Nike did not tie the shoelaces together so there were many complaints from local residents who found shoes for their left foot, but not the mate.)

You can still find Japanese glass fishing floats, though they don't wash up in the quantities they did in years gone by: they were so numerous once that some old-timers used them for target practice. My friend Nate proposed to Charley by carving "Will you marry me" into a glass ball and leaving it on a beach on the west coast of Haida Gwaii where she would find it when they went on a camping trip.

I've found a wooden rifle stock, a sea lion tooth, the bleached bones of a whale (last summer, the unbleached very stinky bones of a whale buried in the sand at Rose Spit); there's a story of a dead killer whale on the beach north of Tlell with the body parts of a pig in its belly. Since the tsunami hit Japan in 2011, we have had a Harley Davidson motorcycle, and enough Styrofoam to fill a landfill the size of Texas wash up on the east coast of Graham Island. On one of his tsunami-debris clean-up sprees, Chris Ashurst found an Afro hair pick adorned with a Black Power fist, Michael König a computer covered in gooseneck barnacles, Dave Unsworth a jar of instant coffee with a silver Cathay Pacific spoon inside, and Kayleen MacGregor found a tin of Double Happiness cigarettes from China.

Toni Smith found several packages of Japanese rations on a west coast beach, with HELP IS ON ITS WAY (in English) written on them. Friends spent a couple of winters caretaking a fishing lodge off the west coast where they retrieved a First Aid kit washed overboard from a Japanese freighter containing 10,000 hits of codeine, "enough for us to party for a week." Ron's girlfriend Betty rescued a whole case of Pond's Face Cream and sent a jar to each of her friends for Christmas. All Ron said he wanted was for Betty to find some teeth. She had two sharp pointed front teeth that hurt him when they "copulated orally."

WASH-UP

"Food comes to you willingly if you are in the right place at the right time."
—Sanne König

Dominic Legault had gone to North Beach for crab. "I have butter at home, garlic in the garden, now all we need is a lemon," he told his companion from Vancouver. A few steps later and there it was at his feet. A beached, sun kissed lemon.

When Götz Hanisch, owner and operator of Rose Harbour Guest House in Gwaii Haanas, was hiking in Gowgaia Bay, south of Tasu, in 1984, he got hungry. He tried to shoot a goose, and missed, and was stumbling over the rocks on the beach to take aim again when he tripped over an industrial sized bag of potato chips. Further down the beach, a 20-pound tin of dehydrated onions. That and a bottle of Suntory Premium Malt's—well, whenever you need something, it's there.

And it's there even when you don't personally need it. I found a baggie of B.C. bud on the beach (apologies for the alliteration). It was above the tide line so technically not wash-up, unless it had been deposited by a rogue wave: for the purposes of this book, it is wash-up. I don't smoke pot but I sold it to finance the publication of this book. (I'm kidding. It's a test—to see if my editor is actually reading the text, not just being stunned by the photographs.)[*]

Wash-up differs from beachcombing in that wash-up is full of tasty things to eat: weathervane scallops, rock scallops cockles, gooseneck barnacles, butter clams and sometimes even "rainbow clams," the code name here for abalone, which are so illegal we dare not speak their name out loud—even having the word in your mouth can get you a life sentence if the Committee on the Status of Endangered Wildlife in Canada finds out.

A few years ago North Beach was covered with hundreds of dead and dying Humboldt squid. I heard some people cooked and ate them like calamari. Others of us used them as halibut bait.

Whether or not we have wash-up depends on the wind. After a northwesterly blows, one that turns round and blows from the southeast after a few days can be a good time. Often if I hear the waves crash on the shore, intermittently, and wait three days, I'll get lucky. Sometimes I just wait until I hear a lot of trucks going past. This is a good indicator: something other than the surf is up.

Wash-up has sea-life in it that may not still be edible, and odd-shaped crimson or turquoise bits, reminiscent of severed genitalia. All mixed in with seaweed and

---

[*] Editor's Note: So where's our cut?

TOP LEFT: The Königs—scallop safari PHOTO BY GUY KIMOLA; TOP RIGHT: Sanne König PHOTO BY PETER SLOAN; MIDDLE LEFT: Wash-up PHOTO BY CHRIS ASHURST; MIDDLE RIGHT: Clam shell PHOTO BY JANIE JOLLEY; BOTTOM LEFT: Cockle PHOTO BY JANIE JOLLEY; BOTTOM RIGHT: Wash-up PHOTO BY ARCHIE STOCKER SR.

TOP LEFT: Humboldt squid and beer can PHOTO BY GUY KIMOLA; TOP RIGHT: The Author beachcombing PHOTO BY STEPH GILLIS; MIDDLE TOP LEFT: Found in wash-up PHOTO BY JANIE JOLLEY; MIDDLE TOP RIGHT: Found in wash-up PHOTO BY JANIE JOLLEY; MIDDLE BOTTOM LEFT: Clam shell in ice PHOTO BY JANIE JOLLEY; MIDDLE BOTTOM LEFT: Found in wash-up PHOTO BY JANIE JOLLEY; BOTTOM LEFT: Doritos wash-up PHOTO BY DONNA BARNETT; BOTTOM RIGHT: Cod in wash-up PHOTO BY PETER SLOAN kelp and old running shoes and woks and drowned birds and a pair of my $900 titanium progressive eyeglasses, which blew off one winter night when I went for wash-up in a gale: I had on a toque, a ball cap, a headlamp, ear-muffs and my new glasses. Everything on my head blew away, except my hair.

Nate Jolley found a bottle of Russian beer on the beach; a bottle of Five Star Whisky, "with a hint of salt," surfaced in Rennell Sound. In the fresh produce department, most of us still reminisce about the Great Green Banana wash-up of 2007 (followed by the Doritos spill of 2009—though I am not sure if Doritos are a bona fide vegetable) and the ravens hopping around with Doritos in their beaks. It isn't uncommon to come across carrots, red onions, and broccoli on the tide line (thrown overboard by fishermen, fed-up with stir-fry, I assume.) Etchi's friend Maggie May found a single piece of sushi sealed in plastic. "It was in perfect condition and seemed so surreal in those days of no electricity or running water."

At TLC, his gas station in Masset, Kirk Thorgeirson has a tome called *The Book of Shame* featuring drivers who drove their vehicles out on the beach and got stuck. One, a trucker with some time on his hands, went for a drive to Tow Hill in his semi—but found nowhere to turn around so headed onto the beach and bogged down. His cargo was potatoes; Paul Bower ate nothing but potatoes for weeks.

ILLUSTRATION BY DEJAHLEE BUSCH

SCALLOPS

So many times Paul has explained
how a south-west wind ninety miles
off shore creates a ground swell
that blows the scallops in on North Beach
but only if there's a northwesterly
and particularly after a southeaster.
So many times: how can I not remember?
—from *Obituary of Light: the Sangan River Meditations* by Susan Musgrave

Farhad and April White and I are parked on the tide line, in their truck, waiting for the tide to fall. On either side of us, as far as you can look, more trucks are parked in the same position. Word is out that there will be wash-up tonight.

The rides look to me like racehorses, lined up at the gate, some champing at the bit (revving their engines), others, like us, alert, watchful, anticipating what lies ahead. We drank a bottle of Chablis, I remember, and listened to Chopin as the sun went down.

Then we left and drove home. No scallops for us tonight. The tide still had a long way to fall, and the bottle was empty.

We find two types of scallops on Haida Gwaii: weathervane and rock scallops. Rock scallops (which, as the name suggests, fasten themselves to rocks and hard surfaces) are smaller and some say tastier, but that hasn't been my experience. The last time there was memorable wash-up I came home with a bag full of rock scallops that had been so beaten up by the storm that they were full of sand, which I couldn't flush out. Scallop meat varies from creamy white to light tan or pink and should have a firm texture, a mild, sweet odor. While sand could be said to have a creamy colour and smell sweet (I guess?) its texture is gritty and coarse.

Weathervanes are the largest of all scallops (growing to shell diameters of 8 inches or more). They are not sedentary, but leap and bound across the ocean floor by clapping their shells and ejecting a jet of water. When they are in shallow water, that is when waves have driven them onto the beach, they are unable to escape back out to sea. I've stood on the shoreline and seen them jump, trying to flap back into deeper water to avoid being stranded by the tide.

The first time I found weathervanes—about 30 of them (I heard stories of those early birds who got to the beach before me, and loaded the backs of their pickups with thousands of scallops)—Tyson Neering and I had the beach to ourselves. Everyone else had been, scored and gone, and 30 scallops were more than enough for me. One scallop equals two meals, maybe even three. The scallop's adductor muscle, the part commonly eaten, is the size of a hockey puck; I cut mine in half and still that can be too much of a good thing.

I remember feeling content, just being there. This is what I love most about food gathering—I can be fully present, living in that shining moment but feel I am accomplishing something, too. No thought necessary. Just bending to scoop up the pink, fan-shaped shell, half-opened on the sand, and feeling it close again in your hands so you know it is still alive.

TOP: Sunset on North Beach PHOTO BY GUY KIMOLA; MIDDLE LEFT: Scallop shells PHOTO BY JANIE JOLLEY; MIDDLE RIGHT: Sunset on North Beach PHOTO BY ARCHIE STOCKER SR.; BOTTTOM LEFT: Weathervane scallops PHOTO BY LYNDA OSBORNE; BOTTOM RIGHT: Rock scallop PHOTO BY CHRIS ASHURST

SHUCKING A SCALLOP: HOW I DID IT

All-seeing scallop eyes PHOTO BY GUY KIMOLA

My first experience with shucking a scallop was traumatic. No one had told me I should stick the knife in under the hinge. The scallop's soft body is surrounded by a thin fold of tissue called a mantle, which lines the inside of the shell. Around the edge of this mantle, dots of iridescent green encircled by rings of turquoise steely blue— I've read 35, 60, more than a hundred—it doesn't matter how many because it feels as if every one of those eyes is looking right at *you* (they *are* real eyes, having cornea, lens, optic nerve).

Where did I stab my knife? Right between at least two of those all-seeing eyes. (In my defense I didn't know they were eyes at the time, so my actions may constitute manslaughter and not first-degree murder in a court of law.) The shell clamped down hard on my knife, and when I tried to pull apart the shell to get my knife out, my hand got stuck inside, too. Somehow I managed to get my hand, the knife and the scallop's soft body surrounded by the mantle and all those crying eyes out of its shell where it started to pulse its way across the kitchen counter. My shrieks brought my friend Tyson into the house. He picked the next scallop out of my bucket and. . .

SHUCKING A SCALLOP: HOW IT IS SUPPOSED TO BE DONE

. . . held the shell in one hand, calmly inserted the knife at the hinge where the two valves meet, and even more calmly cut the tender white muscle loose from both sides of the shell.

Most North Americans eat only the tender white muscle but the entire scallop is (apparently) edible and is eaten with relish by Europeans and Asians. The muscle has a sweet delicate briny flavour. (This is hearsay. After my ordeal I couldn't eat my scallop.)

A scallop at rest, waiting to be shucked. PHOTO BY GUY KIMOLA

COCKLES

Randy Martin shares, but I don't always. At least, I didn't share, once. And I am not proud of it, so this is my chance to confess and say, "I'll never do it again."

I had driven out to North Beach hoping there would be scallops washed up, or at least a cockle or two. A cockle is another type of edible, saltwater clam, described rather fondly in a BC government tract as "a handsome fellow with his light-brown heart-shaped shell and 37 (count them!) strongly radiating ribs"* but there was nothing for miles except driftwood and an eagle and a raven hunkered down in the sand trying to appear casual.

"When ravens find beach kill they act like eagles." PHOTO BY JAGS BROWN

* From "Harvest Beneath the Sea," Commercial Fisheries Branch, Depatrment of Recreation and Conservation, Victoria, BC

The Cockles of the Heart

WHEN THE innermost part of your being feels warmed by a touching story or a movie such as *The Sound of Music,* it is often said to "warm the cockles of one's heart." It's no wonder we associate this warm and fuzzy feeling—the glow of sympathy, pleasure or affection—with the heart, but the cockles in this expression have nothing to do with the edible mollusc or the lonely muscle that beats away, in darkness, inside you, pausing for a fraction of a second after every beat, so that during 70 years of life it has actually been at rest for the equivalent of 40 of these. According to Michael Quinion at World Wide Words, the earliest form of the idiom turns up in the mid 17th century: "rejoice the cockles of one's heart."

It could be that the cockleshell's shape, suggestive of the heart, gave rise to the expression. There's another possible explanation, though: in medieval Latin, the ventricles of the heart were at times called *cochleae cordis,* where the second word is an inflected form of *cor,* heart. *Cochlea* in Latin is the word for a snail (from the shape of the ventricles—also the name given to the spiral cavity of the inner ear); if this is correct we should say something that touches you "warms the snails of your heart."

"When ravens find road kill they act like eagles," a Haida friend of mine says, and the same applies to beach kill. Road, beach, it's all the same to us who live out here at the north edge of the world.

I approached them to see the object of their feigned disinterest: one live (tightly closed) cockle, stranded on the sand.

I didn't leave half (in my defense I didn't have a knife and couldn't have opened it) but took it home, cleaned it, cooked it and ate it. In my defense, again, I did take the parts I didn't eat down to the river for the eagles and ravens to feast upon. But I still feel guilty, especially after Randy's story about sharing, otherwise I wouldn't have remembered muscling those birds for that one cockle on North Beach, January 12, 2012, at 10:43 a.m. PST.

LEFT: Cute cockle PHOTO BY CHRIS ASHURST

RIGHT: Food gathering on the beach PHOTO BY JANE JOLLEY

A SCAVENGER'S FEAST

MENU

Most of the principal ingredients on this menu have been found on the beach,
with the exception of the *actual* ingredients that make up Sea Foam Taffy.

PRE-PRANDIAL DRINK

You choice of Russian Beer, Suntory The Premium Malt's
or Five Star Whisky
Doritos or Potato Chips

HORS D'OEUVRES

Muscled Cockles Alive Alive-O
Shipwrecked Chicken Wings

SALAD

Citrus Salad with Mint

FISH

Rose Spit Halibut with Wild Rose Petals

ENTREE

Sea Lion Lasagne
Beer-Battered Zucchini Blossoms

DESSERT

Sea Foam Taffy

AFTER DINNER INDULGENCES

Instant Coffee
Double Happiness Cigarette (for Persons of Smoke)
Reefer (for Persons of Illicit Smoke)
Codeine

LEFT: Cockles come in all different sizes PHOTO BY ARCHIE STOCKER SR.

RIGHT: Cockle shell PHOTO BY JANIE JOLLEY

THE BOUNTY, THE RECIPES

MUSCLED COCKLE(S), ALIVE ALIVE O!
SERVES 4

In Dublin's fair city,
Where the girls are so pretty,
I first set my eyes,
On sweet Molly Malone,
As she wheeled her wheel barrow,
Through the streets broad and narrow,
Crying cockles and mussels,
Alive alive o!

—"Molly Malone" popular Irish song and unofficial anthem of Dublin, written and composed by James Yorkston of Edinburgh

Purging Your Clams

THE SINGLE MOST important ingredient you need to purge your clams of sand is seawater. This is easy to obtain if you are getting your own clams. Bring a 5-gallon bucket and fill it two-thirds of the way up with seawater before you leave the beach. Note: You cannot purge a clam in fresh water. *Fresh water kills clams.* And you don't want them to die before you get the chance to kill them first.

Why is seawater so important? Because clams live at different salinity levels. If you bring seawater from the beach where you dug the clams, you need not guess at how salty your soaking water should be.

If for some reason you don't live near an ocean (hard to imagine when you live on Haida Gwaii but I guess there is a big world out there without a coastline) buy sea salt—real sea salt, not rock salt, not iodized salt—and dissolve 35 grams of it (about 2 tablespoons plus another teaspoon) in each litre of water. You'll need enough to submerge your clams. (On the other hand, if you live away from the ocean your clams have probably already been purged and you won't have to worry about any of these instructions.)

---

3 lb (1½ kg) cockles

4 garlic cloves, chopped

1 cup (240 mL) white wine

1 cup (240 mL) dry vermouth

¼ cup (60 mL) butter

Handful of chopped parsley

Lemon wedges for garnish

WHAT YOU DO

1   If the cockles are straight from the sea, place them in a bucket of salt water with seaweed in it (See above: Purging Your Clams) for a few hours to purge them. Transfer them to a colander and run cool water over them. Scrub them to eliminate any algae or dirt on the shells.

2   Place the washed cockles in a large skillet or a deep heavy-duty saucepan; add chopped garlic, the white wine and vermouth. Bring to a boil over high heat and let cockles steam open in the wine and vermouth. The cooking time can vary, but the cockles will generally open in 3–5 minutes. Discard any that have not opened after 5 minutes of cooking.

3   As soon as the cockles have opened, remove from the heat and set them aside to cool a little. Pour out most of the liquid, leaving about ¼ cup (60 mL) in the pan with the cockles.

4   Add the butter and finely chopped parsley, then reheat the pan, shaking constantly. When hot, serve immediately, spooning the buttery juices over the cockles.

5   Garnish with lemon wedges.

SHIPWRECKED CHICKEN WINGS SERVES 4
(IN SALTWATER BRINE)

Kelly Ruth (then) PHOTO BY GUY KIMOLA

When it comes to best-time-ever-beachcombing, there's nothing like a wreck. The mind fills with images of Spanish galleons and treasure chests overflowing—copper ingots, bronze cannons and gold coins. The truth is more like beer cans and fishing weights, or, in the case of the *Kelly Ruth*, a troller whose crew was crabbing off North Beach and came in too close and ran aground in 1994—tons of oranges and grapefruit, a rolling pin (that was used at Moon Over Naikoon Bakery until it burned down in 2010) and bags of frozen chicken wings.

Next to Tow Hill itself, the *Kelly Ruth* is North Beach's most famous landmark. "Let's drive up the beach as far as the wreck and catch some crabs for dinner," or "Don't drive farther than the wreck, if you don't have four-wheel drive—after that you hit pea gravel, and you might get stuck," are the kinds of things you'll hear Islanders say to one another, or to visitors from somewhere else. I've watched the *Kelly Ruth* deteriorate until now, 20 years later, there is very little left. Soon we will be saying, "Let's drive up the beach as far as where the wreck used to be . . ."

While looking on the Internet to see what I could find about the wreck of the *Kelly Ruth*, I found this on a blog called Eat Logical Sentences: "The wreck is not on any of the maps; I heard about it from one of the locals. It is about 3 km out along North beach. Apparently Susan Musgrave salvaged some of the wood for use in her home."

Not quite true, though I wish I'd thought of the idea at the time. The wood for our house was beachcombed all right—we have redwood, yellow cedar, yew wood, fir and worm-eaten Honduran mahogany from the beach, but none of it came from the *Kelly Ruth*.

Friends and neighbours were able to salvage some of her cargo, though, before the next high tide. Paul Bower, MB (Master Beachcomber) found the wings, and Juliette Reynolds and Etchi Zaleski cooked them up on a grill in their fire pit.

I have adapted the recipe for those who might not have access to a grill in a fire pit. You can also buy chicken wings in a grocery store, so if there isn't a shipwreck in your hood, do not abandon hope. (The UN estimates there are more than 3 million shipwrecks on the ocean floor, so surely you can find one if you put your mind to it.)

Etchi's wings were naturally brined, but you can easily make your own brine, which will give you a moister and more tender wing. If you add a small amount of vinegar and red pepper flakes to the brine, the vinegar breaks down the heat in the pepper flakes brine carries that flavour into the wings.

LEFT: *Kelly Ruth* (now) PHOTO BY GUY KIMOLA

RIGHT: Tow Hill and *Kelly Ruth* (now) PHOTO BY JANIE JOLLEY

FOR THE BRINE

4 cups (950 mL) water

3 Tbsp (45 mL) salt

3 Tbsp (45 mL) red pepper flakes

2 Tbsp (30 mL) white vinegar

FOR THE WINGS

1 lb (500 g) chicken wings

1 beaten egg

1 cup (240 mL) flour

¼ cup (60 mL) butter (or cooking oil) for frying

FOR THE SAUCE

3 Tbsp (45 mL) soy sauce

3 Tbsp (45 mL) water

¼ cup (60 mL) sugar

½ cup (120 mL) vinegar

Pinch of salt

WHAT YOU DO

1   Preheat the oven to 350°F (180°C).

2   Melt the butter in a medium-size ovenproof skillet and heat until the butter begins to foam.

3   Rinse, and then dry the fillets on paper towels. Season with salt and pepper then lay them, skin side up, in the hot pan.

4   Cook over medium heat for 5 minutes; turn the fillets, than transfer the skillet to the oven.

5   Arrange the rose petals, overlapping, to look like fish scales, drizzle with butter and bake just until the halibut is cooked through, no more than 10 minutes (give or take, depending on the thickness).

6   Using a spatula, gently lift the fillets from the skillet and transfer them to two plates, petal side up. Serve immediately.

STELLER SEA LION LASAGNE
(TRIGGER WARNING: BLOOD, DISMEMBERMENT)

Dolan and Russ (names changed to avoid repercussions[*]) found a freshly dead sea lion on a gravel bar at East Beach, south of Rose Spit, his body still warm, blood pouring from his nose. He had been shot, execution style, in the head—a huge bull, King of the Spit— and Russ has to use a chain saw to sever his head from his body. It took both men to roll the massive head onto a plank and lift it into the back of the truck. (Males can grow to be 11 feet in length and weigh almost 2,500 pounds.) Melody (name changed to avoid same old same old) has the skull.

His skin was two inches thick around his scarred neck, where the two men found a bullet lodged. When they skinned him they found old bullet wounds all over his body. He was a "log of meat"—they took only the neck and canned an "ungodly amount," more than they could eat over the winter, or even give away.

---

[*]   National Marine Fisheries Service listed the Steller sea lion as threatened range-wide under the Endangered Species Act (ESA) in April 1990. Among the many threats to their continued existence was the bounty placed on the species in the early '90s by fishermen who blamed sea lions for stealing their fish. The same day my friends found the King of the Spit they found six more sea lions on the beach that had also been executed.

They ground the meat, they cut it up, cubed it, smoked it and served it on skewers: the sea lion tasted like rich beef, or bear.

Dolan made Steller Sea Lion Lasagne out of the meat he had minced. He used the recipe on the back of the lasagne noodles box, but substituted lambsquarters for spinach, and used Don's (name changed in case, by association, there are repercussions) goat cheese.

SUBSTITUTION

Instead of the recipe on the back of the lasagna noodles box, the one Dolan used, you could make Dafne Romero's Seaweed Lasagne recipe, and substitute beef, which is legal, for the sea lion, which is definitely not.

BEER-BATTERED ZUCCHINI BLOSSOMS

SERVES 4

The first time I ate deep-fried zucchini blossoms was in the south of France, at a small restaurant in the hills above Vence. I was a young writer in mighty company—George MacBeth, the Scottish poet, and John Hawkes, American novelist, both of whom have since died. But that day we were all three hungry and alive: the crunchy saltiness of the crisp golden batter, the flower's sweet delicate taste—I remember feeling as if we were feasting on the wings of an angel.

Choose zucchini (or squash) blossoms that look firm and fresh. Ideally, they should be slightly open. Blossoms are delicate and therefore perishable; use them the day you pick them for the best results. (Some supermarkets and farmer's markets carry zucchini blossoms, but I recommend

Italian Zucchini PHOTO BY GUY KIMOLA

finding a friend who has so many zucchinis they will willingly part with surplus blossoms. That is, if you haven't got space in your own garden to grow some on your own.)

Store blossoms in the vegetable crisper section of your refrigerator until it comes time to cook them. Then wash them gently, pat them dry, and remove the pollen-covered pistils (f) (the yellow, tube-shaped part that can be quite bitter) or stamens (m). You're now ready to proceed.

Beer-Battered Zucchini Blossoms PHOTO BY MICHELLE FURBACHER

Vegetable oil for frying

1¼ cups (190 mL) all-purpose flour

1 tsp (5 mL) kosher salt

12 oz (355 mL) chilled lager-style beer,
club soda or sparkling water

3 egg whites, stiffly beaten

About 2 dozen zucchini blossoms,
pistils or stamens removed

Salt and pepper, to taste

WHAT YOU DO

1 In a large pot, heat about 2 inches (5 cm) oil over medium heat until a deep-fry thermometer reads 350°F (180°C).

2 Combine flour and salt in a medium bowl, then whisk in beer until almost smooth (some small lumps are desirable—don't over whisk or you'll deflate the batter).

3 Beat egg whites separately then fold them into batter.

4 Dredge the blossoms in the batter, two at a time, until completely coated; shake off any excess batter. Gently lower the blossoms into the hot oil. Cook, flipping once with a slotted spoon, until crisp and golden brown, 2–3 minutes.

5 Drain the fried blossoms on a platter lined with paper towels, season with salt and pepper while they are still hot. Repeat with the remaining zucchini flowers.

SEA FOAM TAFFY MAKES 16 SERVINGS

The first couple I married after my appointment as Marriage Commissioner, was Ann and Gordon, from Prince George. After the ceremony at the Blow Hole* the bride and groom wanted to walk on the beach and look for agates. I took them to a good agate patch (Helpful hint to visitors: forget about trying to find agates on Agate Beach. It's like looking for paradise in a place called "Paradise") but the stones on the beach were all covered with sea foam that day.

Sea foam forms when the ocean is agitated by wind and waves, and the dissolved salts, proteins, fats, dead algae and other organic matter get shaken up. I've walked the beach from Cape Ball to Tlell when the foam is knee-deep, or higher—so deep a dog can get lost in it. Haida Gwaii sea foam is not a result of pollutants even though it might appear brownish at times (possibly a result of large blooms of algae decay offshore); as Ann took off her shoes to walk barefoot through the foam, she told me she remembered her grandmother making Sea Foam Taffy. "I have to have that recipe for my cookbook," I said.

I spent the remainder of our walk pondering—how would a person be able to get enough sea foam home before it disappeared in order to make toffee out of it?

LEFT: North Beach and foam
PHOTO BY CHARLOTTE MUSGRAVE

TOP RIGHT: Blow hole PHOTO BY
PETER SLOAN

BOTTOM RIGHT: Sea foam PHOTO
BY CACILIA HONISCH

---

* The Blow Hole is a surge channel that lies at the base of Tow Hill. In the right conditions (big winds and high tide) water is forced upwards from the channel, and sprays all within reach.

CULINARY ALCHEMY

When I was young I was read stories in which faeries and elves magically appeared and then—poof—disappeared again. I accepted this without question: miracles mixed with the mundane were the norm in my daily life. Maybe my early childhood prepared me for how I've spent much of my adult life—in another realm where the supernatural seeps into ordinary, and transforms it: the kitchen.

I saw no logical reason why the sea foam on North Beach could not be used to make taffy. I wish I could say I did not lose the last teaspoon of my innocence that day, when I came home and googled "Sea Foam Taffy" and discovered the truth.

Sea Foam Taffy is familiar to those living on the West Coast, but it has a multitude of otherworldly names. Fairy Food or Angel Food Candy, Sponge Candy, Cinder Toffee, Sponge Toffee, Honey Comb, Puff Candy, Hokey Pokey or Yellow Man. It is even sold commercially under the name Violet Crumble in Australia (though it doesn't contain as much as a ghost of a violet's essence in any form) and, in Britain, Crunchie.

Ingredients vary slightly from place to place. Most use a white and/or brown sugar, corn syrup (light or dark) and baking soda. Those are the basic ingredients. Sometimes it's made with honey; other times apple cider vinegar or molasses are added to increase the acidity.

These are the simple ingredients in the recipe used by Ann's grandmother, Edna Dunlop:

2½ cups (600 mL) brown sugar	½ cup (120 mL) water
½ cup (120 mL) corn syrup	1 Tbsp (15 mL) baking soda

WHAT YOU DO

1   Grease a 10-inch (25 cm) diameter round spring form cake pan with vegetable oil or butter. Trace the bottom of the pan on a piece of parchment paper and line the bottom of the pan with the circle. Line the sides of the pan so that the parchment paper creates a collar that sits 1–2 inches (2.5–5 cm) above the pan. Now grease the parchment paper.

2   In a very heavy, large saucepan add sugar, corn syrup and water. Over medium-high heat bring the mixture to a boil, stirring constantly until sugar dissolves. Continue cooking without stirring until hard crack stage, (i.e. until temperature reads 300°F (149°C) on a candy thermometer.) This should take about 10–15

Trickster Raven

HENRY WHITE went down to the beach at Yakan Point on a day when there was foam covering the sand from the high-tide mark to the water's edge. Henry saw the carcass of a sea lion half-buried in the sand, and a conspiracy of ravens hunched over their find, taking the occasional nip out of its flesh, as if they were testing it for red tide to see if it tingled on their beaks.

Henry is a Raven (from the Raven clan); he watched as a solitary raven plummeted out of the sky into the foam, and rose up again, his black head white.

Then the trickster raven dive-bombed his brothers, who were still hopping around the carcass; they flew off leaving him to feast, until the foam on his head began to dissipate and they recognized him as one of their own—not a bald eagle, after all—and chased him away. He did this over and over again until the others finally cottoned on to his game.

TOP RIGHT: Raven PHOTO BY JAGS BROWN BOTTOM RIGHT: Raven and Moon PHOTO BY JAGS BROWN; **BOTTOM LEFT:** Raven and JuJube PHOTO BY CHRIS ASHURST

minutes. If sugar crystals form on the sides of the pan during the cooking process, brush the sides of the pan with a clean pastry brush dipped in water. It's easy to burn, so don't be impatient and turn up the heat. Watch it closely.

3 Remove from heat and stir in the baking soda; it will foam up high. Mix quickly so you don't lose the foam effect.

4 Pour into a cake pan. Cool quickly and break in pieces.

CHAPTER SEVEN: A Rogue's Galley

ILLUSTRATION BY DEJAHLEE BUSCH

IMAGINE THERE'S NO WOMAN
A WORD ON ROGUES

Ever since I started this book the gender imbalance has troubled me: why haven't I included any women rogues? "Rogue" is not a word normally applied to women, and I can't think of a woman I know, dead or alive, who fits the description. I have concluded this is because women don't have *time* for roguery due to their being in the kitchen, cooking meals for the rogues in their lives. At least that's how it used to be, once upon a time and in the days where words like *rogue* were not applied to large waves or killer whales.

The word rogue has many definitions:

1. a playfully mischievous person; a scoundrel or a scamp:
2. a man who causes trouble in a playful way; a rascal
3. a dishonest, deceitful, unreliable and unprincipled man
4. an elephant or other large wild animal driven away or living apart from the herd and having savage or destructive tendencies.
5. a vagrant or tramp

The men I write about here do not, in any way, fit the description in 3, 4 and 5. I use the word fondly in all circumstances, except when it comes to Mad Mike. I can't vouch for him, having met him only the once. But Hibbie, Paul, Jim, David: there were no finer men.

DAVID PHILLIPS: MASTER CHEF, RACONTEUR, BON VIVANT, FRIEND

"We are all the Players on the Chess Board of Life. These days I am king of the castle, or, as Susan Musgrave called me, 'the Queen at the Crossroads of Infinity'—a name which sticks like butter to my thighs."

—David Phillips

David Phillips PHOTO BY SUSAN MUSGRAVE

"The table is set when the tide is out,*" Louise Dennys recalls David saying when she stayed at Copper Beech House. I have pondered David's words for a long time, and then found a slightly different version on *Haida People, Spirits of the Sea:* "The table is set when the tide comes in." What a difference a tide makes!

David housed, entertained and fed guests from all walks of life. One day you would find Pierre and Maggie Trudeau holding hands, sharing a glass of wine on the deck; the next day a young German traveller wandering through the garden wearing nothing but his yellow thong. He cooked for anyone who dropped by to find his butyraceous form draped in a flowing caftan holding court at the dining room table with "nibbles" for everyone to share.

He cooked for the well heeled and for the lost alike. Denny Boyd, writing in the *Vancouver Sun*, penned an article titled "$100 leftovers beat hangovers on Skid Road" (article undated, from David Phillips' papers):

> *Last week the South Moresby Protection Society and the Haida nation jointly hosted a fundraising salmon barbecue, $100 a plate, in the continuing effort to keep the South Moresby wilderness† safe from mining development. At the conclusion of the buffet dinner, held at the UBC School of Anthropology, the cleanup started after the last guest had left, and it took quite a while. David Phillips, of the Queen Charlottes, an aide to Liberal party president Iona Campagnolo when she was the MP for Skeena, loaded all the leftovers, still in their serving trays, into the back of his station wagon and headed across town.*
>
> *He was at the corner of Hastings and Carrall, down in the skids, when he saw a lot of people wandering aimlessly. Phillips stopped, parked and dropped the tailgate.*
>
> *At 4 a.m. in a part of Vancouver where politicians seldom roam, people kept coming out of the shadows for a paper plate of barbecued salmon, salads, cold cuts and rolls, the dinner that had gone for $100 a few hours earlier. By the time the last plate was scraped clean David had fed 150 street people and given them all a lecture on behalf of the wilderness and the Haida Indian (sic) nation.*

---

*   *"Haida People, Spirits of the Sea,"* virtual museum of Canada website.

†   Now known as Gwaii Haanas National Park, the southern portion of Haida Gwaii. There are no roads within Gwaii Haanas, except to Moresby Camp, a former logging area. Visitors must access this wilderness park by air or water.

He cooked for visiting ambassadors, ballerinas, poets, heads of states, for Adrienne Clarkson when she was Governor General, her partner, John Raulston Saul, and their entourage of RCMP officers for whom the funky, multi-faceted guest house must have been a security nightmare. Who *didn't* he feed? He once turned down a request from John Lennon and Yoko Ono to cook for them in Toronto. "I was already here," he said (meaning home on Haida Gwaii.) "I didn't want to hang out in Toronto."

His dinner parties always included a handful of locals, who ate free and provided entertainment. One time a lawyer from Vancouver, a guest at the house, brought $1,000 worth of his own good wine and port—not content to drink the Australian plonk Masset liquor outlets copiously stock. David invited a fisherman, who had stopped by with fresh halibut, for a drink and he helped himself to a tumbler full of port to swill down with the appetizers. The lawyer, horrified, but trying to be diplomatic, said, "That port isn't for everyone!"

"Oh, I'll drink anything," the fisherman said. "I'm no connoisseur."

He cooked for journalists. Nicholas Woodsworth, in the *London Times:* "When David Phillips asked if I wanted eggs for breakfast it seemed natural enough a question, for what else does a bed and breakfast proprietor ask his guests at 8 a.m. on a summer's day? But when the eggs arrived a few minutes later I saw we had a problem. Herring eggs spawned in a gluey mess on strands of bright green seaweed are a little hard to take this early in the morning.

TOP LEFT: Mile Zero PHOTO BY CHARLOTTE MUSGRAVE

TOP RIGHT: *K'aaw* PHOTO BY MICHELLE FURBACHER

BOTTOM LEFT: Eggs for breakfast. Salmon eggs and *k'aaw.* PHOTO BY MICHELLE FURBACHER

BOTTOM RIGHT: David Phillips' grave, Masset cemetery PHOTO BY GUY KIMOLA

"The herring roe (*k'aaw*) was delicious. We dipped neat little strips into soya sauce and melted butter, and then bit into the tiny, iodine-charged eggs. They burst on the palate with the taste of the sea." (date unreadable on clipping.)

Some secrets of his culinary success: maple syrup (he had been known to drink it by the glass), butter and cream—he especially loved butter. In his last years when he succumbed to technology and bought himself a computer, his password was, true to form, "butterrrrr." He died in September 2010; a year later a visitor to his grave left him a jar of melted butter. Last time I checked it had been consumed.

I can find no agreement as to what David's Haida name, on his headstone, translates as. Roberta Kennedy, who adopted him, thought it meant "Fish that Stands Like a Man" but when I spelled the words for her over the telephone she said that didn't sound right. She was going to check with her mother, Naanii[*] Mary. David himself told me his Haida name translated as "Sweet Hands," but that could have been another name given to him by Naanii Nora, others in the village seem to think. I like the fact that his epitaph is somewhat of a mystery!

David was food personified, the living embodiment of Jean Paul Sartre's definition of a genius. Not someone with a gift, but someone who invented in desperate situations. Things can get desperate on Haida Gwaii when weather sets in. That's when we would stop by Copper Beech House where we knew David would open his fridge at dinnertime and perform his wizardry. He was an alchemist in the kitchen and the feasts he created, night after night, from the most fresh and local ingredients, are legendary: a soup of sautéed chanterelle mushrooms blended with peaches and Island Joe's beefsteak tomatoes; halibut sashimi; poached black cod; smoked peppered sockeye strips; clam fritters with salmonberry–Dijon mustard dip; North Beach scallops steamed with sesame and ginger; Amorous Lemon Cheesecake for dessert.

---

[*]   Naanii is "grandmother" in Haida, Massett dialect.

His motto? "Don't be afraid to try anything."

"I make silk purses out of sows' ears," he once said, with his characteristic exuberant laugh. "It's a necessary skill if you want to survive here."

SAMPLE RECIPE

I never saw David Phillips consulting a cookbook before preparing a meal, though he left me with volumes of well-thumbed Martha Stewarts and stacks of *Saveur* magazine. He improvised, and as far as I know he didn't write many recipes down, preferring always to use the ingredients he had on hand. When company came, which was most nights, David could stretch the chowder by adding seaweed and a tin of asparagus soup, make a little piece of black cod go a long way by whipping egg whites with orange zest and fresh herbs, and serving it in a soufflé served with a baby artichoke sauce.

While I was going through his papers I did find one of his recipes, destined to be faxed to someone called Alexis at Bon Vivant Press. Whether they were ever included in a book, I don't know, but here is a sample, in David Phillips' distinctive script.

JUM DU JOUR WITH MEDALLION OF SPRING SALMON

• JUM/SOUP

WHOLE SALMON (ANY TYPE) FILET BOTH SIDES THEN COOK THE HEAD + BONES WITH 2 QUARTS WATER (MORE WATER IF OVER 6 TO 8 GUESTS) AND 4 CUPS OF CHOPPED (ROUGH) VEGETABLES (CLEAN OUT YOUR FRIDGE) COOK FOR 1 HOUR AT MODERATE HEAT THEN STRAIN.

• SALMON FILETS
SLICE INTO 1" PIECES AND WRAP INTO MEDA IONS, SKIN SIDE IN. PLACE TOUCHING ON A BAKING TRAY WITH A 1/2" SIDE LIP

Jum is the Haida word for seafood stew. PHOTO BY SUSAN MUSGRAVE

HIBBIE GREN, POET AND CARVER

Hilbert Severin Gren, born of Swedish parents on May 17, 1913, grew up in Vancouver and first came to the Charlottes as a deck hand on the troller, *Orca*, in 1929. After joining the navy in World War II he returned to live permanently on the Islands.

Hibbie was a poet, a carver and a man with a great strength for the weakness (i.e. he liked his drink). My friend Helen, who once had a job sorting mail at the Tlell Post Office, found a registered letter for Hibbie, who, by this time, had been dead for 10 years. The postmistress, back then, had decided Hibbie had been too

LEFT: Hilbert Severin Gren
PHOTO COURTESY OF THE DIXON
MARITIME MUSEUM MASSET

RIGHT: Hilbert Severin Gren
PHOTO COURTESY OF THE DIXON
MARITIME MUSEUM MASSET

drunk to be entrusted with important registered mail, so she'd held on to it for 15 years.

Hibbie Gren carved folk art from fishnet floats (made of cork, or treated red cedar, or synthetic cork) and avocado pits. One delightfully malicious rumour is that Hibbie purloined his avocados from Chapman's in Port Clements so he would have the pits he needed.[*] I can only speculate about what he did with the rest of the avocado, which I intend to do (see recipe below).

Of his life and his carvings, Hibbie himself writes,[†] "These are the wild sub-limate projections of one Hibbie to whom we unfairly referred to as 'the town drunk'. There is only a small technical difference. While most of the citizens are discreetly stoned, Hibbie is openly sloshed."

After Hibbie's death on Christmas Day, 1982, the Hecate Press published a slim volume of his poems. If you search Hibbie's name online you will find this collector's item listed with Google Books. The only comment on the page (besides the title of the book and the name of the publisher) is "We haven't found any reviews in the usual places." Hibbie would like that.

WHAT-TO-DO-WITH-THE-GREEN-PART-OF-THE-AVOCADO

SERVES 4

This recipe is adapted from Doňa Vicky of Oaxaca's guacamole (she made a much larger amount.) Geoff Horner, friend and neighbour, was kind enough to share this with me—both the guacamole itself, as well as the recipe.

---

[*] The more likely truth is that his friends saved their avocado pits for him because he couldn't afford to buy the whole fruit. Hibbie sold his carvings to pay for food and drink.

[†] Garth Griffiths (Vancouver) and John Langston (Masset) interviewed Hibbie in 1972 in a pamphlet entitled "Carver of Canada's Misty Isles."

Avocados

I DON'T KNOW how many times I have selected an avocado or two, brought them home, cut them open, and been disappointed to find they are brown and stringy, have black spots like leprosy inside, or smell like month-old work socks that have been balled up, unwashed and left in an unventilated area. Or they are horribly bruised from people poking them with their thumbs to see if they are ripe enough to eat.

How *do* you to tell if an avocado is ripe? Halve the avocado around its equator with a penknife; the bright-green flesh near the skin should be pale to yolk-yellow near the pit. An avocado that is green to the pit will taste grassy. If it's yellow at the core, it will be as creamy as custard.

Obviously you cannot take a knife and split open each avocado on sale at your grocery store. But now that you've read this, don't you wish you could? Just once?

½ cup (120 mL) cilantro, roughly chopped

3 cloves of garlic

⅓ medium onion, chopped in four

3 tomatillos (optional), roughly chopped

1 jalapeño chile, roughly chopped

1 tsp (5 mL) salt

4 avocados, pitted and skin removed (keep two of the pits)

Juice of 2 limes

WHAT YOU DO

1 Wash and prepare cilantro, garlic, onion, tomatillos (if using) and jalapeño; place in a blender with a teaspoon of salt and just enough water to make the ingredients blend.

2 Mash the entire avocado in a large bowl with the smooth bottom of a glass.

3 Mix the blended ingredients into the avocado and add one squeezed lime.

4 Taste the guacamole and add as much of the second lime and more salt as needed for flavour.

5 When ready, place the avocado pits in the guacamole to prevent it from browning.

ASIDE: AVOCADOS (THE PITS)

Gwaii's avocado pit masks PHOTO BY PETER SLOAN

Hibbie was, among many other things, Hluugiitgaa's (Gwaai Edenshaw's) mentor from beyond the grave. Gwaai was born in 1977 to Jenny Nelson, a writer and a teacher (among many other things) and Guujaaw, who (among many other things) has been the famous leader of the Council of the Haida Nation for the past 15 years. Gwaai, as a baby, hung from a pole in Skidegate in his Jolly Jumper while his father made monumental art.

Gwaai began his career by carving avocado pits (I bought two of them a few years ago at a gallery in Masset and no, they are not for sale) and fishing floats, like his mentor, but went on to, in his own wry words, "smaller things such as gold, silver and argillite jewelry and totem poles."

Gwaai told me, "When I first started carving I didn't like avocados so I would get people to save the pits for me. People still save them for me. David [Phillips] did too."

PAUL BOWER, BEACHCOMBER

Paul's home from the hospital:
who would've guessed he could beat
lung cancer! Already he's up
making deals, vying to buy
my old Toyota for parts when I've
driven her into the ground.
—from *Obituary of Light: the Sangan River Meditations* by Susan Musgrave

Stories about Paul Bower abound. At his memorial potluck, the year after his death from lung cancer at the age of 60 on September 7, 2005, woman after woman got up to speak about her relationship with Paul. "Not you, too?" were the most oft-uttered words of the night.

Paul moved to the Charlottes from Nova Scotia in the '70s. He bought a mission vessel, the *Kolberg*, and—always broke—decided to trap octopus, the desired bait for halibut fishermen. In those days a pound of octopus bait was as expensive as a pound of halibut itself.

"He planned to drop a net on the Tow Hill Sasquatch after luring him/her with Green Giant whole kernel corn laced with vodka."

— from *Reward for the Safe Return* by Rich Schultz

LEFT: Paul Bower PHOTO BY MEREDITH ADAMS

RIGHT: Moss-eaten truck PHOTO BY GUY KIMOLA

He read everything he could find about octopus and devised elaborate traps from scrounged material—five gallon pails, cement, boxes, mesh, nets, old inner tubes, bits of metal from rusted-out cars. He took his traps to the west coast of Haida Gwaii, set them out, went back to town, ran out of money, and never retrieved his equipment.

His next venture was to fish crab in Naden Harbour. He needed bait for his small operation, and shot a very large black bear, which had been annoying loggers in a nearby camp; the crab loved it. He took up hunting on a regular basis, using the small Sitka deer as bait, too.

He brought his crabs to Masset where he'd made some contacts with an airline out of Vancouver, and started to ship live crab down south in totes. The airline took most of the seats out of the plane because other crab fishermen followed suit, and there was little to no business in the winter, anyway. Some days there were only two seats left on the plane for passengers.

But the crabs were Paul's nemesis. He began to believe that because he had killed innocent wild animals in order to make money he had brought bad karma on himself. Anita, his wife, left him. He began to drink heavily. Had a fire on his boat. Ran the boat aground. Blew up his truck. Fire followed him wherever he went. He rented a house on North Beach; it burned down. He raised a yurt, cleaned the chimney, burned the yurt down.

He was an anarchist who feuded with everyone. His adopted persona was somewhere between an Andy Capp and a Popeye. Because he did a lot of beachcombing, to some he became known as Relic. He was obsessed with meteorites and the sasquatch. Beachcombed all the wood for my seven-sided house in 1999. I had wanted a pentagon; Paul insisted on the number being seven. And so it was.

I went with him to Rose Spit—the graveyard of the world's driftwood—and watched him chip at logs with his knife, and identify them before the shavings hit the sand: redwood, Honduran mahogany with wormholes (which became my front door), fir, yellow cedar and yew. He hitched huge logs to a winch and wound them on to the back of the latest Toyota pickup he happened to have not blown up. He milled the wood and when my carpenters balked at the price he wanted, got obstinately miffed.

I went to see him, said, "How much do you want for this wood?"

"$600," he said. I wrote the cheque. I thought of him as an artist. Artists should be paid for their work.

In the last 10 ten years of his life he built three or four cabins on the six acres he owned, home of the Rock and Whale Museum, which later transformed into the Moon Over Naikoon Bakery. Visitors to the bakery could eat a bowl of Wendy Riley's yam and coconut soup, or share a cinnamon bun while surrounded by whalebones, fossils, artifacts, agates, glass balls and Paul's own yew wood chopping boards. He rented the cabins he built to a succession of young women, travelers who found their way to his door, always hoping that one—perhaps the one in the cabin named, hopefully, The Spare Girl—might be persuaded to move in with him, at least for the duration of a night. Even on his deathbed he tried to coax Meredith—who had looked after him during his last days—under the covers. "Give a dying old man a kiss. Give him a cuddle."

In his prime, Paul used fish to lure his potential brides. One story involves him picking up one of another local man's girlfriends at the bar, and the two of them

drinking so much that they both blacked out. She recalls waking up on a boat, 50 miles offshore, with Paul on the stern of the boat, fishing.

One of Paul's many "spare girls" recalls early morning raiding parties in the middle of winter with Paul waking them up—a bunch of bleary-eyed, reluctant volunteers piling into his pickup whose headlights would only come on intermittently, whenever he hit a bump—to search for crab pots left stranded when the tide had fallen. Paul, who never left the warmth of truck himself, would instruct his recruits to break into each pot and take the males. This was the etiquette of crabbing back then. "Take the crabs but leave the pots," Paul said.

And then there is my favourite Paul story, from the days when they had exotic dancers at the Singing Surf Motel* in Masset. Paul is said to have offered one of the strippers 50 lb of shrimp to spend the night with him. She turned him down; he drove home and ate the shrimp himself. Unless anyone reading this remembers a different ending to the story, in which case I'd be happy to include it in the sequel to this book.

Paul peeled his own shrimp, so to speak: shrimp, when hand-peeled, have the brightest pink colour and firmest, sweet-tasting meat. Paul isn't around to give us directions, so I have had to exercise poetic license.

THE BEST PEELER

To shell shrimp, you need just your hands.
You grab the fleshy part at the front and peel it off.

SALMON IN BEER AND ALPHABET SOUP[†]

SERVES 4

When your car breaks down on Haida Gwaii, you stick out your thumb. You never know who you are going to meet. The last time I ran out of gas I got picked up by Mad Mike, a former member of a motorcycle social club (as my father would have called it)—a biker who had retired from the Hell's Angels. He'd come here to fish. He sailed his boat, *The Prince Andrew*, up the coast and anchored it in Masset Inlet, where it sprang a leak.

---

*   These days the Masset Waterfont Inn.

†   DISCLAIMER: The author does not advise trying this in your own home. This recipe has not been tested in her kitchen, and never will be.

LEFT: "Breaking Open a Beer." PHOTO BY GUY KIMOLA; RIGHT: *"Prince Andrew* sprang a leak." PHOTO BY GUY KIMOLA

SALMON IN BEER AND
ALPHABET SOUP (CONT'D)

Mad Mike rescued his fishing rod and a case of Campbell's Alphabet soup from below the tipping deck, changed deckchairs, broke open a bottle of Miller Genuine Draft, and began fishing. "I'd come all the way to the Charlottes to fish," he told everyone, afterwards, "and that's just what I intended to do. Fish."

The following recipe has been customized for anyone who does not know how to cook or does not want to cook.

4 salmon steaks, cut 1 inch (2.5 cm) thick.

1 can Campbell's Alphabet Soup

1-12 ounce bottle Miller Genuine Draft

WHAT YOU DO

1   Light a fire on the beach. Ignore the warnings about driftwood being full of carcinogens that are freed into the atmosphere, and your food, when you light a perfect little bonfire on the beach. You only live once. You could die in an earthquake tomorrow, or wash out to sea in a tsunami.

2   Make an oblong cooking tray out of aluminum foil. Stick this on a grill over your fire.

3   Place salmon steaks in center of cooking tray. Pour beer and Alphabet Soup into tray to just below the highest point of the steaks. Cover tray with another piece of aluminum foil to envelope fish completely. Place aluminum tray on grill for approximately 8 minutes or until salmon is just cooked through.

JIM FULTON, MP, SKEENA-QUEEN CHARLOTTE

"Mourning can be very selfish. When someone you love has died, you tend to recall best those few moments and incidents that helped to clarify your sense, not of the person who has died, but of your own self. And if you loved the person a great deal … you will have been clarified many times."
—from *The Sweet Hereafter* by Russell Banks

When I first heard Jim Fulton had "gone into politics" and been elected as our NDP MP, I was afraid he would become less of a rogue. I knew him as the guy who got a Local Initiatives Programme grant in the early '70s so that he and his partner Liz Young and a bunch of their friends could get paid for spending their summer on the beach, drinking beer, smoking dope, picking up garbage and burying it.

The next thing I heard he had become a probation officer. I had pegged Jim as the kind of person who would be reporting *to* a probation officer once a week, not the type who would *be* one. That was the thing about Jim. He defied categorization.

The first time I saw him on television during question period in the House of Commons, he had gained weight, put on a suit, a straight face and Groucho Marx glasses with fake eyebrows, moustache and rubber nose. It was Halloween, but you got the feeling that wasn't the point. There was Jim, the life of the party, terrorizing the federal bureaucracy like no other British Columbia MP had done or has ever done since.

I asked Jim, once, how he got into politics. His first case, when he became a probation officer, involved a bank manager from a rural mainland community who'd been convicted of fornicating with cows. Shortly before he was released from prison Jim went to interview him "to see how his rehabilitation was going" and ask him how he felt about his crime. Jim remembers the ex-bank manager removing his dark glasses, and staring hard into his eyes. "Jim," he said, "have *you* ever looked deeply into the eyes of a cow?"

"I couldn't help him," Jim said. "I knew there was nothing I could do for the man." Later when he relayed the story to friends at Tlell, one of them suggested, "Jim, with your experience of people, you should go into politics."

TOP LEFT: Jim Fulton PHOTO BY MELANIE FRIESEN; BOTTOM LEFT: False nose and glasses ILLUSTRATION BY VEER; TOP RIGHT: Jim and Susan at wreck of the *Kelly Ruth*, Summer 2003 PHOTO BY AGATE ANNIE; MIDDLE RIGHT: Beach Fire, Haida Gwaii PHOTO BY GUY KIMOLA; BOTTOM RIGHT: Creative oil tank PHOTO BY GUY KIMOLA

Jim had an apparent genetic predisposition to exaggerate, to the point where both friends and critics would refer to his most outlandish claims as Fulton Facts. But what is undisputed is that Fulton, who has been compared to Hunter S. Thompson—the gun-toting, drug-consuming gonzo-chronicler of the Hells Angels, American decadence and Richard Nixon—knew how to make an impression. He once pulled a dead 10-pound salmon out of his oversized pants, carried it across the floor, and plopped it on then Prime Minister Mulroney's desk.

Our MP had been battling the Mulroney government over the fisheries department's decision to block a rich sockeye run because of disease concerns. Fulton argued, with eventual success, that the government should provide funds to air-lift enough healthy salmon over the barricade to spawning grounds.

To establish *habeas corpus* (produce the body) Jim had waded waist-deep into the Babine River, which drains into the Skeena, as thousands of migrating salmon struggled to get to spawning grounds:

> *This one sockeye kept coming up and bumping into me, just bump, bump, bump. So finally I just took it and lay it on the bank. And you know what my mind is like.*
>
> *I thought, 'I don't know what I'm going to do with this fish, but somehow I've gotta show people in Ottawa and Parliament that these things are real. These things aren't just cans of salmon.'*

Jim lived with his family in the log house he'd built on the other side of the Tell River on Haida Gwaii, miles from any "conveniences." There was no power or running water, so if a journalist, fellow MP, constituent or friend desperately needed to reach Jim there was a process: you called the bar at the Enlarged Liver Lodge (Jim's name for the Tlell River Lodge—he was feuding, in his own friendly way, with the owner) and offered to buy a patron a drink if he would walk a kilometre down river and bellow out your message to Fulton on the other side.

Every summer our family did the same, shouting from the opposite shore until Jim appeared from the woods ("with his hair and moustache now turned white . . . like one of those mountain gorilla males called silverbacks . . . he commanded respect by sheer physical presence," David Suzuki wrote in his 2006 autobiography) jumped in a canoe, and paddled across to give us all one of his famous lung-crushing bear hugs.

We spent many evenings around a beach fire eating the salmon he'd caught at his "Meat Hole" on the Tlell River, or if it was raining and blowing too hard, around the wood cook stove drinking martinis and eating wild beef by gaslight.

"Have you ever heard of electricity?" our citified daughter, when she was six, asked the Fulton kids, Blair and Katy. "Well, you should *get* it!"

He had nicknames for everyone. David Suzuki was Soozook. My partner was *jefe,* and he called me Soozer. He clarified everyone he met, everyone who loved him, over and over, and there is—selfishly, I know—no one I have mourned more.

RUSTLED BEEF BY GASLIGHT SERVES 8

In the '70s there was still a large herd of what we called "hippy cows" in Naikoon Park, small shaggy feral cattle descended from cows let loose by early settlers. When I spoke to Liz Young, Jim's former partner, she said the cows weren't feral at all; they had belonged to Jimmy Abbott, a local logging company owner. He didn't like them running loose on the road at Tlell so he would round them up and herd them into the park. Jim and Liz's dog Rutabaga would herd the cows back out onto the road again.

Several of Jim's cows did eventually go feral, but the "east coast beef* "has become rarer (no pun intended) in recent years; two of my neighbours went hunting at Cape Ball last fall and the herd has been further reduced by one. There is also a herd of free-range beef cattle near Masset. They are mostly nocturnal, but have a way of shuffling out onto the road on the foggiest days, and if you are not paying attention you can sustain serious damage to your car, not to mention the cow.

Out of the fog a herd of wild
cattle, two heifers locking horns
on the road while I try to steer the truck
around them without getting involved.
I thought I knew where I was going
when I set out, but now
I'm not so sure.
—from *Obituary of Light: the Sangan River Meditations* by Susan Musgrave

When Jim cooked a roast I remember him telling us, with that trickster-gleam in his eye, that we were eating "slow elk," another of Jim Abbott's cows, but this was more likely another infamous Fulton Fact; Liz says when they had meat, it was venison. When Jim had gutted a deer and removed the organs he would bring the warm and throbbing organs to the kitchen, and fry them up (Liz didn't like to eat

---

* East coast of Haida Gwaii, not the east coast of Canada.

the heart and liver while it was "so close to the kill") then hang the deer in the shed for a few days before skinning and butchering it, while Blair, their young son, watched. He had a lot of questions, always, for his dad. "Why don't we eat the fur, too?" he once asked.

Deer, slow elk, wild beef; I never questioned what I was served: I didn't care. Anything tastes delicious when you wait long enough for dinner, and when Jim got into storytelling mode, the night was always young, if not ageless.

When I asked for his recipe, Liz said Jim wasn't much of a cook, that he would have just "thrown the roast in the oven." So I have used more poetic license here, because this is a cutting-edge cookbook, and readers deserve more than just "toss it in the oven. Cook until it stops moving." (Sorry, I can't help myself. It's the closet vegetarian in me.)

Slow Elk PHOTO BY GUY KIMOLA

3 cloves garlic, sliced thin	Vegetable oil for brushing
¼ tsp (1 mL) ground cumin	1 tsp (5 mL) freshly ground black pepper
½ tsp (2 mL) ground thyme	1 tsp (5 mL) smoked paprika
½ tsp (2 mL) ground ginger	3 cloves garlic, mashed
½ cup (120 mL) butter, room temperature	1 tsp (5 mL) salt
3–5 lb (1.4–2.3 kg) leg roast of venison	2 Tbsp (30 mL) olive oil

WHAT TO DO

1   Heat oven to 250°F (120°C). (If you are using a wood cook stove, you are on your own. I didn't watch what Jim was doing; I had had too many martinis.) Cooking at this low temperature means you won't have many pan drippings beyond the melted butter from the drippings, but at least all the moisture will still be in the meat.

2   Mix together sliced garlic, cumin, thyme, ginger and butter to make a filling.

3 With the tip of a sharp knife, make slashes 2 inches (5 cm) apart and ¾ inches (2 cm) deep all over the meat and force some of the filling into the holes.

4 Brush the roast with enough oil to moisten the surface.

5 Mix together pepper, paprika, mashed garlic, salt and olive oil to make a rub and thickly sprinkle over the roast. ("Thickly" and "sprinkle" seem oxymoronic, but I am trying here to recreate the moment, which was one of spontaneity and, oh it was just so much fun being there with Jim and Liz, and our kids all in the bathtub together...)

6 Roast until centre temperature away from the bone is 145–150°F (63–66°C) for medium, 150–155°F (66–68°C) for medium well or 160–170°F (71–77°C) for well done. Jim did not use a thermometer, of course, so he just . . . roasted it until it was done like dinner.

7 Remove from the oven and let sit for at least 20 minutes while you boil some potatoes so that the internal temperature will equalize and juices will be more evenly distributed.

8 Pray that somebody else has thought of vegetables or made a salad. If not, enjoy the meat with potatoes. With another martini, of course.

ASIDE: PAPRIKA

I am chagrined, embarrassed and ashamed to say I have always thought paprika was decorative—for when your dish lacks colour and the recipe says, unimaginatively, "sprinkle with paprika," but mostly flavourless and not something I would take with me on an earthquake evacuation.

Paprika is made from ground, dried fruits of *Capsicum annuum*, either bell pepper or chili pepper varieties or mixtures thereof. The fourth most consumed spice in the world, it is considered the national spice of Hungary and it appears in the country's most celebrated dish, guess what? Goulash. Far from being flavourless, as I so tastelessly suggested, the Hungarians claim it has a *distinct* flavour. Rather, *flavours*. The Hungarians are passionate about their paprika and I wouldn't want to make goulash alongside an unhappy Hungarian.

Throwzini, Hungarian Knife
Holder PHOTO BY KATHLEEN HINKEL

HUNGARIAN PAPRIKA

There are eight grades of Hungarian paprika. If you have a recipe that calls for "paprika" without specifying which kind, you can usually get by with using Hungarian sweet paprika. In fact, most of the paprika sold in grocery stores in this country is simply labeled "paprika;" it tends to be neither sweet nor hot and is a suitable garnish for deviled eggs.

One reason paprika is maligned in North America is that it doesn't store well; its flavour deteriorates quickly. In Europe storage time tends to be shorter, and people sprinkle it with flair on meals; bottles of paprika aren't allowed to languish in the spice rack growing less fresh and less flavourful by the day.

SPANISH PAPRIKA

The two varieties of Spanish paprika, known in Spain as *pimenton*, come from the Comarca de la Vera in Caceres province and a variety from Murcia region. Both were introduced from the Americas, where they originated, by local monks some time in the 1500s. *Pimentón de la Vera* has a deep red colour that spreads through any dish to which it is added, and an intoxicating aroma from the slow oak smoking, and a silky texture from the repeated grinding between stones.

Paprika's flavour is more effectively produced by heating it gently in oil.

Smashed Potatoes PHOTO BY MICHELLE FURBACHER

SMASHED POTATOES

Have too much to drink then cut up some potatoes (leave the skins on; if they have come from the beach (see Wash-Up, page 224) you probably don't have to wash them unless you want to rinse off the salt) and boil them for 20–25 minutes. If you remember to take them off the stove before the water boils dry and the potatoes turn crisp and black, add some evaporated milk, salt and pepper and butter, if you can find it. sprinkle with whatever you have on hand—potato chips, dried onion crisps or even parsley, so you get your vitamins. Eat out of the pan with a communal spoon.

ASIDE: THE PARSLEY RACKET

While prisons are notoriously full of crooks, a lot of crime goes on under the table, too. Ever wonder about that parsley garnish you get with every meal you order at your favourite family restaurant?

It started in New York: restaurants were forced to serve parsley with every meal by organized criminals, and even with a number of mixed drinks. As the Mob jacked up the price of parsley, some restaurants found their parsley bill running as high as their payoffs to the police.

Since most diners push their parsley aside, a few restaurants began trying to cheat the mob by washing the parsley off and reusing it. But suppliers weren't fooled. A count of tablecloths and napkins by Mob-connected laundries proved which restaurants were scrimping on greenery. They were given a warning: a firebombing.

You will notice in this book that many recipes include a sprig of parsley on the plate to accompany a dish or a sprinkle of parsley over the top. It's not that I don't have the imagination to come up with any other garnish, it's just that I am, as they say, connected. For readers who care to know more, please refer to *Montreal's Irish Mafia* by Danny O'Connell. You will find yours truly in the index, or go straight to page 57. When I realized I'd been included in such desperate company I knew I had arrived, in the social sense.

CHAPTER EIGHT: Dinner on the Deck

I call this section Dinner on the Deck but, honestly? There are maybe half a dozen nights a year when the weather is good enough to serve dinner outside in the evenings. If the weather *does* co-operate, the three scourges of summer (the no-see-ums, black flies and mosquitoes) sit down to dine with, and on, my unsuspecting guests. The summer of 2013 was such a bad year for bugs I had to wear white gloves that came up to my elbows (luckily I found a pair at the Thrift Shop) or offer this disclaimer as I brought forth the crab feast: "No, I do not have some unspeakable skin disease—those are no-see-um bites that I have unwittingly scratched in my sleep."

Sometimes, too, an eagle will drop a fish head on the deck: our house is on their flight path back to the trees from the beach where the guests at the fishing lodges fillet their day's catch and toss the remains onto the rocks below. I call it the "Eagle Show;" one evening I counted more than 30 bald eagles standing around waiting for a handout. (The sport of eagle feeding is becoming less popular, however; there are too many fatalities each year when eagles fly into the power lines and are killed.)

Usually we move inside after the bugs have finished their first course. Once we tried burning citronella candles (made in China) purchased at Fields* in Masset, but, alas, these proved to attract every blood-sucking gnat in the neighbourhood rather than repel them.

The Eagle Show PHOTO BY PETER SLOAN

---

* Fields is a brand of Canadian discount stores, established in 1950 in Vancouver, with 64 locations in British Columbia, Alberta, Saskatchewan, Manitoba and the Northwest Territories.

THE RECIPES

DUNGENESS CRAB WITH HIBISCUS FLOWER VINEGAR AND GINGER

MAKES 1 CUP (240 ML)

Hibiscus Flower Vinegar PHOTO BY MICHELLE FURBACHER

For the first few years I served crab at Copper Beech House I did what I thought you were supposed to do: I set out bowls of sweet (unsalted, cultured) melted butter—at least half a cup per person—added chopped garlic and lemon juice, gave a brief demonstration on how to eat crab (without managing to get any past my lips) and let everyone go to it. Then I started overhearing people making comments like, "With crab this fresh you don't need the butter. It's buttery enough by itself." It's true. Crab aficionados say Dungeness meat is so delicious the crab should be boiled in plain seawater and eaten directly as it is picked from the shell with no seasonings or other ingredients to dilute the sweet and delicate flavour.

One evening two guests from Japan showed us how to make a simple sauce of white vinegar and minced ginger—which complemented the butteriness of the crab without taking away from the crab's natural flavours. I went a step further and used hibiscus flower vinegar because I had two bottles in the cupboard and had never known what to do with them. Any vinegar is likely to work (well, maybe not balsamic) but I like the way hibiscus flower vinegar rolls off the tongue. Plus it brings back pleasant childhood memories of when I was three, in Honolulu, in my doll-murdering phase, and you will know all about if you read the section on Nootka Roses (see page 133). I used to ride my tricycle to the end of our garden every morning and pick a hibiscus for my mother. Nancy and Dr. Gillespie were my constant companions. They are still very much alive and here with me today.

| 1 cup (240 mL) Hibiscus flower vinegar | 1 Tbsp (15 mL) minced fresh ginger |

WHAT YOU DO

1   Mince the ginger and add it to the vinegar in a bowl and mix well. Serve with crab, killed and cooked as you like it.

TOP LEFT: Crab feast PHOTO BY SALLY GLOVER; TOP RIGHT: Nancy and Dr. Gillespie (Nancy is the larger of the two; Dr. Gillespie is packing heat.); BOTTOM LEFT: Preparing Crab, for Now and for Later PHOTO BY SALLY GLOVER; BOTTOM RIGHT: Crab dinner PHOTO BY MICHELLE FURBACHER

PAN-FRIED SALMON WITH BEURRE BLANC

I have written about cooking salmon in general (See Cooking Your Fish see page 170). If you can grill your salmon over an alder fire, or any outdoor fire, that is by far the best way to cook it. But sometimes the weather or the bugs force you indoors, and a frying pan on the stove can still produce excellent results.

Bob Fraumeni (Finest At Sea) taught me this, the most important rule of all: *when you are cooking salmon, don't do anything else. Just watch the salmon.* Don't try to make the Beurre Blanc. Do that ahead of time. Don't try to whip the cream for the huckleberry pie, chop garlic for the salad dressing, clean crab, deep-fry razor clams or even churn your Dulce de Leche Buttermilk Ice Cream. *When you are cooking salmon, don't do anything else. Just watch the salmon.* Amen.

Heat olive oil—you want to cook your fish around medium heat, just enough for it to be sizzling, but not too much for it to burn. Lay salmon flesh side down in your pan to sear it (for a grilled look) and to start the cooking process. In about 4 minutes turn the fish so the skin side is down, and continue cooking for another 5 minutes or so, depending on the thickness of the flesh. Add butter to the pan (for flavour) just before you take out your salmon—while it is still raw (or looks to you as if it is.) It will continue to cook. Something else Bob taught me: "When you think it might be done, it is."

BEURRE BLANC MAKES 2 CUPS (475 ML)

Years ago I made everything complicated. I thought the idea was to disguise the taste of fish so I came up with all kinds of sauces to smother it in. I remember inviting Pierre Koffel, the chef at the Deep Cove Chalet in North Saanich, for dinner one night and making a sauce for my salmon from cream, cinnamon and currants. Pierre scraped the sauce off his fish and left it at the side of his plate. "Nev-air put sweet sauce with fish," he said, and went back to reading his *National Enquirer.*

When fish is fresh it has nothing to hide. (This reminds me of a sign I once saw at a fishmonger's in the south of England: "Our fish is fresher than the sea.") Frying it in olive oil, adding butter and salt at the end and maybe a squeeze of lemon juice—you don't need more than that. The flavour is subtle, fragile almost. The way the flakes come apart on your tongue—so very sensuous, until you get a bone stuck in your teeth. (Sorry for ruining the moment. It is my practical, unromantic streak surfacing as I write.)

¼ cup (60 mL) white wine	Freshly ground black pepper, to taste
¼ cup (60 mL) white wine vinegar	1½ cups (375 mL) chilled butter, cut into cubes
1 Tbsp (15 mL) finely chopped shallots	
¼ tsp (1 mL) salt	1 tsp (5 mL) lemon juice

WHAT YOU DO

1   Boil the wine, vinegar and shallots together in a stainless steel saucepan until the liquid is reduced to 2 Tbsp (30 mL). Add salt and pepper.

2   Remove the pan from the heat, and, with a wire whisk, beat in a couple of pieces of butter. When this begins to cream, beat in another piece. Continue in this manner, holding the pan over low heat or warm water, until all the butter is added. The resulting sauce will be creamy and light amber in color. Do not let it get too hot, or it will separate.

3   Stir in the lemon juice and drizzle sauce over the fish.

POTATOES HAIDA GWECCHIO SERVES 6-8

On Haida Gwaii, as you may have ascertained, some of us are all about fusion, necessity being the mother (expletive removed) of invention. This is my version of Potatoes Fontecchio, from *The Silver Palate Good Times* cookbook. Those call for one large or two small bunches of fresh mint, stems removed, leaves finely chopped, and you can do that, if you prefer. I used to pick mint at Chinukundl Creek (Miller Creek) near Skidegate but it has been choked out by the salmonberries and, well, I always have spruce tips on hand because they freeze so beautifully.

Potatoes Haida Gwecchio PHOTO BY MICHELLE FURBACHER

Haida Gwaii and Fontecchio

WHAT DO Haida Gwaii and Fontecchio (a small town in Abruzzo, Italy) have in common? In 2009 the province of L'Aquila was shaken by an earthquake (5.8 on the Richter scale) that left almost 300 dead and many others homeless.

In October of 2012, a 7.7 earthquake shook Haida Gwaii. Unlike the unlucky Italians, we were lucky. The only damage sustained was to my Day-of-the-Dead Elvis figurine, who lost both his arms in a fatal fall from the bathroom windowsill into the sink.

TOP: Victim 153: Skeletal Elvis Earthquake Victim PHOTO BY MICHELLE FURBACHER; BOTTOM: Long Live the King on Haida Gwaii PHOTO BY GUY KIMOLA

5½ lb (2.5 kg) small red new potatoes*	1½ cups (350 mL) olive oil	POTATOES HAIDA GWECCHIO (CONT'D)
8 cloves garlic, finely minced	2 Tbsp (30 mL) coarse salt	
½ cup (120 mL) spruce tips	Freshly ground black pepper, to taste	

WHAT YOU DO

1   Preheat oven to 350°F (180°C).

2   Scrub the potatoes and prick each one with a fork. *Silver Palate* says six times (this may take longer than you think but if you prick each one five times, well, suffer the consequences, people!) Place in a shallow roasting pan and roast for 2 hours.

---

*   I use a mixture of small red, white and purple potatoes but, again, improvise!

2 Cut each potato in half.

3 Toss the potatoes with the garlic, oil, spruce tips, salt and pepper to taste in a large bowl. Let stand for 30 minutes before serving. Serves 8 (at least!)

ASIDE: IN THE EVENT OF AN EARTHQUAKE
INSTRUCTIONS TO GUESTS AT COPPER BEECH HOUSE

"I have suffered many catastrophes in my life. Most of them have never happened."
—Mark Twain

If you wake up and the whole house is shaking (these things are prone to happen when we are soundly sleeping) it is probably only an EARTHQUAKE.

STAY CALM (do as I say, not as I do) and STAY IN BED. Put a pillow over your head (not to smother yourself, but, the seismologist who stayed with us after the 2012 quake, said, to protect your head from possible falling objects.)

If an earthquake happens when you are not in bed, TAKE COVER under the desk or table in your room. (Chances are by the time you find the desk or table, or the presence of mind to *locate* the desk or table, the shaking will have stopped, anyway.)

As soon as this happens you should meet in the living room, the "muster station." Your Copper Beech House host will advise you as to whether a tsunami warning has been issued and whether you should evacuate immediately without waiting for "official notice" which usually comes from Arkansas (in three minutes, as an email) or 45 minutes later by emergency siren or through loudspeaker announcements made by the local RCMP.

If you have a vehicle (always wise to keep your tank topped up, not like me, who prefers to run on empty) drive in an orderly fashion (again, do as I say, not as I do) across the causeway, take a right where there is no light and, as The Boss says, "then, boy, you're on your own." Actually, you are not on your own. Two thousand others will be evacuating and many of them will have been celebrating alcoholically (judging from previous experience) so proceed with care, and drive defensively.

If you don't have a vehicle, someone who does have one (i.e. a staff member) will give you a ride and even let you choose the mix CD you'd like to hear to make your evacuation experience more enjoyable.

Jane Wilson writes, in her column in *The Observer,* "you're supposed to obey the posted speed driving in the southbound lane only, directly to the sand pit at km 13 without stopping." None of us know where the sand pit or km 13 is, so just keep driving until you see cars pulling over at the side of the road. (You will be at the top of what most locals call Garbage Dump Hill, but others insist on calling Deep Creek Hill, though, either way, you won't find any evidence of a sign.)

"North end residents have apparently developed an unusual crisis management plan called, 'Grab a pie and run' after October's earthquake hit during a wedding reception,'" Jane Wilson continues. "'We take our pies seriously here in Masset,' said one resident, who asked to remain anonymous. In the second part of the plan they drive up the hill, and spend their evacuation time walking up and down critiquing the way other people choose to park."

After safely reaching high ground, wait out the warning. (If you tune in to CBC radio for information, you will be up there on the hill until someone in Toronto wakes up at 6 a.m. Eastern time and announces the Breaking News of an earthquake on Haida Gwaii.) Stand down when the all-clear signal is issued or when other vehicles start honking their horns and driving back in the direction of Masset.* (Assume everyone else is getting their updates from Arkansas and that it is safe to return to the comfort and security of your bed at Copper Beech House.) Another catastrophe has not occurred—again. Now you have a story you can tell your friends at home.

PHOTO BY GUY KIMOLA

SAUTÉED SEA ASPARAGUS WITH SESAME

SERVES 4

1½ cups (350 mL) fresh sea asparagus	2 cloves garlic, minced
1 Tbsp (15 mL) olive oil	1 tsp (5 mL) toasted sesame oil

WHAT YOU DO

1   Cover sea asparagus in large bowl of cold water with a teaspoon or so of vinegar. Soak 30 minutes to remove salt; rinse in cold water, and drain.

2   Heat olive oil in skillet over medium heat. Add garlic, and sauté 1 minute, or until golden. Add sea asparagus and cook 5 minutes, or until wilted.

---

*   P.S. Make sure you have a Designated Tsunami Driver on board as the RCMP will have a roadblock at the causeway and will be checking for drunk drivers, valid driver's licenses and insurance, cracked windscreens and rust on the undercarriage of your vehicle.

3   Stir in sesame oil, and serve.

SUBSTITUTIONS

For the sautéed sea asparagus recipe, leave out the sesame oil and garlic. Instead sweat one minced shallot and 3 Tbsp (45 mL) capers, squashed with the back of a spoon, in 2 Tbsp (30 mL) melted better. Do not allow to burn. Add asparagus to pan and sauté for 2–3 minutes. Turn mixture out of the pan, sprinkle with lemon juice and serve.

Alternately use 1–2 tsp (5–10 mL) ginger juice in place of the garlic and toasted sesame oil.

ROASTED SPICED CARROTS WITH POMEGRANATE MOLASSES

SERVES 4

When I grew up in the '50s, the most popular vegetable was peas, and peas came in tins. Other, more suspect (i.e. "gourmet") vegetables (such as broccoli) were put on to boil at two in the afternoon and served up once they were certifiably dead, with the meat and potatoes, at six. I didn't know that broccoli could be green; on my plate it appeared unlike any colour found in nature. So I was never a very big fan of vegetables, not even carrots, which we were made to eat so that we'd be able to see in the dark. No one explained *why* we would need to see in the dark. Mostly we were sent to bed, when we refused to eat our "vegetables" before it got dark.

LEFT: Carrots with Pomegranate Molasses PHOTO BY MICHELLE FURBACHER

RIGHT: Pomegranate seeds PHOTO BY MICHELLE FURBACHER

Now that I have discovered that roasting vegetables makes them taste very close to something delicious and forbidden, like candy, I eat them with relish. That is, I devour them, even as they come out of the oven on their baking trays lined with crisp parchment paper. I once ate a whole cauliflower before it got to the table. Roasted Cauliflower. Can anything be simpler or more flavourful?

Turns out, yes. Roast Cabbage. Roast Onions. Roast Fennel. Roast Just-About-Anything. And of course, the humble star of this recipe, your Roast Carrots.

Roasting any vegetable, and in this case carrots, brings out their sweetness, and when they are roasted in Earthy Spices and drizzled with pomegranate molasses, they hedge on the Divine. Finish with fresh herbs such as basil, mint or cilantro for a bit of brightness. And don't stew if you can't find pomegranate molasses (once I discovered it I bought a case of it at my not-so-local Middle Eastern market, which happens to be in Victoria, on Vancouver Island)—you can easily make your own pomegranate molasses by simmering equal amounts of pomegranate juice and sugar until thick and syrupy. Or substitute balsamic vinegar.

ILLUSTRATION BY DEJAHLEE BUSCH

1 bunch carrots, peeled (approximately 1 lb/500 g)	1 Tbsp (15 mL) pomegranate molasses (or more, to taste)
1 Tbsp (15 mL) extra virgin olive oil	A scatteration of pomegranate seeds (optional)
¼ tsp (1 mL) ground cumin	Salt and pepper, to taste
¼ tsp (1 mL) ground coriander	Sliced mint for garnish (or basil and cilantro or any combination thereof)
Pinch of cayenne pepper	

WHAT YOU DO

1 Preheat oven to 425°F (220°C).

2 Cut carrots in half lengthwise. Cut halves in half to create quarters if carrots are thicker.

3 Toss carrots with olive oil, cumin, cayenne, coriander, salt and pepper.

4   Roast for 10 minutes, flip carrots, and roast for another 5 minutes.

5   Toss carrots with pomegranate molasses (or 2 tsp (10 mL) balsamic vinegar) and optional pomegranate seeds and roast for another 5 minutes until golden.

6   Toss with herbs and serve.

ARUGULA SALAD AND ISLAND JOE'S TOMATOES
(WITH DRESSING BY APPOINTMENT TO THE WHITE HOUSE)
SERVES 4–6

Salad greens—different kinds of lettuces heaped in a bowl—are referred to as "mixed leaves" in Ireland. Something about the term appeals to me—makes me envision kicking my way through an autumnal salad—whereas "lettuce" makes me think of the flavourless, dreary iceberg variety. Iceberg lettuce was originally known as "Crisphead" but got its name change in the 1920s because California growers packed the lettuce on ice for shipping.

I never make the same salad twice (does anyone?) but here is a very simple, delicious one. Always use the freshest ingredients possible. It goes without saying.

½ lb (250 g) arugula, freshly picked

4 large Island Joe's Tomatoes (or any other tomatoes if the cost of catching a ferry to Haida Gwaii to buy Island Joe's tomatoes is prohibitive.)

WHAT YOU DO

1   Heap the arugula on the centre of a large platter.

2   Dress with Dressing by Appointment to the White House (see page 287).

3   Surround with thinly sliced tomatoes—I use Island Joe's because they are local and huge and taste like—tomatoes. (Joe's name is actually George. I suspect he's been asked a million times why he calls his tomatoes Island Joe's, so I couldn't bring myself to be the million and first to ask the same question.)

4   Drizzle a balsamic glaze over your tomatoes. I am particularly fond of the fig balsamic glaze.

NOTES ON TOMATOES

Years ago, on the CBC, I heard, "Canadians are so stupid they keep their tomatoes in the fridge." Since then I have wisened up, and I never keep my tomatoes in the fridge. It robs them of their flavour.

"The Ayatollah" Fraumeni disagrees. (Of course he disagrees. It would be too easy to just agree with me for once.) He did give me a Useful Tomato Tip though: store tomatoes upside down. So for me: upside down and on the windowsill. For Bob, upside down and in the fridge.

DRESSING BY APPOINTMENT TO THE WHITE HOUSE MAKES 1 CUP

In 1997, when we began building our beautiful luminous windy house on the Sangan River, we used to stay at Henry White's beached houseboat at Yakan Point. Henry and Linda and their daughter Shannon had been our neighbours in Sidney for three years, and moved back to Haida Gwaii so they could finish their big house out there on the very tip of the point.

The men went to work all day on our land, building the seven-sided house my husband had been instructed to build by Paul Bower ("Seven was the lucky number," he said) and Linda and I would stay back at Yakan Point and cook the meals. I was happy to have the days to myself, to explore the beach and forest, far away from the construction zone. Carl Jung described a house as an extension of the unconscious, "a kind of representation of one's innermost thoughts." When my house is being renovated, or in this case still being built, my thoughts are in

LEFT: View of Yakan Point from Tow Hill PHOTO BY CHARLOTTE MUSGRAVE; RIGHT: Yakan Point from Agate Beach PHOTO BY JANIE JOLLEY

DRESSING BY
APPOINTMENT TO THE
WHITE HOUSE (CONT'D)

disarray and I feel uprooted, ill at ease. I like my house calm, in order. Just the way I like my unconscious to be.

I was in charge of salads, and Henry particularly liked my dressing. It is part French—oil and vinegar based though it is sweetened by maple syrup, not ketchup, as is traditional—part Italian (I use the best olive oil and the best balsamic vinegar I can find), but the ingredient that makes this worthy of its title, a Dressing By Appointment to the White House, is a trick* my Great-Aunt Polly taught me when I lived with her in Chichester (Sussex, south of England) in the early '70s.

The recipe comes with a disclaimer. I never measure. I have tried to approximate the amounts of the ingredients I use, but my dressing is never the same twice (because I vary the type of oils I use) and I urge you, too, to stop worrying right now: however your dressing turns out it will be 100% better than any store-bought dressing, including Paul Newman's. (If I do say so myself.)

⅔ cup (160 mL) olive oil	2 tsp (10 mL) poppy seeds
2 tsp (10 mL) sesame oil	2 tsp (10 mL) maple syrup
⅓ cup balsamic vinegar	Salt and pepper, to taste
2 tsp (10 mL) Dijon mustard	2 Tbsp (30 mL) "top of milk" or cream

* I add 2 Tbsp (30 mL) "top of milk" (in England—the cream that floats to the top of the milk bottle) or half and half/ whipping cream/evaporated milk. Something to counteract the acidity of the salad and the vinegar.

Iceberg Lettuce

I ONCE saw a man take a bite out of a whole head of iceberg lettuce on a BC ferry headed south from Prince Rupert to Port Hardy. I included him as a character in my novel, *Given,* although he had a somewhat fleeting role.

"I climbed more steps to the solarium where families who hadn't reserved cabins were staking out little nests. An old man, naked except for a pair of happy-face boxer shorts, called out 'There'll be a high tide tonight' as I passed. I nodded to him and carried on past two blonde twins cross-dressing their Barbies, a man in a T-shirt that said 'Will Work for Beer' munching his way through a bald head of lettuce, a woman—her husband and five small boys identically dressed in pyjamas with vertical stripes the colour of stewed rhubarb—reading *All Families are Psychotic,* by Douglas Coupland, and a gang of teenagers on their way to a Marilyn Manson concert in Vancouver."

Possibly my all-time favourite Food Trivia Fact has to do with lettuce. The ancient Romans (the Greeks, too) believed that lettuce was a soporific (to save you a trip to your online dictionary, it caused sleepiness), which is why salad was always served at the end of the meal. The Roman Emperor Domitian might be responsible for the barbaric (I think) tradition of serving salad before the entrée—he liked to test his guests to see who could stay awake during his debaucheries. (I wouldn't want to get a reputation for torturing my guests at my renowned Tow Hill Road orgy parties, so I always serve my salad last.)

WHAT YOU DO

1   Mix all ingredients together. Add the cream last, stir well, and let stand until ready to use.

2   Refrigerate until next time.

VARIATIONS

I use a variety of oils (starting with a base of olive oil)—such as flax seed oil, walnut oil, macadamia nut oil, pistachio oil—just to amp up the flavour. Right now I am obsessed with Blood Orange Olive Oil, but it is almost too exquisite to use in a dressing where some of the other flavours might drown it out.

I use different types of mustard. Lately I've tried pomegranate mustard, but you should feel free to use any kind you are currently excited about

WARNING: Eating poppy seeds in salad dressing, or in cakes, or on bagels, can result in positive test results for heroin for as long as two days after eating the poppy-seed-contaminated food! If you are a prisoner on day parole subjected to urinalysis, you may want to substitute sesame seeds for poppy seeds in your dressing, or on your bagel. If you are a pilot you should avoid poppy seeds, also. If the plane crashes and heroin turns up in your bloodstream, you will get a lot of negative press, albeit posthumously.

8 Pour batter into pan.

9 Bake until cake just rises in center, about 35 minutes. Don't flip out, like I did one time, if a toothpick inserted into center does not come out clean: that one time I baked the cake 5 minutes longer and wished I had trusted my own instructions. How could I not have remembered—the cake goes on cooking in the pan?

10 Cool completely in pan on rack.

11 Cover; chill while making mousse.

WHAT YOU DO FOR THE MOUSSE

1 Melt butter in medium metal bowl set over saucepan of simmering water (do not allow bottom of bowl to touch water).

2 Whisk yolks, cream and vanilla in separate small bowl to blend.

3 Very gradually whisk the yolk mixture into the bowl with the melted butter.

4 Whisk constantly over simmering water until thermometer registers 150°F (66°C), about 6 minutes. The mixture may appear as if it has curdled, but it hasn't. Trust me. All will be well when you . . .

5 Remove bowl from over water; add chocolate and stir to melt. Set aside.

6 Beat egg whites and sugar in large bowl to form medium-stiff peaks. Whisk one-quarter of beaten egg white mixture into warm chocolate mixture, then fold in the remaining egg whites. Pour mousse over cake in pan; smooth top. Chill torte until mousse is set, at least 6 hours and up to 1 day.

7 Run a sharp knife around edge of pan to loosen torte. Release pan sides. Transfer torte to platter. You can optionally whip up cream until peaks form and spread this over the mousse, and then finish with a handful of chopped chocolate. I like to serve my torte with a splattering (or a dollop, take your pick) of Thimbleberry Elderflower Liqueur Coulis (page 293) on the side. I have also served it with Candied Rose Petals (page 136), which was another kind of treat.

THIMBLEBERRY ELDERFLOWER LIQUEUR COULIS MAKES 2 CUPS (475 ML)

½ cup (120 mL) sugar

¼ cup (60 mL) water

2½ cups (600 mL) thimbleberries

(fresh or frozen)

¼ cup (60 mL) Elderflower liqueur (optional)

WHAT YOU DO

1   Heat the sugar and water in a small saucepan over medium heat, stirring from time to time, until the sugar dissolves completely, about 5 minutes. Use a pastry brush dipped in water to brush down any sugar crystals on the side of the pan.

2   Add the thimbleberries and simmer another 5 minutes or until berries have softened and fallen apart.

3   Put the sugar and berry mixture in a blender or food processor and puree.

4   Strain through a fine mesh sieve to remove the seeds and stir in the elderflower liqueur, if using.

5   The sauce keeps well, tightly covered, in the refrigerator for a week and freezes perfectly for several months.

SUBSTITUTIONS

Raspberries, fresh or frozen.

Cake vs. Torte

THE WORD "TORTE" comes from the Italian word "torta," which means a round bread or cake; in Europe, most cakes are called tortes. Some French tortes are called *"gateau,"* which is French for cake, not torte, but anyway . . .

Traditional cakes are made with ingredients mainly consisting of sugar, eggs, butter and flour; the cake's lightness of being comes from of the low gluten content of cake flour, which is made from soft wheat.

A torte, however, calls for little to no flour and the use of ground nuts, such as almond meal, which adds density, through its oils, and nut flavour to the batter as it bakes. The torte is much heavier than the cake in both texture and taste.

WILD ROSE PETAL ICE CREAM SERVES 4

½ cup (120 mL) fresh rose petals

¾ cup (180 mL) sugar

1¾ cups (410 mL) whipping cream

¼ cup (60 mL) wild rose petal syrup (see page 134)

1 tsp (5 mL) lemon juice

WHAT YOU DO

1 Wash rose petals and combine them with the sugar; give this a good shake, cover with plastic wrap and allow to sit in the refrigerator for about 30 minutes.

2 Simmer cream, rose petals and sugar for about 15 minutes. Strain and discard the rose petals and chill the mixture.

3 When ready to make the ice cream, combine the rose petal syrup, rose water and the chilled cream mixture in the ice cream maker, taste and adjust for sweetness, and follow the manufacturer's instructions. Add the lemon juice last, and churn for 5 more minutes. Freeze for at least 6 hours.

4 Garnish with more rose petals before serving.

5 **NOTE:** If you don't have an ice cream maker, simmer the cream with rose petals and sugar as mentioned above. Chill the mix and then fold in the other ingredients and stir gently until the syrup evenly mixes with the cream. Stir in the lemon juice and freeze. When partially frozen, take it out and whisk it again to break up the ice crystals. Freeze until ready to eat.

Wild Rose Petal Ice Cream PHOTO BY SUSAN MUSGRAVE

MENU #2 (HALIBUT)

Smoked Salmon with Spruce Tips, Garlic Scapes and Chevre
Simple Razor Clam Fritters

❊ ❊ ❊ ❊ ❊

Country Rye Bread

❊ ❊ ❊ ❊ ❊

Baked Fillets of Halibut with Sesame Seeds, Butter and Thyme
OR Greg Martin's Halibut Soufflé
Baked Yams with Honey, Butter and Lime
Lambsquarters with Shallots and Capers
Oven Roasted Vegetables: Cabbage and Fennel

❊ ❊ ❊ ❊ ❊

Peach and Huckleberry Almond Torte
or
Buttermilk Ice Cream

THE RECIPES

SMOKED SALMON WITH SPRUCE TIPS, GARLIC SCAPES AND CHEVRE

SERVES 6 AS AN APPETIZER

8 oz (225 g) soft fresh goat cheese, room temperature

4 oz (110 g) cream cheese, room temperature

3 Tbsp (45 mL) minced spruce tips

1 garlic clove, crushed

1 French bread baguette, sliced or 1 loaf

sourdough bread, sliced and toasted

8 oz (225 g) smoked salmon, thinly sliced

½ sliced red onion, thinly sliced (optional)

2 Tbsp (15 mL) capers (optional)

2 pickled garlic scapes

LEFT: Hot-smoked salmon served with spruce tips and pickled garlic scapes PHOTO BY MICHELLE FURBACHER

MIDDLE: Pickled garlic scapes PHOTO BY MICHELLE FURBACHER

RIGHT: Dominic's goat cheese PHOTO BY MICHELLE FURBACHER

WHAT YOU DO

1   Combine goat cheese, cream cheese, spruce tips and garlic in medium bowl. Stir with a fork until well blended. Wrap cheese in plastic and refrigerate overnight (or at least for a couple of hours.)* (Can be prepared 2 days ahead. Keep refrigerated.)

2   Remove plastic wrap from cheese, and set on a plate with baguette, next to a platter of thinly sliced smoked salmon (topped with thinly sliced red onions and capers, if that appeals to you) and garlic scapes. Serve.

ADDITIONS

If your chives have gone to seed, break up one of the beautiful purple flower heads and sprinkle it overtop.

SIMPLE RAZOR CLAM FRITTERS

SERVES 6 AS AN APPETIZER

I suppose you could use other clams (why not?) but razor clams are dug near where I live on North Beach so alas, woe is I, it is what I have. These were better than dessert and I have Steve, a newly acquired (I hope) fisher-friend from Cedar, BC to thank for giving me permission to eat dessert before the rest of my dinner. He read a book that explains if you want to avoid that "full to busting" feeling you get after eating a huge meal and then topping it off with an even huger piece of Double Chocolate Torte you should have your cake and eat it first. Sugar will pass right through you whereas protein takes hours to digest. Problem solved. Eat your cake (or in this case your Razor Clams) first, then the rest will follow. I wish I had known this when I was a kid being told, "Eat your Brussels sprouts or you won't get any dessert."

1 quart (1 L) jar of canned razor clams (or reasonable facsimiles)

1 egg, beaten

Salt and pepper, to taste

1½–2 cups (375–500 mL) panko bread crumbs

¾ cups (190 mL) (approximate) rice flour for coating the clams, or regular flour (but I think the rice flour is what makes them so light)

Oil for deep frying (peanut oil, first choice)

Razor clam fritters PHOTO BY MICHELLE FURBACHER

WHAT YOU DO

1   Dip clams into rice flour, seasoned to taste with salt and pepper, coating evenly.

2   Dip floured clams into lightly beaten egg.

3   Roll egg-coated clams into panko bread crumbs and shake off any excess.

4   Here is the secret for making an as-close-to-perfection-as-it-gets clam fritter. After rolling in panko and before you fry in oil, always put battered clams in the freezer for at least 20 minutes. They can be made ahead and frozen for up to a week before frying. When the panko gets frozen to the egg wash, it sticks like cement and the crumbs never fall off and the results are, tah-dah! (Nothing, however, like cement.)

5   Heat a fair amount of peanut oil or other vegetable oil, to 375°F (190°C). (Use a candy/deep-frying thermometer unless you have an affinity with hot oil and can tell, by looking at it, that it is ready). Fry clams for 1 minute or less. Razors will toughen if overcooked. You want the clams to be perfectly cooked the moment the panko crumbs start to turn golden.

6   Serve with tartar sauce (my favourite at the moment is Alder Smoked Walla Walla Onion Tartar Sauce from the Pike Place Market in Seattle) or the dipping sauce I suggested for Ginger Scallion Crab Cakes (see page 313)—a sauce made of mayonnaise, lime juice, sesame oil and sweet chili sauce.

---

*   It always annoys me when I am told to refrigerate something overnight. That means I'd have to, uh, plan ahead? I skip the "refrigerate overnight" part and make mine right away and eat it, and it tastes fine. More than just fine. Delicious.

ASIDE: PANKO (JAPANESE BREAD CRUMBS)

Panko is a Japanese-style bread crumb traditionally used as a coating for deep-fried foods. The biggest difference between panko and common-or-garden variety bread crumbs is that panko is made from bread without crusts. But here's where it gets interesting. Panko is made by zapping an electric current through the dough. Next the electrocuted crustless bread is coarsely ground into airy, large flakes, which tend to stay crispier longer than other (bread crumbs) because they don't absorb as much grease.

HALIBUT TWO YUMMY WAYS

FIRST WAY: BAKED FILLETS OF HALIBUT WITH SESAME SEEDS, BUTTER AND THYME SERVES 4

A lot of recipes call for halibut (or salmon) steaks. I prefer fillets and I have no idea why. Well, it probably has to do with childhood memories of eating overcooked salmon steaks. I am sure my parents believed fish needed to be cooked until it was thoroughly overdone, because that is how their parents had cooked fish. The word "sushi" hadn't been invented when I was growing up. That is to say, it wasn't in current usage. Well, not on Vancouver Island. Not in our family.

Whenever I cook halibut this way it always comes out "perfectly done."

Four 5 oz (140 g) halibut fillets	Freshly ground black pepper, to taste
Salt, to taste	3 Tbsp (45 mL) toasted sesame seeds
⅓ cup (80 mL) butter, melted	½ tsp (2 mL) whole thyme leaves, crumbled
1½ cups (350 mL) panko	

WHAT YOU DO

1 Preheat oven to 350°F (180°C).

2 Place halibut fillets in a buttered pan. Sprinkle with salt and top each with a dab of butter.

3   Combine the remaining ingredients and cover each fillet with as much of the mixture as you like (I usually have a lot left over, which I freeze for another occasion.)

4   Bake, uncovered, 25–30 minutes or until the fish flakes easily when tested with a fork.

SECOND WAY: GREG MARTIN'S HALIBUT SOUFFLÉ SERVES 4

There are two (unofficial) religious cults on a place Haida Gwaii where we rely on the BC ferry system for our food, our mail and our transportation: the Catchaferrians and the Missedaferrians. I'm a born again Catcheferrian these days, after very nearly missing my ferry one Labour Day weekend when Greg Martin invited me to his house in Queen Charlotte for dinner.

BC Ferries has a rule: you must be in the ferry line-up (to catch a ferry to Prince Rupert) two hours before the ferry sails. Greg thought arriving "early" a waste of time that might be better spent drinking wine together, and he persuaded me to stay until half an hour before the ferry (a five-minute drive from his house) was due to leave. Not only did I lose my reservation, I was moved to the end of the stand-by line. I believe I got on the ferry, but only after being warned by a BC Ferries worker not to take advice from the likes of Greg, whom, he apprised me, marches to the beat of a different accordion.

1 cup (240 mL) Sauternes or Chardonnay	1 tsp (5 mL) lemon juice
¼ tsp (1 mL) salt	¼ cup (60 mL) finely chopped green onions
1 lb (450 g) halibut fillets	Panko*
1 cup (240 mL) mayonnaise (yes, this is the guilty-pleasure secret ingredient!)	Pinch of smoked paprika†
½ cup (120 mL) sour cream	

*   As you've probably figured out by now, I'm a panko fanatic.

†   I seldom used to bother with paprika until I discovered *Pimentón de la Vera* (smoked paprika) and bought it because it came in a little hot red tin. Now I use it on (almost) everything.

Sautéed lambsquarters with lemon PHOTO BY MICHELLE FURBACHER

2   Rinse gently and place them, still dripping, into a large pot with an additional ½ inch (1 cm) of water. Cover and steam over medium heat, turning occasionally, for 5–10 minutes (depending on the amount) or until barely tender.

3   Drain well in a sieve or colander. Rinse under hot water.

4   Heat olive oil and butter in large pot over medium heat. Add shallots and sauté until tender but not brown, about 3 minutes. Add salt and pepper to taste.

Sautéed lambsquarters with capers PHOTO BY MICHELLE FURBACHER

5   Remove the lambsquarters and place in a serving dish. Keep the remaining oil over heat.

6   Add the capers to the remaining oil and fry for 30 seconds, or until they begin to pop.

7   Scoop the capers out of the pan and gently combine with the lambsquarters and shallots.

8   Drizzle with lemon juice.

OVEN-ROASTED VEGETABLES

Until I discovered how easy it was to roast vegetables, as I have already confessed, I was not much of a vegetable enthusiast. If they are fresh out of the garden, then yes, but if they are fresh-frozen, fresh-canned, or even freshly purchased from the fresh produce section of my grocery store I would rather eat cake. I would rather eat cake anyway; cake goes straight to the pleasure centre of the brain, whereas vegetables go to the eat-your-vegetables-if-you-know-what's-good-for-you part of the brain associated with cake-deprivation and other disciplinary actions.

These days I love my vegetables. As long as they are roasted.

BAKED CABBAGE WITH COCONUT OIL

SERVES 2–4

3 Tbsp (45 mL) coconut oil

1 medium head cabbage

Salt and pepper, to taste

1 tsp (5 mL) caraway or fennel seeds
(optional)

WHAT YOU DO

1   Preheat oven to 400°F (200°C). Brush a rimmed baking sheet with 1 Tbsp (15 mL) coconut oil.

2   Cut one medium heady cabbage into ½ inch (1 cm) thick rounds and lay these on a baking sheet. Brush with 2 Tbsp (30 mL) coconut oil. Season with salt and pepper and sprinkle with caraway or fennel seeds, if desired. I never do this because my desire does not run along seedy lines, so to speak.

3   Roast until cabbage is tender and edges are golden, 35–40 minutes.

SUBSTITUTE

Olive oil for coconut oil, if you prefer. Use parchment paper instead of brushing the baking sheet with oil.

ROASTED FENNEL SERVES 2–4

I've heard fennel described as tasting like a cross between celery, cabbage and licorice. Roasting, however, brings out an entirely new pine-nutty taste. I like to keep my method as simple as possible (no addition of balsamic vinegar or parmesan cheese for me, though these can be delicious—it's all a matter of taste, isn't it, and your mood on any given evening.)

2 fennel bulbs (thick base of stalk)

1–2 Tbsp (15–30 mL) olive oil

Salt, to taste

WHAT YOU DO

1   Preheat oven to 400°F (200°C).

2   Halve the fennel bulbs, lengthwise, then cut lengthwise in 1 inch (2.5 cm) thick
    pieces.

3   Rub just enough olive oil over the fennel to coat. Lay the fennel pieces on an
    oiled baking tray, or one lined with parchment paper, sprinkle with salt and
    roast for 35–40 minutes, or until the fennel is cooked through and beginning
    to caramelize.

PEACH AND HUCKLEBERRY ALMOND TORTE (ADAPTED FROM *VEGETARIAN PLEASURES: A MENU COOKBOOK* BY JEANNE LEMLIN)

SERVES 8

FOR THE TORTE

½ cup (120 mL) butter, softened	2 eggs
1 cup (240 mL) sugar	½ tsp (2 mL) almond extract
½ cup (120 mL) ground almonds	3–4 (depending on size) ripe peaches, peeled and sliced ½ inch thick
½ cup (120 mL) all purpose white flour	¾ cup (180 mL) fresh or frozen huckleberries (optional)
1 tsp (5 mL) baking powder	

FOR THE TOPPING

1 Tbsp (15 mL) butter	2 Tbsp (30 mL) all-purpose white flour
1 Tbsp (15 mL) sugar	½ tsp (2 mL) cinnamon

WHAT YOU DO

1   Preheat oven to 350°F (180°C). Butter the bottom of a 9-inch (23 cm) spring-
    form pan.

2   In a large bowl or food processor (which is what I use) cream the butter and
    sugar together until blended. Add the almonds, flour, baking powder, eggs and
    almond extract; beat until smooth and fluffy.

Peach and Huckleberry and Almond Torte PHOTO BY MICHELLE FURBACHER

3 Scrape the batter into the springform pan and smooth over the top. Arrange the peach slices on top in one layer. (They don't have to be neat, which is what I *also* like about this recipe!) Sprinkle huckleberries over the peaches.

4 In a small bowl make the topping: Toss together the butter, sugar, flour and cinnamon. Cut the butter into the mixture until it is the texture of coarse crumbs. Sprinkle evenly over the peaches.

5 Bake for 50–60 minutes, or until golden brown all over. Cool on a wire rack for 10 minutes, then remove the sides of the pan. Serve warm or at room temperature.

BUTTERMILK ICE CREAM SERVES 4

Kayley Redgers introduced this ice cream, from Deb Perelman's Smitten Kitchen blog, in the summer of 2012 when she worked at Copper Beech House. I have turned on countless guests, friends and family members to Deb's blog. I also bought multiple copies of *The Smitten Kitchen Cookbook* last Christmas and gave them as gifts. My niece, Catherine, has taken fiendishly to baking as a result of Deb's astoundingly awesome (and wonderfully uncomplicated) recipes.

Deb herself acknowledges having adapted this recipe from Claudia Fleming's "astoundingly awesome woefully out-of-print, *The Last Course* but I have it on good authority that if you call The North Fork Table and Inn (where she now 'pastries'), they have a small supply and might even send you a signed copy."

I have further adapted the recipe by doubling the amount of vanilla. You can never have enough vanilla, I always say.

1 cup (240 mL) heavy cream	1 cup (240 mL) buttermilk
¾ cup (180 mL) sugar (divided)	1 Tbsp (15 mL) vanilla extract
6 large egg yolks	Pinch of salt

WHAT YOU DO

1 In a large, heavy saucepan, combine the heavy cream and ½ cup (120 mL) of the sugar and bring to a simmer over medium heat.

2 In a large bowl, whisk egg yolks and remaining ¼ cup (60 mL) of sugar.

3 Remove the cream mixture from the heat and drizzle a small amount into the yolks, slowly, and whisking constantly to keep the eggs from curdling. Do this a few more times to warm up the yolks before pouring the yolk mixture back into the cream, whisking non-stop.

4 Cook over low heat until the mixture is thick enough to coat the back of a spoon.

5 Strain the mixture and whisk in the buttermilk, vanilla and salt. Cool completely and freeze in an ice cream maker according to manufacturer's directions.

VANILLA EXTRACT ONE 12 OZ (375 ML) BOTTLE

When I moved to Port Clements in 1970, I couldn't find pure vanilla extract on the shelves of the general store. (They also had a shipment of left-footed gumboots that fall. I asked about the likelihood of buying a matching pair in the future. "It's what we get," the clerk said.)

I thought I had arrived at the end of the world. I could live without a right-footed gumboot, but not without pure vanilla extract.

I asked if I could special-order some, at which point the store owner came out and took me into the back where he opened a small safe. His wife, I learned, was another Islander with a great strength for the weakness, and he had to keep the pure extracts locked up so she wouldn't drink them all. (Commercial vanilla extracts are 35% alcohol, by law, and usually have simple syrup (sugar water) added to it to give it a sweet aftertaste.)

It turns out that it is one of the easiest things in the world to make your own vanilla extract. All you have to do is buy a bottle of vodka, add vanilla beans, shake occasionally, and let age in a dark cool place. Homemade vanilla can be used after 4 weeks, but the extraction will continue for 6 months and even after that the vanilla, like a good wine, will continue to mature indefinitely.

6 vanilla beans	12 oz (375 mL) bottle 40% vodka

WHAT YOU DO

1   Sterilize a bottle and lid.

2   Use kitchen scissors or a sharp paring knife to cut lengthwise down each vanilla bean, splitting them in half, leaving an inch at the end connected.

3   Lay your cut bean flat, exposed side up. Run a clean butter knife tilted at a

Homemade vanilla extract
PHOTO BY MICHELLE FURBACHER

Vanilla Beans

THERE ARE well over 200 varieties of vanilla beans. Knowing the differences may make you a vanilla snob, but isn't life too short to drink bad vanilla extract? (Forget that I wrote that. Tasteless joke.)

Each vanilla bean comes from a hand-pollinated vanilla orchid (the only orchids that produce an edible seed). Once the vanilla seed pod has developed, it must be handpicked as well. After picking, the curing process takes several months, which is why vanilla extract, and especially vanilla beans, can be so expensive.

45° angle along the bean so that it scrapes up all the black stuff (also called caviar) from the inside of the pods.

4   Insert the cleaned bean skins and the caviar into your bottle.

5   Fill the bottle with vodka.

6   Week 1: Shake the bottle vigorously every day. Seeds and cottony fibrous chunks will swirl in the bottle, this is normal. By the second or third day the extract should be a bit darker. Open it up and take a sniff.

7   Weeks 2–4: Shake the bottle a few times a week.

8   Week 5: You now have a very raw vanilla extract that you can use in any recipe that calls for it. If you want vanilla seeds in your recipe give the bottle a shake before pouring. Top up the bottle with additional vodka if you expose any vanilla beans.

9   After 2 months, extraction has pretty much finished. The extract keeps for years.

TIPS

I make vanilla sugar by drying the pods I've used to make my extract and putting them in a container of granulated sugar. This infuses the sugar with yummy vanilla flavour for baking.

When buying vanilla extract make sure it is labeled "pure," not "Artificial Vanilla Flavouring." The imitation vanilla extracts are synthetic, made from glycoside found in the sapwood of certain conifers or from coal extracts, and leave a bitter aftertaste.

MENU #3 (VENISON)

Crab Cakes for Crab Lovers
or
Ginger Scallion Crab Cakes for All Others

❀ ❀ ❀ ❀ ❀

Elderflower Sorbet

❀ ❀ ❀ ❀ ❀

Multi-Grain Sourdough Bread

❀ ❀ ❀ ❀ ❀

Venison and Mixed Onion Stew with Chanterelles and the Creature
Mashed Potatoes with Roasted Garlic and Coconut Milk
Baby Kale with Macedonian Feta
Beets Margaret Atwood

❀ ❀ ❀ ❀ ❀

Quinoa and Grilled Sourdough Salad

❀ ❀ ❀ ❀ ❀

Pear, Cranberry and Vanilla Crumble
or
Dulce de Leche Buttermilk Ice Cream

THE RECIPES

CRAB CAKES FOR CRAB LOVERS

SERVES 4–6 AS AN APPETIZER

If you experiment long enough with different crab cakes recipes you may make an amazing discovery—crab cakes are best when they are made of crab. That is, if you are overly generous with the crab and hold back or eliminate all the other ingredients.

4 cups (950 mL) of crabmeat	1 cup (250 mL) or more as needed panko
1 egg, beaten	

WHAT YOU DO

1   Mix beaten egg into crabmeat, combine thoroughly and, with dampened hands, shape into 1¼ inch (3 cm) balls.

2   Chill in the fridge for a few hours so they will firm up and won't fall apart when they are cooking.

3   Heat the fat in your deep fryer to 375°F (190°C), roll the crab cakes in panko and fry for about 3 minutes.

If you prefer the taste of crab to be disguised, so you don't even know you are eating it, try the following recipe.

GINGER SCALLION CRAB CAKES FOR ALL OTHERS SERVES 2-4. DEPENDING ON HOW BIG YOU MAKE THEM, YOU SHOULD GET BETWEEN 8–12 PATTIES.

6 Tbsp (90 mL) olive oil, divided	1 Tbsp (15 mL) grated fresh ginger
2 garlic cloves, minced	1 bunch scallions, chopped
1 shallot, minced	¼ cup (60 mL) cilantro, chopped
	INGREDIENTS CONTINUED . . .

½ tsp (2 mL) red pepper flakes

1 large egg, lightly beaten

½ jalapeno, minced (or more, if you like it hot)

1 tsp (5 mL) salt

¼ cup mayonnaise

1 tsp (5 mL) freshly ground black pepper

Dash of sweet chili sauce

1 cup (240 mL) panko

Juice of 2 limes

1 lb (500 g) fresh crabmeat

1 tsp (5 mL) tamari

WHAT YOU DO

1 Heat a couple of tablespoons of olive oil in a medium-sized skillet over medium heat, and add the minced garlic, shallots and ginger. Sauté for 2 minutes, just until they start to get a bit of colour and release an aromatic smell. Remove from heat and pour (along with oil) into a large bowl.

2 To the bowl, add the scallions, cilantro, jalapeno, red pepper flakes, mayonnaise, sweet chili sauce, lime juice, tamari, egg, salt and black pepper. Mix until well combined.

3 Fold in the panko and crabmeat and gently mix together. Be careful not to break up the crabmeat too much.

4 Use a large spoon to scoop up ¼ cup servings of the crab mixture, and shape into patties with your hands. Place on a parchment paper-lined baking sheet and let rest for about 10 minutes.

5 Pour a ¼ cup of olive oil into a heavy bottomed skillet—the oil should come up the pan about a ¼ inch—and heat over medium heat. When the oil is hot, use a spatula to gently slide the patties into the oil in batches. (I do 2–3 at time, max).

6 Let fry on the first side for about 2–3 minutes and then flip using the spatula. Let fry on the other side for another 2–3 minutes or until crisp and golden brown. Remove from oil and let drain on a paper towel lined baking sheet.

7 Continue with the rest of the patties. You can also just make a few of them and

leave the rest covered with plastic wrap in the fridge for up to 2 days. There is no rule saying you have to eat them all in one go. It's hard to stop eating them, though. You have been forewarned.

8   Serve immediately on a bed of dressed mixed greens with a sauce for dipping made of mayonnaise, lime juice, sesame oil and sweet chili sauce. Sorry, I don't have a recipe for this. I just add the ingredients until it looks and tastes right.

ELDERFLOWER SORBET SERVES 4–6

Fresh elderflowers, enough to fill a quart jar	1½ cups (350 mL) sugar
1 quart (1 L) water	Juice of 2 lemons, rinds reserved

WHAT YOU DO

1   Pick enough flowers of the Red Pacific Elderberry to loosely fill a large brown paper or canvas grocery bag. Pick when the flowers are fully open and are light, fluffy and vibrant, as their aroma fades once the afternoon sun hits the flowers. On Haida Gwaii we don't often have to worry about the hot afternoon sun hitting *anything*, especially in May, and I often wait until the end of an overcast day to go down the road with my scissors and harvesting bag in hand: my syrups are as intense as I would wish them to be. Note that flowers that have not opened or turned brown do not give a good flavour so don't bother picking them.

Elderflower Sorbet PHOTO BY MICHELLE FURBACHER

2   Many elder species have cyanide-like compounds in the green umbel stems. This won't kill you but it will add an unwanted bitter almond flavour and scent to the sorbet. To avoid this you will need to pick the individual flowers off the stem. This can take several hours to get enough to make one quart (or litre) of sorbet. It can be a tedious task, a meditational one or busy work for your hands while drinking last year's elderflower wine with friends.

3   Fill a quart jar with the flowers. Pack down gently. Set aside.

4   Mix the lemon juice, water and sugar in a heavy saucepan. Add the lemon rinds and bring to a boil. Immediately turn down to a simmer. Cover and let simmer for 10 minutes.

5 Remove from heat and strain fluid into jar of elderflowers. Cover jar and let cool to room temperature, then refrigerate until cold. Line a bowl with clean muslin. Pour the contents of the jar into muslin. Now gather up the edges of the muslin and twist the top so the flowers mush is on the bottom. Squeeze out as much of the elderflower syrup as possible.

6 Place the strained syrup in an ice cream maker and freeze according to manufacturer's instructions. (That's what they always say in recipes but I lost the manufacturer's instructions to my Donvier way back when. It's done when it is done. You have to watch it carefully.)

7 Serve softly frozen. This sorbet has a strong, somewhat elusive flavour, and needs to be savoured on its own, but I've read that the addition of a little bit of tequila when served gives it a certain *je ne sais quoi.*

VENISON AND MIXED ONION STEW WITH CHANTERELLES AND THE CREATURE*

SERVES 4

You see he'd a sort of a tipplin' way
With a love for the liquor he was born
And to send him on his way each day,
He'd a drop of the craythur every morn'
—from *Finnegan's Wake* by James Joyce

1 Tbsp (15 mL) Worcestershire sauce	3 shallots, peeled and quartered
1 cup (240 mL) or more sautéed chanterelle (or other) mushrooms	4 garlic cloves, thickly sliced
	a handful of garlic scapes (optional)
1 medium leek, white part only, halved lengthwise, washed, dried and sliced	2 celery stalks, sliced into 1-inch (2.5 cm) pieces
1 medium onion, halved and sliced	INGREDIENTS CONTINUED . . .
2 carrots, diced	

* Creature: a contracted form of "Creature-comfort." A drop of the creature, or, as they say in Ireland, "a drop of the craythur."

TOP LEFT: Onion Basket PHOTO BY MICHELLE FURBACHER; MIDDLE LEFT: "Good Feed" Chanterelles PHOTO BY CHRIS ASHURST; TOP RIGHT: Garlic and Scallions PHOTO BY MICHELLE FURBACHER; MIDDLE RIGHT: Chopping leeks PHOTO BY MICHELLE FURBACHER; BOTTOM: Venison stew PHOTO BY MICHELLE FURBACHER

BABY KALE WITH MACEDONIAN FETA

SERVES 4

Almost everything tastes better when it's a baby, which is why we have laws. It is considered more socially acceptable to let animals grow up before slaughtering them (I am not talking about cows and sheep here, but wild creatures, like deer. I remember the Unborn Fawn Burgers at a Tlell potluck, circa 1972. The pregnant mother has been shot, by mistake; the experience scarred me into writing *The Charcoal Burners,* about a commune of cannibals living off a commune of vegetarians in the northern bush.)

Barb Sly, at Green Gaia, orders large bags of baby kale and sometimes I buy it all. It is that good. The leaves are harvested before they mature, when they are mild tasting, tender and sweet, not chewy and bold like their parents. Baby kale is similar to baby arugula (with less of a bite).

You are of course free to use any variety of kale (or a mix of varieties) in this dish. Green, red or Tuscan kale (sometimes called *lacinato,* black or dinosaur kale) would all work, though I use baby kale whenever I can get it.

12 Tbsp (30 mL) butter	Salt and pepper, to taste
3 lb (1.5 kg) baby kale	⅓ cup (80 mL) (or more) Macedonian feta*

WHAT YOU DO

1   Heat butter in a frying pan and add the kale. Cook until it is reduced in size, its colour has intensified and it is softened (5–10 minutes). Stir in feta. Keep stirring until the feta begins to melt, season with salt and pepper, and serve piping hot.

SUBSTITUTION

If you are using another type of kale you should remove and discard the thick bottom stems and center stems, roughly chop the kale.

If you can't find Macedonian feta, or can't be bothered going out of your way to look for it, substitute the rubbery stuff that comes in tubs.

---

*   A sheep's milk feta that is incredibly creamy and not too briny. Once you have tasted this you will not ever want to go back to eating the rubbery stuff that comes in tubs. Trust me on this one.

BEETS MARGARET ATWOOD SERVES 4

I found a recipe for Beets Dauphinoise many, many years ago in a *Gourmet* magazine. I cut it out and lost it, many years ago, so it is safe to say this recipe comes from my head. How I choose to make it depends on whatever else is competing for attention in my head on any given day, but I am giving you my best shot here. Since "dauphinoise" (usually a potato dish baked in milk, cream and cheese) means that it comes from the Dauphiné area of France, near the Italian border, I have decided to call my dish something closer to home. When Margaret Atwood and Graeme Gibson stayed at Copper Beech House, I made this dish, and Margaret asked for this recipe. It seemed fitting that I name it in her honour.

3 lb (1.5 kg) beet roots	Salt and pepper, to taste
½ cup (120 mL) chicken or vegetable stock	2 cups (475 mL) grated Gruyere or Emmental cheese
2 cloves garlic, minced	⅓ cup (80 mL) panko
2 scallions, diced fine	Daubs of butter, to taste
2 cups (475 mL) heavy cream	⅛ tsp (1 mL) freshly grated nutmeg

WHAT YOU DO

1   Preheat over to 375°F (190°C).

2   Scrub beets and slice them into the tiniest (1/8–inch/3 mm thin) slices you can manage. I have purchased a mandolin which makes the job easier, but then you have to wash it without cutting your fingers off, so ease, as always, comes with a price. Layer the slices in a gratin dish and press them down with the back of a spoon. They should come to just below the top of the dish.

3   Mince the garlic, dice the shallots and add to the dish.

4   Bring stock, heavy cream, garlic and scallions to a simmer in a large saucepan and pour this mixture over the beets. The cream should come to just below the top layer of beets (top up with more cream if necessary).

DINNER ON THE DECK   *321*

5 Sprinkle with grated cheese, breadcrumbs and daubs of butter. Place on a rimmed baking sheet (in case of overflow) and bake until bubbly and golden brown on top, 40–45 minutes.

6 Remove from oven and grate nutmeg over top just before serving.

QUINOA AND GRILLED SOURDOUGH SALAD SERVES 4

Here I thought I could get away with writing a whole cookbook without once mentioning quinoa,* and then my friend Angie Long returned to the Spare Girl cabin on Meredith's land at Moon Over Naikoon and I loaned her my copy of Yotam Ottolenghi's vegetarian cookbook, *Plenty*. Angie cooked dinner for me at her Café of Monumental Simplicity (not open to the public, I am sorry to say) and included this recipe. I could have eaten the whole salad, and I think I might have done so. Angie used pieces of the sourdough loaf I had given her once it was a few days old. Now I have a use for all the ends-of-the-loaves I had been previously feeding to the ravens and eagles.

I have adapted this recipe by adding a few more ingredients, such as the red and yellow peppers, and the Macedonian feta. The best part about the original recipe is that it only calls for a quarter of a cup of quinoa so the ubiquitous grain doesn't dominate the salad and I don't have to feel I am jumping on any kind of food faddist bandwagon.

¼ cup (60 mL) quinoa	½ small red onion, very thinly sliced
4 slices of day old (or more) sourdough bread	¼ cup (60 mL) chopped cilantro
Olive oil to brush the bread	1½ Tbsp (23 mL) chopped mint
1 large ripe tomato (or two small), diced	2 Tbsp (30 mL) chopped parsley
½ sweet red bell pepper, seeded and diced	¼ cup (60 mL) olive oil
½ sweet yellow bell pepper, seeded and diced	1 Tbsp (15 mL) lemon juice
½ small English cucumber, diced	1 scant Tbsp (14 mL) sherry wine vinegar

* DISCLAIMER. I cannot tell a lie. I did mention the Andean "renowned super-grain" being a cousin to our own lambsquarters, and Third World economies, the butterfly effect, chaos and much much more, earlier in the book.

2 small garlic cloves, minced

Salt and pepper, to taste

¼ cup (60 mL) Macedonian feta or goat cheese

WHAT YOU DO

1   Preheat the oven to 400°F (200°C).

2   Place ¼ cup (60 mL) quinoa in saucepan, add ½ cup (120 mL) water or stock and bring to a boil. Simmer until tender, about 15 minutes. Set aside.

3   While the quinoa is cooking, brush both sides of the bread with a little bit of olive oil and sprinkle with a few pinches of salt. Lay the slices on a baking sheet and bake for about 10 minutes, turning them over halfway through. The bread should be completely dry, and crisp. Remove bread from the oven and allow to cool, and then break by hand into bite-sized pieces.

4   Dice the vegetables and herbs and place in a large bowl. Gently fold in the quinoa and sourdough croutons and add salt and pepper to taste. Sprinkle Macedonian feta or goat cheese over the top, and serve.

PEAR, CRANBERRY AND VANILLA CRUMBLE SERVES 8

I first came upon a version of this recipe in *The Sweet Kitchen* by Regan Daly. Every one of her dessert recipes is fabulous. (If you like to bake, get her book, while quantities last.)

   The pears are sweet enough, and the cranberries, well, they are tiny and tart. It makes for a great juxtaposition (one of my favourite long words—one I actually know the meaning of!)

   I make this dessert year round because I pick the cranberries myself and freeze them. Pears are one thing you can usually buy in Masset, even if you have to buy them a week before they are ready to use.

¾ cup (180 mL) all-purpose flour

¾ cup (180 mL) old-fashioned (slow-cooking) rolled oat flakes

¾ cup (180 mL) loosely packed dark brown sugar

INGREDIENTS CONTINUED . . .

¾ cup (180 mL) butter, cold, cut into small pieces

Seeds of 1 vanilla bean, hull reserved for another use*

¼ cup (60 mL) loosely packed light brown sugar

¼ cup (60 mL) granulated sugar

1 Tbsp (15 mL) cornstarch

¼ tsp (1 mL) ground mace

5–6 medium-sized ripe but firm pears (Bartlett or Anjou)

3 cups (700 mL) fresh cranberries†

WHAT YOU DO

1   Preheat oven to 375°F (190°C). Butter a large 2½ quart (2.5 L) shallow baking dish, preferably ceramic. The trick to the best crumble topping, I read somewhere, is in the fingers. Use your fingers—the warmth of your skin will melt the butter into the right size bits.

2   To make the topping, combine the flour, oats, brown sugar and butter in a mixing bowl and cut together until the largest pieces are about the size of the oats. Use your fingers to rub the ingredients together until the mixture forms crumbly dough. The crumble can be made up to 2 days ahead of time and stored in the refrigerator. (Here we go again with the refrigerator. Why do recipes always say this? Can anyone wait *that* long for dessert?)

3   To make the filling, in a large bowl, stir together the vanilla seeds (or powder and/or extract) sugars, cornstarch and mace.

4   Peel and core the pears and cut them into eighths. Add the pears and cranberries to the mixing bowl with the filling in it, and toss gently to thoroughly coat the fruit.

---

*   I put the used hulls in my sugar container, thus having vanilla-sugar on hand for just about everything I bake. I have substituted vanilla powder in this recipe for the seeds—about ½ tsp (2 mL) with 1 Tbsp (15 mL) vanilla extract. I can never have enough vanilla—so whatever combination you decide to do, depending on your taste for vanilla—will work. (See page 309 for Vanilla Extract).

†   I use wild cranberries from the Haida Gwaii bogs: they are about ⅛ the size of commercial cranberries—like tiny red rubies that are (almost) too exquisite to eat. But the big fat commercial ones work just as well.

5 Scatter the fruit mixture in the baking dish, then crumble the oat mixture over top, distributing it evenly.

6 Bake the crumble for 35–45 minutes for a shallow dish, 45–55 minutes for a deeper casserole, or until the top is crisp and golden and the filling can be seen bubbling up through the cracks.

7 Cool at least 15 minutes before serving, then serve warm or at room temperature with a scoop of ice cream. I'd suggest *Dulce de Leche* Buttermilk Ice Cream. (See recipe page 326)

SUBSTITUTIONS

Regan suggested, "tightly packed brown sugar" but I have changed it to "loosely." I like the word "loosely" better, and I also prefer my desserts on the looser, more tart side.

LEFT: Pear, Cranberry and Vanilla Crumble prep PHOTO BY MICHELLE FURBACHER

TOP RIGHT: Pear, Cranberry and Vanilla Crumble PHOTO BY MICHELLE FURBACHER

BOTTOM RIGHT: Sign (we suspect) courtesy of Ken and Lucille at Haida Rose Café in Old Massett PHOTO BY MICHELLE FURBACHER

Dulce de Leche BUTTERMILK ICE CREAM

SERVES 4

I have combined Smitten Kitchen's Buttermilk Ice Cream and *Dulce de Leche* Ice
Cream recipes to come up with a recipe that is the best of both worlds.

1 cup (240 mL) heavy cream

¾ cup (180 mL) dulce de leche
(purchased, or homemade, see page 327)

6 large egg yolks

1 cup (240 mL) buttermilk

1 Tbsp (15 mL) vanilla or one whole
vanilla bean, scraped and simmered with
the cream

Pinch of salt

Sprinkling of edible gold flake

WHAT YOU DO

1   In a large, heavy saucepan, combine the heavy cream and *dulce de leche* and
bring to a simmer over medium heat.

2   In a large bowl, whisk egg yolks.

3   Remove the cream mixture from the heat and drizzle a small amount into the
yolks, slowly, and whisking constantly to keep the eggs from curdling. Do this
a few more times to warm up the yolks before pouring the yolk mixture back
into the cream, whisking non-stop.

4   Cook over low heat until the mixture is thick enough to coat the back of a spoon.

5   Strain the mixture and whisk in the buttermilk, vanilla and salt. Cool completely and freeze in an ice cream maker according to manufacturer's directions.

6   Serve topped with a sprinkling of edible gold flake.

Dulce de Leche ONE CAN = 1¼ CUPS (300 ML) *DULCE DE LECHE.* I PROCESSED 4 CANS AT ONCE AND GOT 5 CUPS (1.2 L) AND—WHAT ELSE?—FROZE WHAT I DIDN'T USE, FOR FUTURE USE.

When Argentines move to another country, one of the things they miss, aside from their family, is *dulce de leche* (pronounced "DOOL-seh deh LEH-cheh," meaning *candy of milk* or *milk jelly* in Spanish)—a creamy sweet, caramelized milk-and-sugar concoction found in almost every Argentinean pantry. There are many different ways of making it—in a saucepan, in a double boiler, in the microwave, in the oven, in a pressure cooker—the simplest being to heat a tin of sweetened condensed milk in a saucepan of water on top of your stove. The Russians call it "Boiled Condensed Milk" but that's not nearly so poetic as *dulce de leche*.

Dulce de leche is said to have originated in 1829 in the providence of Cañuelas in Buenos Aires (though the French have their own version of its origin dating back to Napoleon's day.) It's a long story involving a war, a couple of generals, a treaty and a maid who forgot the milk boiling on the stove. When things end up burnt in my kitchen there isn't usually a happy ending. My burnt messes never end up starring in a *Winning Desserts of the World* cookbook. They go over the cliff onto the riverbank where the ravens and eagles do daily fly-bys hoping for a fiasco in my kitchen.

300 mL (1¼ cups) can of sweetened condensed milk

WHAT YOU DO

1   Remove the label from the can of condensed milk. If you leave it on, you'll get a papery mess in the water. Yuck.

LEFT: Two eagles PHOTO BY JAGS BROWN; RIGHT: Two ravens PHOTO BY JAGS BROWN

DULCE DE LECHE (CONT'D)

2 Pierce two holes, on opposite sides of the can, with a can opener. Do not skip this step. Without these holes, the can may bulge and there is the danger of it exploding.

3 Place the can in a small saucepan and fill it with enough water to come up to 1 inch (2.5 cm) from the top of the can. You will need to add more water during the cooking process to make sure water doesn't go below this level as it evaporates. Don't let the water come higher than ½ inch (1 cm) from the top of can, though, as you don't want any getting on the top of the can and seeping into the holes you pierced. Another mess in the water. Yuck again.

4 To prevent the can from rattling in the water (which I would find extremely annoying considering it is likely to be rattling for at least 3 hours) put a cloth (a face cloth will do) under the can.

5 Place the pot on your stove and turn it on to medium-high heat. Watch the water closely until you see it come to a simmer.

6 Lower the heat to hold the water at a simmer. Some of the condensed milk might escape through the holes. If this happens, scoop it off with a spoon. Try not to let any spill over into the water. (Remember how I warned about a mess?)

7   Wait. And wait some more. How long you wait depends on the type of *dulce de leche* you want. A soft *dulce de leche* takes about 3 hours. A firm *dulce de leche* will take up to 4 hours.

8   Remove the can with tongs and place on a rack to cool.

9   Open the can carefully with a can opener and pour into a bowl. The top will be more fluid, and there will be thicker, darker chunks at the bottom that will need to be scraped out. When everything is in the bowl, whisk together to make it homogeneous and smooth.

ASIDE: EDIBLE GOLD LEAF

"Gold to airy thinness beat."
—from *Clockwork Prince* by Cassandra Clare

Gold leaf is typically sold either in sheets or as flakes. I use the flakes to sprinkle over ice cream and over icing on cakes. It makes me feel decadent to toss a handful (well, okay, a pinchful) on top of some unprepossessing dessert, such as Wild Rose Petal Ice Cream. (Of course, there is nothing unprepossessing about Wild Rose Petal Ice Cream. I admit, I am possessed.)

If you are worried about ingesting heavy metals, gold is considered "biologically inert," meaning it passes through the digestive tract without being absorbed. When selecting your gold leaf, make sure to get gold that is as pure as possible—at least 22–24 carats. Personally, I prefer mine to be 100 carats. I don't think they've made a gold that pure yet, but I remain ever hopeful.) Gold leaf with a smaller carat value has more impurities and is less safe to eat. If you buy gold leaf that is clearly labeled as "edible" and has 22–24 carats, eating gold leaf is not likely to shorten your lifespan. In fact, you will probably live even longer due to the sheer state of bliss into which your body will slip after ingesting as-pure-as-possible edible gold flake.

MENU #4 (VEGETARIAN)

Kale Three Ways:
Kale Crunch, Wilted Kale Salad with Hazelnuts, Cheesy Kale, Chips
Cauliflower Popcorn

❋ ❋ ❋ ❋ ❋

Copper Beech House Chowder

❋ ❋ ❋ ❋ ❋

Fig, Anise, Hazelnut and Gorgonzola Sourdough

❋ ❋ ❋ ❋ ❋

Pasta with Squash, Leeks, Cranberries and Spruce Tip Citrus-Cream

❋ ❋ ❋ ❋ ❋

Crunchy Cabbage and Sugar Pea Salad with Sesame Miso Dressing

❋ ❋ ❋ ❋ ❋

Haida Gwaii Three Berry Pie
and/or
Cream Cheese Sorbet

THE RECIPES

KALE THREE WAYS

KALE CRUNCH SERVES 4 AS A SNACK OR APPETIZER

1 bunch kale	Sprinkling of salt
1 Tbsp (15 mL) olive oil	⅓ cup (80 mL) grated Parmesan or more

WHAT YOU DO

1   Preheat over to 375°F (190°C).

2   Rinse the kale and pat dry with a tea towel. Regular, mature kale works perfectly well in this recipe. Save the baby kale for salad or substitute it for lambsquarters in dishes such as Lambsquarters with Shallots and Fried Capers page 303, where you want a smoother-textured green. Remove the insufficiently succulent stems and slice the rest into smallish pieces. Massage the pieces to make them more tender, if you wish.

3   Toss with oil and salt.

4   Roast in oven for 15 minutes.

5   Sprinkle cheese over kale.

6   Bake for a further 10–15 minutes. Cheese should be melted, and the kale slightly browned and crispy.

SUBSTITUTION

Most of the time I use grated Parmesan, but found that Havarti with dill gives the kale an extra lift so now use it instead when I have it on hand.

WILTED KALE SALAD WITH HAZELNUTS SERVES 4 AS A SNACK OR APPETIZER

1 bunch kale	⅓ cup (80 mL) hazelnuts
Salt and pepper, to taste	¼ cup (60 mL) olive oil
2 tsp (10 mL) balsamic vinegar	

WHAT YOU DO

1 Rinse the kale and pat dry with a tea towel. Remove the stems and chop the rest into smallish pieces.

2 Put the chopped kale in a bowl and sprinkle with salt, pepper and the balsamic vinegar. Toss well.

3 Roughly chop the hazelnuts.

4 Heat olive oil in a frying pan and let the nuts sizzle until they begin to brown. Pour the hot oil and nuts over the kale and give it another toss until the kale wilts: guaranteed you will eat this right out of the bowl before it even gets to the table.

CHEESY KALE CHIPS SERVES 4 AS A SNACK OR APPETIZER

Shirley and Gord Kricheldorf and their family went on a raw food diet for a while after watching a video about factory farming they found at the library. Shirley invited me for a raw pizza night and I was expecting, well, uncooked pizza dough with celery and carrot sticks on top and wondered how I was going to get through the evening (I took several bottles of wine for courage and fortification.) I needn't have worried. Shirley made some of the best food I had ever tasted. Every bite was an explosion of flavour in the mouth and I would have turned to raw food myself except that Shirley said it had taken her three full days of preparation to not-cook our meal that night.

Shirley's Cheesy Kale Chips (which has no cheese in it, by the way—the "cheesy" flavour comes from nutritional yeast) is the snack Gord takes with him to the beach (along with a flask of rum and cranberry juice for health purposes) when we go on a tsunami-debris collecting party, or when he goes with the men to cut firewood or shoot a deer on East Beach.

1 large bunch of kale

1 cup (240 mL) cashews, (soaked 2 hours, then drained)

1 red bell pepper, seeded and chopped

¼ cup (60 mL) olive oil

3 Tbsp (45 mL) freshly squeezed lemon juice

1 Tbsp (15 mL) agave or honey

⅓ cup (80 mL) nutritional yeast

¼ tsp (1 mL) turmeric powder

½ tsp (2 mL) salt

¼–½ cup water (60–125 mL)—enough to make thick but creamy consistency

WHAT YOU DO

1   Rinse the kale and spin dry. Remove the stems and tear into bite size pieces. Let the kale air out as much as possible before coating so the seasoning-mixture will stick to the leaves. (As in the other recipes, pat dry with a tea towel.)

2   To make the seasoning mixture, blend all the other ingredients in a food processor until smooth.

3   Transfer kale and blended ingredients to a large bowl and mix well using your hands to ensure the leaves are thoroughly coated.

4   Place the kale on dehydrator trays; dehydrate at 115°F (46°C) overnight (8–12 hours).

5   If you don't own a dehydrator, or can't borrow one, preheat your oven to its lowest setting. Line several baking sheets with parchment paper. Place kale pieces on baking sheets allowing space between each piece so they do not touch or overlap. Reserve any remaining kale and refrigerate, covered, until first batch has finished baking. Bake kale until crisp and completely dry, between 2 and 4 hours. Check after the first hour and turn leaves over, and after that check periodically. Chips will be ready when crunchy and stiff and topping doesn't feel chewy or moist.

TIP: To keep your Kale Chips crunchy, take a small fabric bag or a piece of cheesecloth and fill it with uncooked rice (if using the latter make sure the rice is tied up in the cheesecloth so none of it can escape.) Place it and the kale in an airtight glass container and seal with a lid. The rice soaks up any extra moisture in the container.

CAULIFLOWER POPCORN

SERVES 2–4 AS A SNACK OR APPETIZER

Cauliflower from Lynda Osborne's garden PHOTO BY MARK BRISTOL

I found this recipe in Bob Blumer's delightful *Surreal Gourmet Bites*. Bob suggests serving this dish in an empty movie popcorn container but a) we have no movie theatres on Haida Gwaii, b) even if we did I would not buy popcorn because it is too expensive and c) even if I could afford to splurge on popcorn I would almost certainly not remember to take home the empty movie theatre popcorn container to serve my cauliflower in.

I usually open the oven door, slide the cauliflower out onto a plate, and start picking away, usually burning my fingers in the process, but not feeling the pain. There is no point making this dish as an accompaniment to a main dish; it will definitely not last that long once your roasted cauliflower is out of the oven and anywhere within taste-sight, if you know what I mean.

1 head cauliflower	1½ tsp (7 mL)* salt
¼ cup (60 mL) olive oil	

WHAT YOU DO

1 Preheat oven to 450°F (230°C).

2 Trim the cauliflower: Pull off any outer leaves and cut off the protruding stem end close to the head. Cut remaining cauliflower into florets the size of golf balls, or smaller, which I often do because I don't like the idea of eating anything to do with golf.

3 In a large bowl add the cauliflower, oil and salt. Toss thoroughly.

4 Spread cauliflower on a baking sheet lined with parchment paper. Roast 45 minutes if the florets are small, 60 minutes if golf-ball size, or until each floret has become golden brown. The caramelization process will convert the dormant natural sugars into sweetness, into "sweet, lip-smackin' candy bombs" (thanks, Bob!). The browner the florets, the sweeter they will taste. Turn 2 or 3 times during roasting.

---

* Bob suggests 1 Tbsp (15 mL) salt. I have tried it that way because I really like salt, but I think it is just as good with a little less. I suppose if your head of cauliflower is huge, something closer to a tablespoon of salt would be good. But organic heads are usually much smaller, and of course more expensive, especially on Haida Gwaii. It is crucial to cultivate friends with gardens.

COPPER BEECH HOUSE CLAM (OR WITHOUT CLAM) CHOWDER SERVES 8–10

"Chowder breathes reassurance. It steams consolation."
—from *Charles Wysocki's Americana Cookbook* by Clementine Paddleford

Chowder is one of those things that never tastes the same twice. Or shouldn't, in my view. If we wanted a soup that tasted "the same" each time we would buy Campbell's Clam Chowder in a tin, wouldn't we? Not that there is anything wrong with Campbell's soups: my favourite for years was Campbell's Cream of Asparagus. My old dad would arrive in time for lunch (usually when I was in the middle of a really tricky scene in some novel I was beating myself up over) with a can of Asparagus Soup in a brown paper bag, and we would sit and eat and not have much to say except how much we both enjoyed a good bowl of Campbell's Cream of Asparagus soup. I think it cost thirty-seven cents in those days.

But my family never "splurged" on store-bought soups. These were the days when, once a week, all the leftovers in the fridge were dumped (I use the word advisedly) in the stockpot and cooked until what remained of the flavours were gone. I believe the recipe was called the Cleaning Out the Fridge Soup. My great-aunt Polly used to save all her vegetable water to make her soups, and one day I came home from my short-lived day job in the south of England (I was let go for allowing a young man to try on a sequined cat suit and model it for all the other shoppers over my boss's lunch break) to find there was nothing for lunch that day because Aunt Polly had mistakenly added the water, in which she boiled her handkerchiefs, to the split pea soup.

Back to the chowder. "Clam chowder is one of those subjects, like politics or religion that can never be discussed lightly. Bring it up even incidentally, and all the innumerable factions of the clam bake regions raise their heads and begin to yammer," wrote Louis P. De Gouy, in *The Soup Book* (1949) (a book my mother might have received as a wedding gift—my parents were married in 1949—and quite possibly the source of the Cleaning Out the Fridge Soup, come to think of it.) (Thanks, Louis P. De Gouy, for a wrecked childhood.)

I intimated (in the title) that this was going to be a Clam Chowder, or that it could be—if you have razor clams handy, or the small juicy clams scarcely bigger than hazelnuts, the ones Herman Melville enthused over in *Moby Dick*. But I prefer my chowder without seafood, so I add the optional smoked salmon, clams, halibut and things that other people like, at the end. Recipes should be suggestions or guidelines (much as I view stop signs) not rules—especially when it comes to making soup.

Chowder PHOTO BY MICHELLE FURBACHER

Kayley Redgers first made a version of this clam chowder in the summer of 2012 at Copper Beech House (she added the smoked paprika, among other things). She found a recipe online, from the famous Red Fish Blue Fish restaurant in Victoria, British Columbia, my granddaughters' favourite place to eat fish tacos. I have cut back on the heat (hot sauce and chipotle puree) because some people don't like spicy food. (The original recipe called for ¼ cup chipotle puree!) But the heat, the spice, is what makes this chowder so different from any other I've tasted.

¼ cup (60 mL) olive oil

2 Tbsp (30 mL) canola oil

2 Tbsp (30 mL) toasted ground cumin

2 Tbsp (30 mL) toasted ground coriander

1 tsp (5 mL) salt

Freshly ground black pepper, to taste

3 cups (700 mL) diced potatoes

6 cloves of garlic, chopped fine

3 cups (700 mL) carrots, diced

3 cups (700 mL) celery, diced

3 cups (700 mL) leeks and/or onions, chopped

1 bunch cilantro stalks, minced

¼ cup (60 mL) garlic scapes (optional)

½ cup (120 mL) sweet chili sauce

1 Tbsp (15 mL) Worcestershire sauce

1 Tbsp (15 mL) smoked paprika

1½ tsp (7 mL) hot sauce

½–1 tsp (2–5 mL) chipotle puree (optional)

1 12-oz can (350 mL) corn niblets

1 cup (240 mL) clam nectar (optional)

3 tins coconut milk or coconut cream

¼–½ lb (110–250 g) whitefish (cod or halibut) chopped into small pieces (optional)

¼ lb (110 g) smoked salmon, chopped into pieces (optional)

1 cup (240 mL) clams (or more) cut into small pieces

2 cups (475 mL) fresh sautéed chanterelles, or 1 cup (240 mL) previously frozen and thawed

¼ cup (60 mL) cilantro and/or green onion for garnish

WHAT YOU DO

1   Toast (brown) cumin and coriander in olive oil and canola oil mixture. Add sea salt and pepper. Set aside.

2   In a separate pot, parboil potatoes and set aside.

3   Sauté onions and/or leeks, celery, carrots and cilantro stalks for 5–10 minutes in oil. When vegetables are slightly soft, clear a space in the middle and add your minced garlic. Cook for another 30–40 seconds until you can smell the garlic. Stir all the vegetables together, along with the toasted spice mixture.

4   Add sweet chili sauce, Worcestershire sauce, smoked paprika; hot sauce and chipotle puree (if you are using it). Add all remaining ingredients.

5   Simmer for half an hour or longer.

6   Ten minutes before serving, add the optional cod or halibut, smoked salmon—or sautéed chanterelles. And, of course, finely diced razor clams. Or any kind of clams you have on hand. Simmer for 10 minutes.

7   You can use leftover, previously cooked fish, too, but you don't want the seafood overcooked, so sprinkle it over the top of the soup before serving. Garnish with the cilantro leaves and green onion.

TIP: One of my Haida friends makes the best chowder I've tasted (next to this one.) His secret? He adds to his chowder the biggest can of Campbell's Cream of Asparagus soup money can buy.

PASTA WITH SQUASH, LEEKS, CRANBERRIES AND SPRUCE TIP CITRUS-CREAM
ADAPTED FROM THE *REBAR MODERN FOOD COOKBOOK*
SERVES 4

When I was a kid, pasta was not called pasta; it was called spaghetti, even if it was linguine, fettuccine, penne or what my own kids came up with when I experimented with different kinds of pasta in the '80s: *vermincelli*. The exceptions were

Geoff Horner's ravioli PHOTOS
BY GEOFF HORNER

macaroni and cheese, which my mother made from scratch, and ravioli, which came in a tin and had the exotic, European sounding name of Chef Boyardee. I didn't know you could make your own spaghetti, and that the Italians had been doing so for thousands of years. The spaghetti I grew up with was dry and came in a box. If you ate it raw it would absorb all your stomach juices and you would blow up. Same thing with another ethnic food: rice. So we were warned.

Knowing that I might explode and make a terrible mess for my mother to have to clean up stopped me from sneaking into the cupboard for a handful of raw rice when I felt peckish, but I admit I sometimes thought of experimenting on my siblings.

A person with more time on their hands would make their own pasta* but it ain't me, babe. I have my limits. (I don't make homemade marshmallows, either, remember?) I'd rather be out in the woods picking wild mushrooms than stuck in a kitchen stuffing my booty into little squares of ravioli. (That didn't come out right. I think "booty" nowadays conjures up something that wouldn't easily be stuffed . . . nevermind . . . on to the recipe.)

2 cups (475 mL) butternut squash, ¼ inch (6 mm) dice	2 Tbsp (30 mL) dried cranberries or ¼ cup wild cranberries
	INGREDIENTS CONTINUED . . .

*   After I had written these words I got a text from my friend and neighbour Geoff Horner inviting me to dinner to try his homemade ravioli. Later in the day, Meredith Adams, who lives off-the-grid and doesn't have a pasta maker, called to say she was making homemade ravioli: teach me to make brash statements about time on one's hands and having limits! I suggested my friends bring their creations to my house for a ravioli-fest. Geoff's ravioli included calendula and nasturtium petals rolled into the dough, a technique he learned from an Italian friend who had used rose petals: another use for Nootka roses in the spring!

1½ cups (350 mL) white wine or vermouth, divided

1 lb (500 g) assorted mushrooms*

1 Tbsp (15 mL) butter

2 Tbsp (30 mL) olive oil, divided

1 tsp (5 mL) + a pinch of salt

4 garlic cloves, minced

2 large leeks, white and light green parts only

4 shallots, chopped fine

1 bay leaf

Juice of 1 orange

Juice of 1 lemon

Zest of 1 orange

1 tsp (5 mL) freshly ground black pepper

1½ cups (350 mL) whipping cream

3 Tbsp (45 mL) spruce tips

3 Tbsp (45 mL) minced chives

1 lb (500 g) pasta (*Rebar* suggests wild mushroom ravioli†)

¼–½ cup (60–125 mL) grated Parmesan

¼ cup (60 mL) hazelnuts, roasted, skinned and chopped

WHAT YOU DO

1   Lightly steam the squash until just tender. Place the cranberries in a small bowl and add the ¼ cup (60 mL) wine or vermouth. Set aside.

2   Dry cook the mushrooms in a skillet until most of the water has evaporated, then add butter, 1 Tbsp (15 mL) oil and a pinch of salt. Stir, cover the pan and let the mushrooms continue to cook down. Remove the lid; add the garlic, and sauté until the mushrooms are golden. Transfer to a bowl and set aside.

3   Heat the remaining olive oil in the skillet and add leeks, shallots, bay leaf and remaining salt. Sauté until soft. Next add the wine or vermouth, citrus juices and zest and pepper. Reduce the liquid by half; add the cream and bring to a full simmer.

*   You can use any combination of bolete, oyster, shiitake, hedgehogs or just chanterelles.

Spaghetti

BIG JIM Colosimo (1871–1920) was head crime lord of Chicago for a time, providing protection for a couple of whorehouse madames. When a problem arose Big Jim would arrive juggling jars of spaghetti and his own homemade tomato sauce. While the girls gave him the 411, he would make them a pasta they couldn't refuse. Then he sat down with them to "swallow the clothesline."

ILLUSTRATION BY DEJAHLEE BUSCH

4   When the sauce has thickened slightly, add the steamed squash, cranberries (with liquid), sautéed mushrooms, spruce tips and chives and allow them to heat through. Season with additional salt and pepper. Cover and keep warm.

5   Heat a large pot of water for the pasta. When the water has boiled, *butta la pasta* ("throw in the pasta") and cook until *al dente* ("to the tooth").

6   Drain pasta, toss with olive oil or butter to lightly coat. Serve topped with sauce, grated Parmesan, hazelnuts and extra spruce tips or chives.

SUBSTITUTIONS

You can use sage in lieu of spruce tips.

CRUNCHY CABBAGE AND SUGAR PEA SALAD WITH SESAME MISO DRESSING

4–5 SERVINGS

There are many versions of this Asian-influenced salad on the Internet and in cookbooks. This recipe is lightly adapted from the *Smitten Kitchen Cookbook*, which, as you may have guessed, is a favourite source of mine.

---

†   The authors of *Rebar* say wild mushroom ravioli is available at specialty markets. Nothing like that here on Haida Gwaii, though I have found fresh butternut squash, spinach, and three cheese ravioli at the Co-Op: move over, Chef Boyardee! When the fresh pasta has sold out, I have substituted all different kinds of shapes and sizes of pasta for this recipe. Recently I used La Tour d'Eiffel shaped pasta when I cooked for my daughter Charlotte, who has had a life-long love affair with Paris.

FOR THE TOPPING

¼ cup (60 mL) butter

¼ cup (60 mL) sugar

½ cup (120 mL) flour

WHAT YOU DO

1 Combine graham cracker crumbs with melted butter. I don't add sugar, as most recipes suggest you do. I do add cinnamon, but only if I'm in the mood.

2 Pat into pie plate and set in freezer to chill until ready for use.

3 Preheat over to 400°F (200°C).

4 Mix the sugar, cornstarch, lemon juice and cinnamon and toss the berries in this mixture until they are evenly coated. Let this sit for 15 minutes or more. The sugar will coax the juice from the berries and create liquid which will dissolve the cornstarch.

5 Whilst the juice is being coaxed from the berries, whisk together the heavy cream, sugar, eggs and pinch of salt.

6 Mix these wet ingredients into the berries.

7 Pour into chilled crumb-crust, dot with butter.

8 Combine butter, sugar and flour and sprinkle over the top of the filling.

9 Bake at 400°F (200°C) for 20 minutes.

10 Turn oven down to 350°F (180°C) and bake until topping is nicely browned and the filling appears set, another 40–45 minutes.

CREAM CHEESE SORBET MAKES 1 QUART

I first tasted this at the Emerald Lake Lodge in the Rocky Mountains—served with a wedge of Bumbleberry Pie. I asked the chef for the recipe and he

More Pie, Please

"I had a vision that a man came unto us on a flaming pie, and he said, 'You are Beatles with an A.' And so we were."
—John Lennon

"Picture your grandmother in Hell, baking pies ... without an oven."
—George Carlin

"Another day, another dollar. I'm tired and I want pie."
—Unknown

obliged—but the amounts were enormous—20 pounds of cream cheese, that sort of enormous—so I have scaled it so you end up with a quart of creamy bliss, not a walk-in freezer full.

2 cups (475 mL) sugar	Juice of 1 lb (500 g) limes or ½ cup (120 mL) lime juice
2 cups (475 mL) water	1½ tsp (7 mL) vanilla extract
2 lb (1 kg) cream cheese, room temperature	½ tsp (2 mL) salt

WHAT YOU DO

1 Place cream cheese in a bowl and beat vigorously with a wooden spoon until smooth. (You could also put it in a food processor, but there's all that cleaning afterwards.)

2 Bring sugar and water to a boil in a 2-quart (8 L) saucepan over high heat, and cook, stirring, until sugar dissolves.

3 Remove from the heat and slowly drizzle into cream cheese, whisking constantly to avoid lumps.

4 Stir in lime juice, vanilla and salt until smooth; chill for 1 hour.

5 Process in an ice cream maker according to manufacturer's instructions.

MAIN COURSES

Farhad-fairly-caught-fillets of Wild Halibut
with Sesame Breadcrumb Topping
Served on a Bed of Sangan River Sea Asparagus
Roast of Venison
Prepared by Archie Stocker Sr.
Chipper's Venison Surprise:
Name the Ingredients and Win $5,000 Award*
Vancouver Island Kentucky-Blue Green Beans
Rick Grange's Tow Hill Road Carrots-in-Their-Infancy
Gourmet Potato Salad with Caramelized Onions by Charlotte

DESSERTS

Miss Wyoming's Mango Fandango
Sophie's Sweet as Apple Pie
Hand-Flagellated Cream Infused with Orange Flower Water

CHEESE

Comox Camembert with Sangan River Coulis of Thimbleberry
Soft Surface Ripened Moonstruck Organic Baby Blue
English White Stilton with Lemon
French Morbier
Daniel's Organic Impressively True to Nature Dark Orange Chocolate

There isn't space in this book to include all the recipes from this typical Haida Gwaii feast, but there is one I will share here because it is a good way to end a book. A interviewer once asked me, "What would you like to be remembered for?" My answer was—my red pepper jam.

---

*   Pepsi Cola—no one guessed.

RED PEPPER JAM 4 PINTS (1.9 L)

3 large red bell peppers

5½ cups (1.3 L) sugar

1 cup (240 mL) apple cider vinegar

⅓ cup (80 mL) freshly squeezed lemon juice

One 3-oz pouch liquid pectin

WHAT YOU DO

1   Wash and cut into quarters 3 large red peppers. Dry them off, remove seeds and then grind the pieces in a food processor.

2   Place in heavy saucepan with sugar and apple cider vinegar. Heat until boiling, stirring constantly.

3   Remove from heat. Let stand 15 minutes.

Moon over Naikoon PHOTO BY GUY KIMOA

4   Reheat to boiling. Add lemon juice. Boil 2 minutes.

5   Add liquid pectin.

6   Remove from heat. Stir for 5 minutes.

7   Seal in sterilized jars (important) (I don't use a hot water bath to process—the vinegar ensures this doesn't get mouldy, but make sure the jars and lids are very very hot.)

ADDITIONS

For spicier jam add hot chili sauce, crushed red pepper flakes or diced jalapeños to taste.

EPILOGUE

AN EXCLUDED SORT OF PLACE

As I crumple an old newspaper to light a fire in the wood stove, an item catches my eye. Every day a teacher, Yang Zhengxue, treks an hour and a half up and down craggy peaks in a remote corner of southern China to reach his students who live high on a mountain ridge in a limestone cave, "an almost prehistoric habitat without electricity, running water or any other amenity that would identify it as a home for residents of the 21st century."

Sounds like home sweet home to me. The newspaper is dated December 11, 2003, but the news hasn't changed much. Weapons of mass misery, genocide, political blunderings—the so-called real world seems a long way from these misty,

mystical isles. Here, in the wilderness, I encounter a different sense of time, where my days fail to follow orderly paths, unfolding instead in unpredictable ways. I reset my body and mind to a cosmic time frame, plan my activities around the incoming and outgoing tides, the rising and setting sun.

There is no such concept as *mañana* on Haida Gwaii; no word exists for that kind of urgency. A tourist once stopped for Buddy—a local character who spent his days walking the five miles, back and forth, between Skidegate and Queen Charlotte

Race in progress PHOTO BY GUY KIMOLA

City (as it was called before it lost its "city" designation due to not having a large enough population)—and asked him if he needed a ride. "No thanks," Buddy replied, "I'm in a hurry."

There's limited cell phone service here, few schedules to keep. Pockets of these Islands missed the last ice age, but some of my technological pioneering friends have recently joined the 21st century and bought transistor radios, so they can find out the current time by tuning in to the CBC.

Truth moves to the heart as slowly as a glacier, and that's how time moves here, also. I've been waiting at the side of the road with a garbage bag full of dirty laundry for most of the morning (my truck has a dead battery); the first fisherman to come by in his half ton, stops. I settle into a pile of gill nets on the seat beside him, and then ask if he has the time.

"I used to wear a watch," he says, "but I lost it in the winch." He shows me an empty sleeve.

A school bus full of llamas, their heads poking out the open windows, draws up in front of the Laundromat, where the fisherman deposits me. Nobody gives the llamas a second look—they're used to it, just as people are used to living with wild and unpredictable weather.

"But doesn't it rain *all* the time up there?" a friend, planning a visit from Vancouver, writes. Well, yes, it raineth. In fact the rain falls so hard here, sometimes, it bounces off the ground then goes back up.

It's no surprise that the windshield wipers on my pickup have a life of their own. Even if the rain lets up, and I reach to switch them off, they don't miss a beat.

There'd be no point trying to get the wipers fixed. Once when my father came to visit from Victoria, we ended up having the inevitable discussion about "island time." Dad said even on Vancouver Island these days you couldn't expect to get anything done in a hurry. He had taken his radio to an electrician two weeks ago and he still hadn't got it fixed. "That's nothing," said my elderly neighbour, Frieda Unsworth. "I took my car to a mechanic in Masset seven years ago and I haven't got it back yet."

Masset's the kind of small town where you recognize everyone by the vehicle they drive. The Government Liquor Store employees can tell you what anybody in town drinks, also, and whether they've been drinking too much, lately, for their own good. When I first moved to the Islands, in the early '70s, the Masset Liquor

Store had a guest book, and visitors were asked to sign the book after purchasing their commodity, "Sometimes I sign it twice a day myself," a friend, working at Copper Beech House said. (Comments in the Guest Book ranged from "excellent liquor" and "Drunk, 7-24-98 10:23 a.m. Wolf Parnell" to "The wine here is cheaper than the gas.")

When people find out where I live they often ask, "Don't you feel isolated, living out there, away from it all?" I even had a taxi driver in Toronto ask me if I came from an "excluded" sort of place. (I should add from the point of view of a Haida Gwaiilander, it is the *rest of the world* that is remote. Perhaps that is being Haida Gwaii-centric?)

Living in seclusion, or exclusion if you like, does have advantages. People are forced, by circumstances, to be polite to one another. You can't risk running the local undertaker off the road because he turns in front of you without signalling: you may need his expertise one day.

Chances are you know where he's headed, even if he forgets to indicate. Living on an island you never *have* to use your turn signals: everyone knows where you are going, anyway.

On Haida Gwaii everybody knows where you've *been*, also. They know what you do for a living, and who you are married to—at the moment. For this reason I always try to behave myself when I go to town. I'm especially well behaved in the post office, because the last person I want to alienate is the person who sorts my important registered mail.

At the north end of the world, home to any number of social misfits who have fled from the normal stresses of 21st century living, the barter system is alive and well. If you want *all* your garbage hauled away, you leave a reefer on top of your can as an incentive for the local collector.

Life is simple, here, pared down to the bare necessities. There is only one traffic light, for instance, and few other signs giving directions. There *is* a sign announcing WIGGINS ROAD AHEAD, a few meters before you come to Wiggins Road itself, and that tells you something about the frequency of side roads off the highway connecting Queen Charlotte with Masset. And then there was the WILDLIFE VIEWING sign underneath the one indicating "Masset Cemetery Road." From

Masset Cemetery PHOTO BY MICHELLE FURBACHER

what I remember of the people who are now permanent residents in the graveyard, "wild life" viewing would be an understatement.

The graveyard is one of the places I like to spend quiet time, though. The trees drip moss, the graves themselves are overgrown with salal, salmonberry bushes and more moss. I haven't chosen the precise spot, but one day I expect to take up residence there myself. "Everybody loves that graveyard," said my friend Henry White, as I helped him undecorate his Christmas tree on the Ides of March. "One guy even *hanged* himself in there."

The simple life gets busy here. Between cleaning crabs, gutting deer, canning razor clams and picking huckleberries for pie, I finally find time to finish the article about Yang Zhengxue and the limestone cave dwellers. The only modern appliance they possess is a battery operated red plastic alarm clock. Twice a day its owner lets it chirp on and on, for 45 minutes or more—"not to tell the time, but to entertain, like music from a Stone Age radio."

Those cave dwellers sound too high tech for me. But no place to me compares to living where can you see multiple rainbows in the sky, or count 25 eagles perched on the same rock, or lie out under the stars in August and watch the Perseids meteor shower, the Northern Lights *and* forked lightning all at the same time. When the storms start howling and the plane doesn't come in, and the ferry is stuck in Prince Rupert and supplies are running low in the Co-Op and the Government Liquor Store, there's no place on this earth I'd rather be.

Stephen Reid, the solemnizer's husband, finally released from prison, August 2014, Yakan Point PHOTO BY GUY KIMOLA

FOR FURTHER READING

CHAPTER 1: FOR STARTERS

"Haida Gwaii: Where is it?" virtualmuseum.ca

The Raven Steals the Light by Bill Reid and Robert Bringhurst.

"Ondaatje on the Hook: The Poet as Restaurant Critic" can be read in its entirety in *You're in Canada Now . . . Motherfucker: A Memoir of Sorts* by Susan Musgrave.

Stalking the Wild Asparagus by Euell Theophilus Gibbons.

"Foraging for Food," *Martha Stewart Living*, August 2011. www.marthastewart.com

Wild Harvest: Edible Plants of the Pacific Northwest by Terry Domico.

The Wild Table: Seasonal Foraged Food and Recipes by Connie Green; recipes by Sarah Scott.

Fat of the Land: Adventures of a 21st Century Forager by Langdon Cook. fat-of-the-land.blogspot.com

Edible Wild Plants: Wild Foods From Dirt To Plate by John Kallas.

"A Bushel and a Peck" by Patricia Marx. *The New Yorker.* January 12, 2012.

CHAPTER 2: BREAKFAST AT COPPER BEECH HOUSE

"The Copper Beech House, 92 years later" by April Johnson. *The Observer.* September 14, 2006

Jeff in Venice, Death in Varanasi by Geoff Dyer.

"Cilantro Haters It's Not Your Fault" by Harold McGee ("The Curious Cook"), *The New York Times.* April 13, 2010.

"Beneath the Salt" *The Oxford Companion to Food* by Alan Davidson.

Various Articles under "The Yoghurt Wars" tag by Hamilton Nolan. gawker.com

The Penguin Cookery Book by Bee Nilson.

Extra Virginity: The Sublime and Scandalous World of Olive Oil by Tom Mueller.

CHAPTER 3: FROM THE FORAGE OF THE OVEN

King Arthur Flour's blog, *Flourish.* kingarthurflour.com/blog/

Tartine Bread by Chad Robertson.

Obituary of Light: the Sangan River Meditations by Susan Musgrave.

The Boreal Gourmet: Adventures in Northern Cooking by Michele Genest.

CHAPTER 4: FOOD GATHERING THE YEAR ROUND

Common Edible Seaweeds in the Gulf of Alaska by Dolly Garza.

"Snipping seaweed for nutrition and profit" from *Northword Magazine*. April 7, 2011.

"Sea Asparagus" by Jacqueline M, Newman, writing in *Vegetables and Vegetarian Foods. Spring Volume: 2007.*

Plants of Haida Gwaii by Nancy Turner.

The Boreal Herbal: Wild Food and Medicinal Plants of the North by Beverley Gray.

Falling Cloudberries: A World of Family Recipes by Tessa Kiros.

During My Time: Florence Edenshaw Davidson, A Haida Woman by Margaret Blackman.

Wild Berries of the Northwest by J. Duane Sept.

Eating Wildly: Foraging for Life, Love, and the Perfect Meal by Ava Chin. www.avachin.com/eating-wildly/

How to Be a Domestic Goddess by Nigella Lawson.

To the Charlottes: George Dawson's 1878 Survey of the Queen Charlotte Islands by George Mercer Dawson.

The Outer Spores: Mushrooms of Haida Gwaii by Paul Kroeger, Bryce Kendrick, Oluna Ceska and Christine Roberts.

CHAPTER 5: HARVESTING THE LAND AND THE SEA

The Beginner's Guide to Hunting Deer for Food by Jackson Landers.

Cargo of Orchids by Susan Musgrave.

Pain and Possibility: Writing Your Way through Personal Crisis by Gabriele Rico.

The Green Shadow by Andrew Struthers.

The Joy of Cooking by Irma S. Rombauer, Marion Rombauer Becker and Ethan Becker.

Stalking the Blue-Eyed Scallop by Euell Gibbons.

A Cook Book with a Difference: Good Food, Memories, Drawings from George Mercer Dawson Secondary School in Masset.

Camus: West Coast Cooking Nuu-chah-nulth Style by The Nuu-chah-nulth Tribal Council.

Salmon and Woman: the Feminine Angle by Peter Behan, Wilma Paterson.

The Fishes & Dishes Cookbook: Seafood Recipes and Salty Stories from Alaska's Commercial Fisherwomen by Kiyo Marsh, Tomi Marsh and Laura Cooper.

The Salmon Recipes: Stories of Our Endangered North Coast Cuisine, edited by Luanne Roth.

CHAPTER 7: A ROGUE'S GALLERY

Montreal's Irish Mafia by Danny O'Connell.
The Mafia Encyclopedia by Carl Sifakis.

CHAPTER 8: DINNER ON THE DECK

The Rituals of Dinner by Margaret Visser.
The Silver Palate Good Times Cookbook by Julee Rosso, Sheila Lukins and Sarah
    Leah Chase.
Rebar Modern Food Cookbook by Audrey Alsterburg and Wanda Urbanowicz.
Given by Susan Musgrave.
All Families are Psychotic by Douglas Coupland.
The Charcoal Burners by Susan Musgrave.
Vegetarian Pleasures: A Menu Cookbook by Jeanne Lemlim.
The Smitten Kitchen Cookbook by Deb Perelman and the Smitten Kitchen Blog.
    smittenkitchen.com
Plenty by Yotam Ottolenghi.
In the Sweet Kitchen: The Definitive Baker's Campanion. By Regan Daley.
Surreal Gourmet Bites by Bob Blumer.
Moby Dick by Herman Melville.

EPILOGUE

Haida Dictionary, Volumes 1 and 2, compiled by John Enrico.

ACKNOWLEDGEMENTS

Putting this book together has been a humbling experience. As soon as I began to write about anything we eat, I learned how little I know. I realized how much I counted on others (who could, of course, being human, be fallible, misguided, or misinformed) and not on just knowledge gleaned from the numerous books (which, being written by humans, could be fallible, misguided or misinformed) I devoured in an attempt to "get things right."

In a few cases I have included the Haida names for the plants, animals and fish who have been foraged or feasted upon in this book. I have found many different Haida spellings and refer readers to Todd deVries haidalanguage.blogspot.com: Íihlxaadas húus xíinaangslaang, which includes a page on "how to pronounce Haida." ("We Haida's are coming alive again.") Nancy Turner is the authority, in my opinion, when it comes to the Haida names of plants; please refer to her *Plants of Haida Gwaii*. John Enrico's 2 volume *Haida Dictionary* is also a treasure trove.

I have found that Haida spellings change, and have changed quite radically in the 40-odd years I have been here. It is certainly not my intention to offend or upset anybody by spelling a word "the wrong way," and I apologize, in advance, if this has happened. Yahguudang. Respect.

Material in this book has been previously published in the following newspapers, anthologies, magazines, and books (all works by Susan Musgrave unless otherwise noted):

"Ondaatje on the Hook: The Poet as Restaurant Critic," was first published in the *Globe and Mail*. It was also included in *You're in Canada Now, Motherfucker: A Memoir of Sorts* (Thistledown).

A Condensed History of Copper Beech House is adapted from "The Copper Beech House, 92 years later" by April Johnson, *The Observer*, September 14, 2006.

"All the Comforts of Home," "Wild Salmon Don't Do Oxytetracycline," "We Don't Eat That Kind of Food" (extracted from "The Dying Art of Tent Raising") were published in *You're in Canada Now . . . Motherfucker: A Memoir of Sorts* (Thistledown).

Poems (first lines) "How empty the white bowl;" "So many times Paul has explained;" "Paul's home from the hospital;" and "Out of the fog a herd of wild. . ." were first published in *Obituary of Light: the Sangan River Meditations* (Leaf Press). They were also included in *Origami Dove* (McClelland & Stewart).

"Picking Cloudberries by Moonlight;" published in *What the Small Day Cannot Hold: Collected Poems* (BeachHolme)

The quotation beginning, "I have always been nervous around shellfish," is from the novel *Given* (Thistledown).

An extract appears here from "Silent in its Shout: A Long Weekend in Sicilia," which won first prize in *Accenti* magazine's creative non-fiction contest in 2012.

It was reprinted in *Conspicuous Accents: Accenti Magazine's Finest Stories of the First 10 Years* edited by Licia Canton. Longbridge Books.

Many thanks to:

Dejahlee Busch for her drawings of Raven that appear throughout this book and the ornaments used for section breaks.

Gwaai Edenshaw for permission to reproduce his drawings, "David Rowing" and "Gogeet."

David Shrigley for his postcard, "Mushrooms."

Dafne Romero for permission to reprint the seaweed lasagne recipe that appears on her packages of Giant Seaweed Lasagne.

Patsy Aldana for hunting down the lovely cover of Matt Cohen's *Peach Melba.*

Michael König for allowing me to use his photograph from 'The Diary of One who Disappeared' by Leoš JanáÐek —Opéra National de Paris.

Garth Griffiths (Vancouver) and John Langston (Masset) interviewed Hibbie Gren in 1972 in "Carver of Canada's Misty Isles." Reprinted with kind permission of the Dixon Entrance Maritime Museum in Masset, BC. Special thanks to Barb Rempel and Peter Rempel for helping me access the material.

And thanks to all the photographers whose work has taken this book into another dimension. Their photographs have been reproduced here with their kind permission. Michelle Furbacher, art director at Whitecap. Peter Sloan. Guy Kimola. Charlotte Musgrave. Jags Brown. Janie Jolley. Archie Stocker Sr. Kathleen Hinkel. Kimberley French. Chris Ashurst. Evelyn Lavrisa. Marlene Liddle. Langdon Cook. Farhad Ghatan. Bob Fraumeni. Lisa Froese. Ginelle Taylor. Lynda Osborne. Geoff Horner. Max Mitchell. Sally Glover. Shannon Lythgoe. Randy Martin. Cacilia Honisch. Elin Price. Johanne Young. Byron Dauncey. David Anderson. Melanie Friesen. Julia McNamara. Mark Bristol. Annie VerSteeg (Agate Annie). Meredith Adams. Steph Gillis. Donna Barnett. Tarynn Lloyd. Soren Poulsen. Till Geiger. Misty Betham. Judith Musgrave. Barrett and Nate. William Gibson. Daniel Rabu. Ricardo Toledo. Greg Martin. Robert Musgrave. Liz Stocker. Jayne Mason.

And last but by no means least, my editor, Jordie Yow. For once I am at a loss for words, and I imagine, for that, he is grateful.

INDEX